Beyond Bogotá

Beyond Bogotá

*Diary of a
Drug War Journalist
in Colombia*

Garry Leech

Beacon Press
Boston

Beacon Press
25 Beacon Street
Boston, Massachusetts 02108-2892
www.beacon.org

Beacon Press books
are published under the auspices of
the Unitarian Universalist Association of Congregations.

12 11 10 09   8 7 6 5 4 3 2 1

Text design and composition by Yvonne Tsang
at Wilsted & Taylor Publishing Services

Library of Congress Cataloging-in-Publication Data

Leech, Garry
  Beyond Bogotá : diary of a drug war journalist in Colombia / Garry Leech.
    p. cm.
  Includes index.
  ISBN 978-0-8070-6145-9
  1. Drug control—Colombia. 2. Drug control—United States. 3. Colombia
—Foreign relations—United States. 4. United States—Foreign relations—
Colombia. 5. Drug traffic—Economic aspects—Colombia. I. Title.

HV5840.C7L43 2008
070.4'4936345092—dc22
  [B]   2008007621

For my son, Owen

Contents

A note from the author

The idea for this book emerged during an eleven-hour detention I endured at the hands of Colombia's largest guerrilla group in August 2006. More specifically, it evolved from thoughts that washed over me during that ordeal about my three-month-old son, Owen. I couldn't stop thinking that if anything happened to me, either during that detention or at any other time in Colombia, I wouldn't be around to explain to Owen, when he grew up, what sort of work his father did. Sure, he could read my articles and books and discover my views on U.S. policy in Colombia. But those writings do not explain how I conduct my work. They don't describe the challenges and adventures involved in carrying out investigative journalism in Colombia's remote rural conflict zones. And they don't depict the moments of terror or those of inspiration that I have experienced in my encounters with Colombians from many walks of life. Most importantly, they don't shed light on why I do this sort of work and the path that led me to become a drug war

journalist. Consequently, *Beyond Bogotá* is the story of my
work in Colombia—a sort of memoir, if you will.

Naturally, my story cannot be separated from the larger
drama in which the principal protagonists are Colombians who
are living and dying every day in the midst of the country's
decades-old civil conflict. Colombia is the world's leading pro-
ducer and exporter of cocaine, and its illegal drug trade has fed
the habits of drug users in the United States for more than three
decades. As a result, we Americans are directly linked to
Colombia's violent drama, both through ever-rising levels of
personal cocaine use and through the war on drugs that our
government has been waging in this South American country.

I have tried to place my personal story within the larger
contexts of the U.S. war on drugs and Colombia's civil conflict.
I have drawn from my experiences working in various parts of
Colombia over the past eight years in an attempt to portray, as
comprehensively as possible, both my personal story and the
struggles of those rural Colombians who are caught in the middle of the violence. There are not enough pages in this book for
me to include all of the Colombians I have met or even to reflect
on every region of the country in which I have worked. Therefore, I have selected those people and places that I hope will
provide the reader with a relatively comprehensive portrayal of
life in Colombia's rural conflict zones. Woven throughout are
accounts of the most profound and personal of my own experiences in Colombia. Sadly, for their own safety, I have had to
change the names of some of the protagonists. I have not, however, altered the names of those Colombians who are already
public figures or visible spokespersons for governments, organizations, communities, or armed groups.

Ultimately, this book is an account of the U.S. war on drugs
and Colombia's civil conflict as seen through the eyes of a journalist. Colombia's civil conflict and the war on drugs are complex issues, and I don't for a moment pretend that I fully grasp
all of their intricacies or that I have sufficiently addressed them

in these pages. What I have tried to do is to recount my experiences and observations as accurately and honestly as possible. *Beyond Bogotá* is not a journalistic work, but rather the personal story of a journalist's search for meaning in the midst of violence and poverty.

The First Hour

10:00 a.m., August 16, 2006

They order me to sit in a white plastic chair. One of the guerrillas remains behind to guard me while the other two rebels depart in a maroon Toyota SUV. My guard sits across from me in a similar white plastic chair and shows no interest in engaging me in conversation. He appears to be in his late fifties, with shoddy gray hair and a weather-beaten face that suggests he has endured many years of hard living. He is wearing a frayed red dress shirt and beige pants. A revolver in a leather holster is slung low on his right hip, giving him the appearance of a gunslinger in an old cowboy movie. Propped against the wall next to him, within easy reach, is a fully locked and loaded AK-47 assault rifle.

I'm sitting in a wooden shack on a remote farm. It has three rooms, each extending from the front to the rear of the small house. From my chair in the central room, which is open to the outside on both ends, I can see a middle-aged woman cooking in the outdoor kitchen behind the house and a teenage girl minding a small baby.

My guard passes the time listening to an old black plastic radio that he holds in his lap, occasionally shifting its position to ensure continued good reception. He does not engage in channel surfing; instead, the radio remains firmly set on one station. That station is called Radio Resistencia, and it is broadcast by my guard's rebel group, the Revolutionary Armed Forces of Colombia, better known by its Spanish-language acronym, FARC (Fuerzas Armadas Revolucionarias de Colombia). Although the FARC claims to be fighting for political, social, and economic justice in Colombia, the U.S. State Department has listed the group as an international terrorist organization since 1997.

Last night I arrived in the town of Vista Hermosa in eastern Colombia. My objective was to investigate the consequences in La Macarena National Park of the recent aerial fumigations of coca, the plant whose leaves are the raw ingredient of cocaine. The story is important because the fumigations mark an escalation in the war on drugs, since it is the first time the Colombian government has succumbed to pressure from the Bush administration to spray coca crops cultivated in one of the country's biologically diverse national parks.

Early this morning, after spending the night in a basic but clean hotel room, I hired a driver named Javier and his four-wheel-drive jeep to take me into La Macarena. On the way out of town, we stopped at the final police checkpoint in the government-controlled part of this region. When I told the officer that I was going to La Macarena to investigate the fumigations, he asked me to step out of the jeep and to follow him into the local base of the National Police. Inside the base, officials told me to sign a waiver stating that they had warned me that I was entering guerrilla country and that the National Police wouldn't be held responsible for anything that might happen to me. The waiver served two purposes for the authorities. It helped protect them if I were to be kidnapped or, worse yet, killed by the rebels. It also allowed them to track the movements of people in the region. I wasn't completely comfortable with this, but agreeing to sign the waiver was the only way through the checkpoint.

After leaving the checkpoint, Javier and I made our way across the river into FARC-controlled territory. We drove past cows grazing lazily in the fields, with the lush green hills of La Macarena half-hidden behind a thin, mystical layer of fog to our right. The road was rough, wet and muddy from recent rains, and in many places only wide enough for one vehicle. We crossed numerous streams and rivers, some via primitive wooden bridges, others by utilizing the vehicle's four-wheel drive to wade through the flowing waters. We saw few dwellings along our route into the park, save for a couple of tiny villages consisting of a handful of simple wooden houses.

La Macarena National Park is situated east of the Andes Mountains in Meta—one of Colombia's thirty-two departments, or territorial divisions—where the wide open plains of the north, known as Los Llanos, meet the Amazon rainforest to the south. The park itself is a spectacular mountainous outcropping covered in lush rainforest and filled with rivers and canyons, much of which is inaccessible to all but the hardiest of travelers. In 1989, the Colombian government finally designated this natural wonder a national park, and the United Nations Educational, Scientific and Cultural Organization (UNESCO) declared it a "heritage of humanity" site. While the interior of the park is mostly uninhabited, several thousand peasants who colonized the region in the thirty years prior to the park's creation continue to live within its confines.

Those peasants came in the early 1960s, fleeing government repression that originated in a period known as *La Violencia,* or the Violence. On April 9, 1948, Jorge Eliécer Gaitán, a dissident member of the Liberal Party, was gunned down on a street in Bogotá, the Colombian capital. Gaitán had become a champion of the poor by calling for land and labor reforms and was considered to be the favorite to win the 1950 presidential election. His assassination led to an orgy of violence throughout the country that lasted for over a decade and took more than two hundred thousand lives.

During the early years of *La Violencia,* the ruling Conservative Party mobilized the army against Liberal Party supporters and anyone perceived to be a communist. But as the fighting raged on, the elites in both the Conservative and Liberal parties became concerned that the sectarian violence might evolve into a social uprising by the country's poor majority. Colombia's two dominant political parties signed a power-sharing pact that led to a coalition known as the National Front. Under the pact, the Conservative and Liberal parties alternated four-year terms in the presidency and divided all government positions evenly between themselves. The National Front lasted until 1974, when the two parties again fielded candidates against each other.

Meanwhile, during *La Violencia* and the National Front years, the army waged a war against peasant communities in central Colombia that were demanding political, social, and economic reforms. Some of these communities became self-declared independent republics and formed self-defense movements to protect themselves against government repression. The Colombian military responded by intensifying its campaign against them, with support from the U.S. government, which viewed the conflict through a Cold War lens and considered the peasants to be communists. The military forcibly displaced many of the communities, and the peasants fled the Andean highlands and resettled in Colombia's Amazon region. By 1964, the peasant self-defense movements in areas like La Macarena had evolved into the FARC. More than forty years later, the Marxist-oriented FARC guerrillas still control La Macarena National Park and its environs.

Two and a half hours after leaving Vista Hermosa, Javier and I arrived in the small town of Santo Domingo. The local inhabitants unabashedly stared at the *gringo* in the white jeep that was slowly making its way along the dirt main street. Several people later told me that they could not recall the last time either a *gringo* or a journalist had entered this remote region.

Javier pulled over in front of a general store, and we climbed out of the jeep to ask a woman where we could find fumigated coca crops. We had barely finished posing the question when a young man—he couldn't have been more than nineteen years old—pulled up on a dirt bike and ordered me to step out into the middle of the street. He told me to stand with my arms held straight out and my legs spread apart.

"Who invited you here?" he asked sternly.

"Nobody," I responded. Certain that he was a FARC guerrilla, I added, "I am a journalist, and I would like to request permission to investigate the effects of last week's fumigations."

"But who invited you?" he asked again, intent on making sure I understood that he would dictate the terms of the conversation.

"I didn't know how to obtain an invitation, so I came here to ask for permission." The fact that this young guerrilla was clearly unhappy with my unannounced arrival in Santo Domingo was making me nervous. I noticed people beginning to gather in front of the buildings to watch this encounter occurring in the middle of the street.

The young man frisked me for a weapon and ordered me to empty my pockets. I pulled out a tape recorder, notebook, pens, extra batteries, passport, press card, and other odds and ends, including a blue poncho in which he wrapped my belongings after inspecting them. I then extracted my digital camera from its case on my belt and handed it to him. Meanwhile, another young man, who had just finished searching the jeep, brought over my backpack. The two of them stepped aside and whispered to each other, then turned and ordered me to sit in a chair at a table in front of a nearby café.

And there the three of us waited. I had no idea what we were waiting for, and my welcoming committee had absolutely no intention of volunteering that information. I decided that, given their unfriendly demeanor, any attempt to question them might only aggravate them. I waited quietly, trying to conceal my nervousness.

The wait was less than fifteen minutes. It ended when a white jeep containing three men dressed in civilian clothes pulled up outside the café. All three, who appeared to be in their early to mid thirties, poured out of the jeep and walked over to me, making no attempt to conceal the 9mm semiautomatic pistols tucked into their waistbands. One of them grabbed my backpack while another took my poncho and its contents. The driver ordered me to get into the front passenger seat before planting himself behind the steering wheel. The other two climbed into the back, carrying my belongings. We turned off the main street and made our way into the countryside on a dirt road that was far more treacherous than the one Javier and I had taken earlier that morning to get to Santo Domingo.

Behind me I heard the distinctive metallic sound of a slide on a gun being pulled back to shift a bullet into the chamber. I froze. For a terrifying second, I held my breath and waited for the crack of a gunshot. It never came, and I slowly exhaled. But then the thought crossed my mind that the guerrillas might be taking me out into the countryside to shoot me and ditch my body by the side of the road. I tried to put my mind at ease by telling myself that they wouldn't be likely to make such a rash decision regarding the life of a foreign journalist without first seeking authorization from higher-ranking FARC commanders.

My fears were partially alleviated thirty minutes later when we turned in at a small farm perched atop a hill. The terrain in that area was more rugged, and an increased density of rainforest replaced the grazing cattle. The small farm that had been cut out of the jungle was one of many scattered throughout the region.

The jeep came to a halt in front of a small wooden house, and I was ordered to get out. Six partly uniformed guerrillas were awaiting our arrival. They appeared to be a little younger than the three in the jeep, who immediately departed after handing over my belongings and me. My new guardians were adorned in various combinations of camouflage jackets and pants, blue jeans, and T-shirts. They all carried AK-47 assault rifles, and one held a two-way radio. Two of the guerrillas sifted through my belongings while the others stood watching both my stuff and me.

"Do you have a gun?" one of them inquired.

"No," I replied.

One of the rebels inspecting my belongings began flicking through the pages of my U.S. passport.

"Are you a member of the U.S. military?"

"No, I'm a journalist seeking permission to investigate the recent fumigations in this region."

I answered numerous questions over the next several minutes, informing them that I wrote for the online publication *Colombia Journal* and various magazines in the United States. One of the guerrillas asked me to show him the photos on my digital camera, which were merely some scenic views from the drive that morning. At the conclusion of the interrogation, one of the rebels brought a green plastic chair from the house, placed it in the shade under a tree, and ordered me to sit down. The rebel with the two-way radio strolled out of hearing range and began communicating with someone whom I assumed to be his commander.

I sat under the tree, scanning the scenery. There were a variety of food crops being cultivated in the fields surrounding the farmhouse, and beyond them nothing but rainforest. I had yet to see any coca fields. One guerrilla brought me a cup of coffee while others periodically asked me innocuous questions about life in the United States. The mood relaxed a bit. Suddenly one of the guerrillas stared me in the eyes and calmly stated, "You know, if you are not who you say you are..." He finished the statement by pointing two fingers to the side of his head and jerking them upward to imitate the firing of a gun. I nervously reassured him that I was exactly who I claimed to be, and hoped to hell that they believed me.

About twenty minutes later, three more armed guerrillas pulled into the farm in a maroon SUV. The driver appeared to be in his late thirties and wore a black T-shirt and camouflage pants. He got out of the SUV and walked over to two of my guards; his demeanor suggested that he was of superior rank. After a few words with the other rebels, he strode over to where I was sitting and, as I pulled myself up out of the seat, offered his hand in greeting. He asked how I was doing and then told me to get into the passenger seat of the SUV. The other two guerrillas who had arrived with him climbed in the back with my belongings, and we made our way down a narrow dirt road toward the rear of the farm.

We drove for about fifteen minutes before pulling into another farm, which was similar to the one we had just left, but with one significant difference: this farmhouse stood in the midst of coca fields. I was taken into the wooden house, which was surrounded by a circular eight-foot-high wire fence, and told to sit in a white plastic chair. Two of the rebels, along with my passport, backpack, and everything else I had brought with me, departed in the SUV. The oldest of the three guerrillas remained behind to guard me.

The Second Hour

11:00 a.m., August 16, 2006

I've been sitting here with my guard for almost an hour listening to Radio Resistencia. The male voice emanating from the black box rails against the "fascistic and militaristic" policies of Colombia's president, Alvaro Uribe. I feel an overwhelming sense of impotence as a result of being detained and held at gunpoint. At times like this, I wonder why the hell I do the type of work I do. The time is passing interminably slowly. The option to change my mind, to simply walk away, no longer exists. I am now at the mercy of the FARC. Some distant rebel commander will be my judge, jury, and if things take a real turn for the worse, my executioner.

The possible outcomes of my predicament begin racing through my mind. In short, my future depends on the response of a FARC commander to my request to investigate the aerial fumigations of coca crops. As far as I can figure, there are four potential responses to my request. The best response would be the FARC giving me the green light to go ahead with my work. The next best would be a refusal to let me work and an order to leave the region. The remaining two potential scenarios are the most worrisome. The FARC could decide to kidnap me and hold me for ransom, a tactic they have routinely used to fund their insurgency. Such a scenario could entail several years of captivity in the jungle. The final option would simply be to kill me.

I repeatedly mull over these potential fates. I feel relatively confident that the outcome will prove to be one of the first two, as most of my writing has been critical of U.S. drug war policy in Colombia. Therefore, in my mind at least, I don't pose a significant threat to the FARC's political, social, or economic interests. The second possible outcome—ordering me to leave —is the most likely one, given that I showed up in the region without any prior permission. Nevertheless, the last two options continue to haunt me. And while the more likely of these two is the kidnapping scenario, I am fully conscious of the fact that the FARC detained and killed three American human rights workers in 1999. The more I think about the possibility of death, the more I realize that it's not actually death itself that terrifies me. I am more afraid of missing the life that I live. A subtle difference, perhaps, but a crucial one for me, as it drives home just how much I love my wife and son.

As the Spanish lyrics of a revolutionary song ring out from Radio Resistencia, I reminisce about the labyrinthine road that brought me here. I'm a forty-six-year-old captive of an armed group in the midst of a civil conflict being waged between leftist guerrillas and a U.S.-backed military. Over the past twenty-four years, so much has changed in my life. And yet certain things feel deeply familiar. Back in March 1982, I was also detained in the midst of a civil conflict. On that occasion, it was the U.S.-backed military in El Salvador that imprisoned me, under suspicion of being a mercenary fighting for leftist guerrillas seeking to overthrow the Salvadoran government.

I was a naive twenty-one-year-old backpacking through Central America. My appetite for Latin America had been whetted during an eighteen-month enlistment in the U.S. Marines. Thirteen of those months were spent in the Panama Canal Zone. During that time, I participated in the U.S. Army Special Forces jungle warfare program, which was once administered by the infamous School of the Americas, an institution that provided counterinsurgency training to Latin American militaries. However, at the tender young age of nineteen, it wasn't the military life in Panama that appealed to me, but the nightlife. I spent most of my off-duty time in the bars of Panama City, chasing local women who preferred *gringos* to their male compatriots.

Meanwhile, my military activities on base mostly involved hours upon tedious hours of guard duty, painting palm trees for some unknown reason, cleaning already spotless rifles, participating in litter detail, and many other mind-numbing, time-filling chores. I quickly grew to detest the dehumanizing, desensitizing, and tedious nature of military life and responded to it by becoming increasingly disobedient of my superiors. When a thirty-five-day stint in the brig failed to curb my insolence, the commanding officer of the marine detachment in Panama offered me a general discharge for, as he clearly stated, "the good of the service." Naturally, I immediately accepted his offer, for the good of me.

Many years later I would come to realize just how oblivious I was of the political and social realities in Panama. Reflecting on my marine deployment, I began to understand to what degree the presence of tens of thousands of U.S. military personnel in Panama City had dramatically, and disturbingly, influenced many aspects of the local culture and economy. Still, I became enthralled with Panama's natural beauty and its people and developed a curiosity about Latin America in general. So, shortly after my discharge, I decided to explore Central America and set off with my brother, Don, on a three-month expedition.

Both of us were excited to experience Central America, but

woefully ignorant of the political situation in the region. While my upbringing hadn't fostered an awareness of U.S. foreign policy or many other global issues, it did lie at the root of my love for travel. I was born in Coventry, England, but moved to Manchester—where I spent most of my formative years—when I was eight. When I was fifteen, my family left England and moved to Detroit, where I felt like a perpetual outsider. Nevertheless, I became the quintessential post-Watergate, apolitical, alienated, bored, middle-class American suburbanite.

Shortly after graduating from high school, I sought to escape my suburban doldrums by heading to the West Coast in search of adventure. While living in Los Angeles in 1979, I decided to enlist in the U.S. Marines in the hope of being deployed to some exotic foreign country. Panama proved to be that exotic destination, and eight months after being discharged, I returned there with Don.

Shortly after reaching Panama City, Don and I separated and he returned home. I decided to visit the Darién Gap, a rugged, remote region of jungle, swamps, and mountains in eastern Panama. Once my money supply had dwindled to an uncomfortably low level, I left Panama and began my long journey back home, traveling by bus through Costa Rica and Nicaragua and into Honduras. In early March 1982, I took one of the many old, dilapidated, but colorfully decorated buses that constituted the public transportation system along the Honduran stretch of the Pan-American Highway to the border with El Salvador. I maneuvered my way through the typical border chaos, paying the equivalent of two dollars to obtain the necessary exit stamps in my passport, and then set out on foot across the border bridge, arriving a few minutes later at the Salvadoran checkpoint called El Amatillo.

I wanted to get through customs and immigration as quickly as possible, because it was late in the afternoon and I knew that the civil war had made it extremely dangerous to travel after dark. I entered the guardhouse and handed my passport to one border official and my backpack to another. The latter proceeded to empty out my belongings onto a table. Leafing through a book of poetry written by Patti Smith, the border guard noticed a black-and-white picture of the author holding a walkie-talkie and, unable to read English, assumed it to be revolutionary literature. I tried to convince him otherwise, but after another official noticed my old, beat-up, military-looking black boots, they decided to take me up a nearby hill to the buildings that overlooked the border crossing. As I was led up the hill, I demanded to know what was going on. One of my two escorts told me I was going to see *"el comandante."*

We reached the top of the hill, only to find that their commander had left and wouldn't return until later that evening. I was placed in an outdoor cell that consisted of three brick walls, a roof, and a steel gate. There, staring out over the border crossing, I waited patiently for the commander to return. Perhaps it was naiveté, but I wasn't overly concerned about my predicament at that moment. I figured that the commander would send me on my way once he heard my explanation. But apparently he did not return that evening. Or if he did, he chose not to speak with me. Nightfall came and, realizing that I was stuck there, I settled in as best I could on the hard cement floor.

At that time, all I knew about the Salvadoran civil war was that the United States supported the Salvadoran army in its battle against Marxist guerrillas. Having been thoroughly socialized to believe that western democracies, particularly the U.S. and British models, represented all that was good in the world, I logically assumed that the U.S.-backed Salvadoran army must therefore represent the force for good in that war. I had no idea that the Salvadoran army was in fact responsible for the overwhelming majority of human rights abuses being inflicted on the Salvadoran people. In hindsight, my ignorance probably served me well, because that knowledge would surely have had a negative effect on my state of mind during the ordeal that was just beginning. It was an experience that would mark the dawn of my long, slow political awakening.

The next morning, two soldiers removed me from the cell and led me to a waiting pickup truck. They placed handcuffs on my wrists and pushed me into the rear bed of the truck, all the while ignoring my repeated requests to speak with their commander. In the back of the truck, along with the two soldiers and me, was a middle-aged Nicaraguan woman who was also handcuffed. We were driven to a military base in the city of La Unión, where I was pulled out of the truck. Someone removed my handcuffs and replaced them with a shoelace that tied my thumbs together behind my back. The soldiers sat me on a bench just inside the gate and left me there to stare at the lime green paint peeling off a wall two feet in front of my face.

I sat patiently, listening to the frequent movement of soldiers entering and leaving the base, but every attempt to turn my head to observe the activity resulted in a sharp blow to my back from a rifle butt. I lost all sense of time, aware only that it was still daylight. At one point, my thumbs were untied and I was served rice, beans, and a tortilla, the same meal that I would eat every day of my detention. As soon as I finished eating, my thumbs were retied, and I was once again awash in boredom.

I had no idea what was going to happen; the situation had obviously evolved beyond the point where a simple explanation was going to secure my release. I was becoming increasingly concerned. Oddly, although I envisioned several potentially unpleasant scenarios, the possibility of death never seriously entered my mind. In hindsight, I believe that was due to a combination of the psychological component of my military training and my ignorance regarding the brutality of the Salvadoran army.

At some point during the afternoon, an army officer came

to interrogate me. It was then that I discovered the reason for my detainment. I had been accused of being a mercenary working with the guerrillas.

The officer began asking questions: "What is your name?" "Where do you live?" "Why are you in El Salvador?" "What were you doing in Nicaragua?"

The Nicaraguan stamps in my passport must have aroused their suspicions, although at the time I had no idea that Nicaragua's leftist Sandinista government was ideologically aligned with El Salvador's Farabundo Martí National Liberation Front (FMLN) guerrillas.

The questions kept coming: "What is your father's name?" "What is your mother's name?" "Where do they live?" "What kind of work do they do?"

I answered all of the officer's questions, though I neglected to mention my military service for fear that it might incriminate me in light of the mercenary accusation. Eventually the officer departed, and I was left alone to ponder the fact that I was a suspected mercenary. Still, I managed to remain relatively optimistic, believing they would soon sort out the misunderstanding and set me free.

Shortly after nightfall, a group of soldiers came and placed a blindfold over my head. They stood me up and pulled me along by my arms, which was intensely painful for my thumbs because they were still tied together. I struggled to maintain both my calm and my footing as the soldiers led me blindfolded through a maze of unannounced obstacles, including stairs and several low doorways. As a child, I had played games with my brother and friends in which I was blindfolded and led around a house that I was familiar with, and I found the experience unnerving. But being led blindfolded through that base by soldiers who viewed me as their enemy was absolutely terrifying.

At the end of that brief but nerve-wracking trek, the soldiers released my arms and pushed me to the floor. I heard footsteps receding and then the door being slammed shut and locked. The blindfold had served its purpose, for I had no idea where I was or how to get out of there.

After a few minutes, I began rubbing the side of my head against the wall and successfully removed the blindfold. The room was approximately twelve by twelve feet, with light blue stucco walls, a red tile floor, and no furniture. There was one window, with wooden shutters but no glass; it was the source of what little light penetrated the room. There were two doors, the one through which I had entered and another that opened into a bathroom containing a toilet and a brass pipe running up the wall, which was meant to serve as a shower. Lying motionless in the corner of the main room was the Nicaraguan woman who had traveled with me from the border. She was blindfolded, with her thumbs tied together behind her back.

I was obviously there for the night, and I was becoming increasingly concerned that my situation was deteriorating quickly. Still, I tried to remain optimistic and get some sleep, but it was impossible to find a comfortable position on the unforgiving tile floor. Lying on either side or on my back soon put my arms to sleep. And lying on my stomach only caused me pain due to the weight of my arms pulling my thumbs apart and causing the ties to cut into my skin. I spent the night sitting upright in the corner, where I drifted in and out of sleep.

The following morning, three soldiers brought us breakfast and, to my relief, were unconcerned with the fact that I was no longer blindfolded. Like most of the soldiers I saw during my detention, they were young men in their late teens. They removed the Nicaraguan woman's blindfold and both of our thumb ties before leaving us alone to eat.

After finishing her breakfast, the Nicaraguan woman made her way into the bathroom. The three soldiers returned while she was in there. Upon realizing where she was, they retied my thumbs and disappeared through the bathroom door. I heard a woman's muffled cries and men's laughter from behind that closed door, leaving little doubt about what was taking place. I felt so helpless sitting there while they raped her. I thought of shouting for help, but realized that it might only result in more soldiers joining in on the abuse. I felt sick to my stomach.

After a while the three soldiers emerged from the bathroom, laughing, obviously full of themselves. They picked up our breakfast dishes and left. Through the open bathroom door, I could hear the woman sobbing, but I couldn't decide whether to try to comfort her. Would my presence simply instill more fear in her? I decided to give her some space. A couple of hours later, she emerged from the bathroom and settled back into her corner. When I asked her whether she was all right, she ignored me. She was as alone and terrified as any person I had ever seen, and I felt powerless. Thankfully, for the remainder of the time that I spent with her she was subjected to only verbal taunting, which she endured in silence.

Shortly after lunch, several soldiers brought in a table and two chairs. They untied my thumbs and ordered me to sit in one of the chairs. The Nicaraguan woman was removed from the room, and I was left face-to-face with a different army officer than the one from the previous day. He began asking me the same questions I'd been asked before. After answering them, I asked to speak with the British embassy. Even though I had lived in the United States for six years and had served in the U.S. Marines, I had yet to become a U.S. citizen. The officer simply responded, *"Mañana."*

After the officer left, the soldiers brought the Nicaraguan woman back into the room and, much to my dismay, removed the table and chairs, leaving us only the floor to sit on. They didn't retie our thumbs, which was a great relief because when they were tied, the only position I had found to be relatively pain-free was standing up. The fact that the officer had asked the same questions as the day before was disconcerting, but my optimism was buoyed at the thought of speaking to the British embassy.

Dinner came and went without incident, and the Nicaraguan woman continued to ignore any attempt I made to communicate with her. I never did learn her name. In fact, she never uttered a single word to me during our time together. That night, with my thumbs finally free, and exhausted from the stress of the previous couple of days, I actually slept well.

On the third morning of my detention, I heard raised voices from outside the room. Peering through the shutters, I saw a naked man who looked to be in his twenties performing calisthenics in the dirt courtyard. Soldiers stood on both sides of him, and every time he failed to perform to their expectations, they beat him with sticks. Cheered on by their comrades, they whipped him until tears streamed down his face and blood down his back.

Eventually the semiconscious man was carried from the courtyard and taken into what appeared to be a room similar to ours. I wondered whether I was going to endure a similar punishment. But in spite of having just observed that senseless abuse, I still thought it inconceivable that such a thing could happen to me. My attitude was undoubtedly influenced, rather naively, by the belief that my captors would never subject a foreigner who lived in the United States to such treatment. After all, I reassured myself, the United States was their ally. I was oblivious to the fact that Salvadoran soldiers had brutally raped and murdered four female American missionaries only a year before my detention.

That afternoon there was another interrogation session, which turned out to be a welcome relief from the boredom. When I asked about my earlier request to speak to the British embassy, I was again told, *"Mañana."* I knew that the Salvadoran government was legally required to notify the embassy of the arrest of any British citizen, and the growing realization that my captors had no intention of doing so made me suddenly feel very isolated. I'd last contacted my family when I was in Nicaragua, and all they knew was that I was somewhere between Nicaragua and the United States. It was becoming more and more difficult to remain optimistic. The uniformity of each day offered little in the way of hope, and for the first time I began to believe that an extended detention was a real possibility.

My fourth day began with the usual breakfast, but shortly afterward a group of soldiers came for both the Nicaraguan woman and me. My thumbs were again tied together behind my back and a blindfold placed over my eyes. I was led out of the room and after a few minutes walked into something solid, which I quickly determined to be the tailgate of a pickup truck. I was pulled up, to a large extent by my hair, onto the bed of the truck and forced to lie down among other live bodies. It was creepy to lie on top of the wriggling bodies of people I could not see and who were most likely in the same predicament as I was. Who were they? What had they done? What would happen to them? What would happen to all of us?

A short drive terminated next to a helicopter, and I was deafened by the sound of its engine. Amid the nerve-wracking noise and commotion, I was pulled out of the truck and stumbled into some steps. My guards again pulled me up by my hair, this time into the helicopter. Once aboard, I was pushed down to the floor, where I lay on my stomach next to the other prisoners. The helicopter took off and remained airborne for about thirty minutes. During the flight, I suddenly felt a sharp pain in my left ear. A soldier had just ripped my gold hoop earring out.

When we landed, I was placed into the rear of a van. Following a very short drive, I was pulled out of the van and the thumb ties were replaced with handcuffs. When I stumbled climbing some steps, one of my guards began beating me with what I assumed to be his rifle butt. Most of the blows struck me on the right hipbone, causing me to wince in pain and to curse at the soldier in English. While he probably didn't understand the words, he certainly recognized the tone, which only caused him to intensify the beating. I recognized that my response was stupid, but I was impulsively and desperately trying to gain some control over my situation.

Shortly after I finally reached the top of the steps, the blindfold was removed, and I found myself in a large warehouse with eight other prisoners, all male Latinos. We were evenly spaced around the walls, and there were more than enough soldiers present to deter any thought of escape. I was ordered to sit on the floor, a task that proved painful due to the beating I had just endured. I watched a group of soldiers slowly work their way around the building as they questioned each prisoner in turn. I had no idea where I was, but actually found myself relieved at the potential change in my circumstance, although I didn't yet know if it would be for better or worse.

When my turn finally came, the interrogation was exactly the same as the experience in La Unión. I gave the same old answers to the same old questions, but this time my request to contact the British embassy was greeted with silence.

After the soldiers had finished with me, they again placed the blindfold over my eyes and led me out of the warehouse. When they brought me to a halt and removed the blindfold, I found myself standing inside a barred gate. On my left ran a wall about twelve feet high. Opposite it, to my right, were three jail cells. The soldiers took me to the barred door of the third cell, unlocked and opened it, removed my handcuffs, and placed me inside.

The cell was about twelve by fifteen feet with gray cement walls. A built-in cement seat ran around the walls, and a ceiling of steel bars hung several feet below the roof. In one corner were the now familiar brass pipe shower and a white porcelain toilet without a seat. The cell was occupied by ten Latino men, all of whom seemed surprised that their new cellmate was a *gringo*.

Entering that cell, I envisioned all kinds of horrors. But my fears were soon alleviated when most of my new cellmates displayed nothing but friendliness toward me. One of them was a twenty-year-old university student named Carlos, who claimed he'd been arrested, along with two friends, for drinking in a parked car outside the international airport. With the aid of a Spanish language *Reader's Digest,* which he had somehow managed to procure, the two of us spent much of the next three days giving each other Spanish and English lessons. Most of the other prisoners also claimed to be students who had been arrested for trivial reasons, although there were two prisoners who were unwilling to tell their stories and who kept mostly to themselves.

Shortly after my arrival, the Nicaraguan woman was brought through the outer gate, but she wasn't placed in a cell; instead she was seated on the ground in the alleyway that ran between the cells and the wall. After only one night she was removed, and my cellmates told me that she had probably been transferred to a women's prison. I hoped she'd be safe.

I discovered that I was in the capital, San Salvador. Over the next few days I learned that Carlos, my Spanish teacher, had been in jail for over a month. He had not seen his friends since the night of their arrest, and he had not been allowed to contact his family, who, as far as he knew, remained unaware of his predicament. Both of his thumbs had ugly red wounds, about a quarter of an inch deep, where ties had cut through his skin. It was several months before I regained the full feeling in my thumbs, so I imagine he suffered permanent damage.

There was barely enough room for all of us to lie down and sleep on the cement floor, which in the early hours of the morning became uncomfortably cold. The blue tank top and beige cotton pants I had been wearing since my arrest offered little in the way of warmth. Each meal consisted of rice, beans, and a tortilla, and as the days passed I began to lose my appetite. Whether this was due to worry or inactivity I'm not sure, but other prisoners happily ate my leftovers. We could take showers only in the morning hours, since there was no drain and the flooded floor, which also served as our bed, required most of the day to dry. It was when they showered that I noticed several of my cellmates had brutal-looking scars across their backs, undoubtedly a result of beatings similar to the one I had witnessed in La Unión. For me, though, the most unpleasant aspect of life in that cell was the fact that eleven men were using a toilet that had no real flushing mechanism. At first the daytime heat and humidity made the stench unbearable, but to my amazement its oppressiveness diminished with each passing day as I became accustomed to the foul odor.

There was a very vocal prisoner in the next cell, who would get my attention by yelling, "Hey, *gringo*!" He would then proceed to question me about the United States and, being full of good humor, wanted to know whether I was enjoying my stay in El Salvador. We communicated in this manner daily, our voices carrying through the barred ceiling, until a guard eventually told us to be quiet.

The next three days passed without any further interrogations. The time dragged. Boredom and increasing concern became the dominant factors in my detention. I could see no way out, and a new fear emerged. It wasn't a fear of being physically hurt, but rather a fear of the psychological torture that would inevitably result from a prolonged imprisonment. I also couldn't stop thinking about my parents and the endless torment they would have to endure once they realized I had gone missing.

And then, late in the afternoon of the seventh day, my salvation arrived in the form of the International Committee of the Red Cross. Several Red Cross workers were engaging in a random inspection of the jail and were startled to find a *gringo* prisoner. After I related my story, they told me that they didn't have the authority to get me released, but they agreed to notify the British consulate.

They then turned their attention to the other prisoners. To my amazement, not one of my cellmates registered a complaint about their predicament or their treatment. These were people who had been victims of abuses resulting in crippled thumbs, brutally scarred backs, and certainly much more. As if that were not bad enough, they had no doubt also endured psychological torment and been denied any form of contact with the outside world, including their families. After the Red Cross workers departed, I asked Carlos why none of the prisoners had spoken out about their treatment.

"If we complain, there will be repercussions against us and our families," he explained.

He went on to reassure me that because I was a foreigner, the Red Cross visit would most likely result in my release. This news left me feeling truly optimistic for the first time in almost a week, and yet somewhat ambivalent about the favorable treatment I appeared to be receiving.

Carlos was proved right the next morning when two guards came to take me away. I hastily bid farewell to my cellmates. As I left with the guards, who for the first time did not blindfold me, I was overcome with a strange mixture of sadness and relief. I wondered what lay in store for Carlos and the others I was leaving behind. I couldn't avoid feeling guilty about the fact that my government had the power to gain my release, whereas their government was the party responsible for their dilemma.

In the ensuing years, I learned about some of the gross violations of human rights perpetrated by the Salvadoran military against both Salvadorans and foreigners during the two years prior to my detention. In March 1980, former Salvadoran soldiers trained by the U.S. military assassinated Archbishop Oscar Romero, who had been using his pulpit to plead with Salvadoran troops to stop killing their brothers and sisters. In December 1980, members of the Salvadoran military raped and murdered four female missionaries from the United States. Three months later, while attempting to flee across the Lempa River to neighboring Honduras, thousands of Salvadoran refugees were bombed by the Salvadoran air force while the army simultaneously attacked them with machine gun and mortar fire. Dozens of unarmed peasants were killed. In December 1981, troops from the Salvadoran army's elite Atlacatl Battalion, which was created, funded, trained, and armed by the United States, massacred more than nine hundred peasants in and around the village of El Mozote. Most of the victims were women and children.

Six weeks after the El Mozote massacre, and one month before my detention, President Ronald Reagan certified that El Salvador had complied with the human rights conditions required for receiving U.S. military aid, a certification that Reagan would sign every six months for the remainder of his presidency. The U.S. government provided more than four billion dollars in military and economic aid to El Salvador during the 1980s, funding the largest U.S.-supported military operation since Vietnam—and with a similar goal of quashing communism. The Salvadoran army used that military aid to slaughter the very population it was supposed to be defending. It was not so much a war against communism as a war against peasants who sought to escape the repression and poverty they were enduring under a brutal regime. The decade ended as it had begun when on November 16, 1989, soldiers from the Atlacatl Battalion massacred six Jesuit priests, their housekeeper, and her daughter. By the end of the twelve-year war against the specter of communism, more than seventy thousand Salvadoran civilians had been killed.

As the guards led me through the outer cell gate, I was utterly unaware of how lucky I was to still be alive after spending eight days in the custody of the Salvadoran army. We crossed a large open courtyard and entered a small office building. A Salvadoran army officer was seated at a desk in one of the offices, and a very British-looking elderly gentleman sat across from him. The officer introduced the man to me as Mr. William Chippendale, the British honorary consul. The officer then returned my backpack, my passport, and to my surprise, my money. The Patti Smith book and the poetry I had written during my travels were not among my belongings. Chippendale suggested that I not make an issue of the missing items if I wished to get out of there in the near future, and I took his advice. The Salvadoran officer said that I was free to go on the condition that I leave the country immediately and never return. It was a condition that I gladly accepted.

The consul and I left the office and made our way to the front gate of the base. I cannot describe the overwhelming sense of relief that I experienced as we walked through that gate and out onto the street. I inhaled what seemed to me the freshest air on the planet. We climbed into Chippendale's car, and he explained that he hadn't known of my existence until the Red Cross contacted him earlier that morning. He asked me a few questions about my ordeal and said that he would be filing an official protest regarding the failure of the Salvadoran authorities to notify him of my arrest. The consul then drove me to the bus station, where I thanked him and boarded a bus to the Guatemalan border.

I had one final scare before leaving El Salvador. At the border, the guards noticed that my passport didn't contain the required entry stamp, and as a result they assumed that I had entered El Salvador illegally. This was a problem that, in the excitement of my release, I had failed to foresee. After I explained my situation to the border guards, one of them disappeared into an office to call headquarters in the capital. I was left standing there with a sinking feeling that I was about to relive the entire ordeal. But after several agonizing minutes, the guard reappeared and stamped my passport with the appropriate exit stamp. I walked out of the guardhouse and, with an enormous sense of relief, made my way across the border to Guatemala.

I didn't fully realize it at the time, but for eight days I had experienced a minuscule amount of the terror that many Salvadorans endured for over a decade. I was lucky enough to get out of there alive; more than seventy thousand Salvadorans weren't.

The Third Hour

12:00 p.m., August 16, 2006

I glance at my watch and see that only two hours have passed since I arrived at this farm. Looking over at the primitive kitchen, I see my guard talking to the women, who are busy preparing a meal. The teenage girl picks up the baby and carries her into the house and then into the bedroom to put her down for a nap. My thoughts immediately drift back to my son Owen. He was born almost three months ago and is my first and only child. I picture his thin layer of light brown hair and toothless smile. I feel a shiver run down my spine at the thought of possibly being kidnapped and not seeing him or my wife Terry again for several years. The thought is unbearable. I curse myself for getting into such a predicament.

Throughout my twenties and well into my thirties, I had no desire to have children. My rationale for not wanting them was that they would infringe upon my freewheeling lifestyle. But my feelings about becoming a father shifted as I got older, and now I cannot imagine life without Owen. I've lived an exciting life full of amazing experiences, but not one of them remotely compares to that of becoming a father. For years I listened to parents tell me about the wonder of having a child, and I'd dismiss them as people who simply didn't understand how full and rich my life was. But now I realize that it was I who never understood how amazing and magical their lives were.

The fear of being kidnapped comes and goes in waves. When I think that I might not see Terry and Owen for who knows how long, that I might not be there to see my son grow up or to hold my wife in my arms, the anxiety reaches an unbearable level. The only thing in the world that I want is to be with Terry and Owen again. Please, God, make that happen!

I continue to fight against the rising anxiety by trying to convince myself that the FARC isn't going to harm a foreign journalist. After all, I've depended on that immunity in all my past dealings with Colombia's armed groups, and so far it has served me well. Nevertheless, being detained in Colombia has always made me feel much more afraid than I was during my detention in El Salvador. There are three reasons for the difference, I think. The first is that I've consciously worked hard to rehumanize myself in the years since the Marine Corps effectively trained me to bury my emotions in some deep, dark hole. Second, I understand the potential dangers in Colombia far greater than I did in El Salvador. And finally, there is always the possibility that someone in a position of authority might not be happy with my coverage of Colombia's armed conflict and decide to retaliate against me.

But on this occasion, thinking of the worst-case scenario is even more terrifying than it was during previous detentions I've endured in Colombia. The reason has little to do with my own well-being and more to do with the sense of responsibility that comes with being a father. Whereas Terry is an adult and was aware of the work I do when we met, Owen hasn't entered into a relationship with me by choice. Is it fair to Owen that I put myself in the position that allowed me to end up here? Should I take advantage of my privileged position as an American and find a safer alternative to the work I'm currently doing? Or should I continue with my work in the hope that it sets some sort of positive example for my son as he grows up? I try to believe the latter—that by doing this work, I'm setting an example for Owen—but I'm not completely convinced.

I force myself to think of things other than my family in an attempt to alleviate the anxiety. I steer my mind back to November 1989 and my first trip to Colombia. I wasn't working as a journalist then, but rather was once again on a three-month backpacking trip. I had flown from the United States to Costa Rica and was backpacking from there to the Ecuadorian Amazon, stopping in Panama on the way.

The situation was tense in Panama City at the time, when the game of political one-upmanship between the U.S. government and Panamanian dictator Manuel Noriega was reaching its zenith. For much of the 1980s, Noriega had been a CIA asset, supporting the U.S.-backed Contras in their attempt to overthrow Nicaragua's Sandinista government. He was also involved in cocaine trafficking, something that the Reagan administration overlooked while it needed the Panamanian strongman's support. But by the end of the decade, Noriega was exhibiting signs of independence, and the winding down of the Contra war had made him dispensable. Even though the tension in Panama City was palpable and a nighttime curfew had been enacted, I never imagined that a month after I left Panama, the U.S. military would invade, overthrow Noriega, and ship him to Florida to face drug-trafficking charges. The human cost of catching this single drug trafficker was immense; more than four thousand Panamanians were killed in the invasion. The Panama invasion marked the first time that the war on drugs was used to justify direct U.S. intervention in a Latin American nation. The threat of communism had collapsed along with the Berlin Wall, but Washington now had a new post–Cold War justification for militarily intervening in what it considered its own backyard.

As for me, I was no longer the naive, apolitical, callous youngster that had been jailed in El Salvador seven years earlier. Although I didn't realize it at the time, following my release from jail I dealt with my survivor guilt by ignoring the political and human rights realities of the Salvadoran civil war. But by the end of the 1980s, I'd begun to educate myself about the political situation in Latin America and was slowly coming to terms with U.S. policy in El Salvador and in the rest of the region. I was beginning to understand the political and economic links between people, communities, and nations. I came to understand that the plight endured by those Salvadorans with whom I had shared a cell seven years earlier was linked to my life and the lives of everyone else in the United States—and to conscious policy decisions made by my government.

As that decade drew to a close, I prepared to leave Panama for my trip to the Ecuadorian Amazon. In order to get to Ecuador from Panama, I had to first pass through Colombia.

Nearly everyone I encountered in Panama warned me to be careful in Colombia because it was a very dangerous country. Many suggested I fly to Ecuador in order to bypass Colombia entirely. It wasn't only drug violence I had to be concerned about, they warned, but also leftist guerrillas and common criminals. But given my tight budget, taking an international flight was out of the question. And so I set off on a grueling journey that involved taking a small Cessna airplane from Panama City to a remote Caribbean fishing village, then two small fishing boats transporting contraband smugglers along the Caribbean coasts of Panama and Colombia, and finally an eighteen-hour bus ride from the small Colombian port town of Turbo to Medellín, Colombia's second-largest city.

Thirty-four hours after leaving Panama City, I arrived in Medellín. Utterly exhausted, I checked into the Hotel Inter-Americana in the center of the city. It was noticeably nicer than the dives I normally stayed in and represented my first concession to those who had warned me to be extra careful in Colombia. After showering, I made my way up to the rooftop café for dinner and a cold beer. The view from the roof of that twelve-story building was spectacular. The sun was setting behind the mountains and the lights of the city were beginning to shine, as though they were reflections of the stars emerging in the sky above. At that moment, it was difficult to believe that Medellín had become synonymous with bombings and violence.

The perpetrator of much of that violence was the city's most infamous son, Pablo Escobar. Escobar was head of the notorious Medellín cartel, which was responsible for most of the Colombian cocaine that was being shipped to the United States. In less than a decade, starting in the mid-1970s, Escobar had evolved from a petty criminal to Colombia's most prominent drug trafficker. He amassed a fortune of more than five billion dollars, landing him on *Forbes* magazine's list of the world's richest men. Along the way he bought police officers and judges, ruthlessly disposed of his enemies, and formed paramilitary death squads to fight against the country's leftist guerrilla groups. He even got elected to Colombia's congress in 1982 by building a Robin Hood–like image among the poor of Medellín —he spent millions of dollars building houses, schools, and recreational facilities in impoverished neighborhoods, where he is revered as a folk hero to this day. Meanwhile, on the political front, Escobar actively campaigned to have the government outlaw extradition to the United States, calling it a violation of Colombian sovereignty.

In 1986, U.S. president Ronald Reagan declared that drugs were a threat to national security. Three years later his successor, George H. W. Bush, expanded the war on cocaine by shifting the focus from interdiction at U.S. borders to intervention in drug-producing nations. The Bush administration demanded that the Colombian government arrest Escobar and other drug traffickers and extradite them to the United States to stand trial. Under intense pressure from Washington, the Colombian government agreed to go after the drug baron. Escobar and his associates, calling themselves the Extraditables, retaliated by launching an all-out offensive against the state. They planted hundreds of car bombs that killed some five hundred people, and they blew up an Avianca airliner in mid-flight, taking the lives of all 119 passengers and crew on board. In December 1993, with the help of U.S. intelligence and U.S. Army Special Operations units, Colombia's state security forces finally tracked Escobar down and killed him on a Medellín rooftop.

Almost four years to the day before Escobar's death, I was eating a fried fish dinner on a different Medellín rooftop, oblivious to the fact that I was about to sample some of the wild contradictions that epitomize life in Colombia.

Upon finishing my meal, I decided to shoot a little pool by myself before retiring to my room to catch up on sleep. I had been playing for only a few minutes when a man strolled over to me.

"Good evening," he said as he extended his right hand. "My name is Roberto. Would you allow me to buy you a beer?"

I hesitated for a moment, recalling the repeated warnings I had heard before coming to Colombia. I shook his hand and, figuring that the hotel was as safe a place as any in which to engage with strangers, replied, "Yes, thank you."

When Roberto returned with our beers, I invited him to join me in a game of pool. He was in his early thirties, about five feet seven, with wavy black hair and a thick moustache. He was attired in a blue dress shirt and jeans and shot lousy pool. Roberto explained that he was a businessman from Bogotá who had just completed his work in Medellín and was planning to return home the next day.

A couple of games and the same number of beers later, Roberto said he would like to buy me another beer in a little bar just around the corner from the hotel. Again I hesitated. I was just about to explain that I had been traveling for a day and a half with little sleep and really should get to bed, when I thought to myself, "What the hell. Why not experience a little bit of the city." I reacted as I usually did when traveling in Latin America, which was to make decisions about people based on my gut instinct. However, while my gut told me that Roberto was okay, my rational mind still remained wary as we exited the hotel and made our way around the corner to the bar.

Roberto insisted on paying for the drinks because, as he kept telling me, I was a guest in his country. The soccer game on the television behind the bar led us to talk about the "beautiful game," as it is known in Brazil, before moving on to a discussion about life in the United States. When we had finished another round of beers, Roberto suggested that we take a taxi to a bar near a university in another part of the city. I again agreed, although I was becoming suspicious of this stranger who was so eager to pay for all my drinks. After all, this was Colombia; despite my positive feeling about Roberto, part of me was still anticipating the worst.

A couple of rounds at the next bar led to another taxi, this time to a nightclub in a large warehouse-like building. It was after midnight when we entered the club, which was packed with Colombians in their twenties and thirties. The music was loud, the dance floor was full, and the overwhelming majority of the women were stunningly beautiful. We found ourselves a table and ordered beers under the watchful eye of the other patrons, who were no doubt curious about the presence of a *gringo*. Or they could simply have been taking notice of our overly casual attire, which stood in stark contrast to everyone else's immaculate sense of fashion.

Roberto and I partied until four o'clock in the morning before catching a cab back to the hotel. As we rode in the cab, I wondered what the catch might be to this wonderful night. Roberto had spent no small sum of money on our entertainment, and I couldn't help but think that the other shoe was about to drop. It seemed unlikely that he planned to rob me, given that he appeared to have plenty of disposable income.

Could it be that he was gay and intended to hit on me when we got back to the hotel? We clambered out of the taxi and staggered drunkenly into the hotel lobby. The moment of truth had arrived.

"Thank you for everything," I said, extending my hand.

"You are welcome," he replied as we shook hands. "Like I said, you are a guest in my country. I hope you enjoy the rest of your stay."

And with that, he released my hand, turned, and disappeared down the hallway. The moment of truth had come and gone in a flash. And the truth was that Roberto had simply exhibited a degree of warmth and generosity that I later realized is not uncommon among Colombians. As for me, I entered my room burdened with shame for having harbored so many suspicions throughout the night.

I awoke the next morning feeling invigorated, despite a nasty hangover, by what a wonderful country Colombia appeared to be. Little did I know that another Colombia was about to rear its ugly head.

I made my way to the immigration office in order to obtain an arrival stamp for my passport. I hadn't gotten one in Turbo, the port where I entered Colombia, based on the advice of the Panamanian official who had given me my exit stamp in the small fishing village of Puerto Obaldía. He had told me there wasn't an immigration office in Turbo. He advised that I should get my passport stamped as soon as possible in the first major city that I visited, or I'd be considered an illegal immigrant.

At the immigration office in Medellín, I explained to a woman seated at a desk just inside the door exactly what I needed, and she told me to take a seat. Less than five minutes later, I was ushered into an office and seated in front of a desk occupied by a man in his mid forties who was dressed in a military-style uniform.

"How can I help you?" he asked in a friendly tone.

"I need to get an entry stamp in my passport, because I entered the country through Turbo," I explained.

"Why didn't you get it stamped in Turbo?"

"I was told there is no immigration office in Turbo."

"Well, there is, and that is where you should have had your passport stamped. You are in Colombia illegally." His demeanor had shifted from friendly to accusatory.

"I was unaware of that. Could I please get it stamped here?" I pleaded.

"Come back and see me at four o'clock this afternoon, and I will see what I can do."

And with that, I was summarily dismissed.

I spent the next five and a half hours exploring the city, doing my best not to think about my immigration predicament. Central Medellín contained numerous modern high-rise buildings, most of which appeared to be banks. No doubt they were built with, and stocked full of, drug money. After all, Pablo Escobar had to keep his billions somewhere. The streets were full of activity, belying the fact that the city was in the midst of a wave of bombings and assassinations recently initiated by the Extraditables. I purchased a brightly colored hammock from a street vendor and ate lunch, which was more a desperate attempt to alleviate my hangover than a response to hunger.

I returned to the immigration office a little before four o'clock and was again told to have a seat. This time the wait was well over an hour. Finally the woman led me into the same office as before, and I sat in the same chair across from the same uniformed official. I waited silently while he finished his paperwork. After a few minutes, he put down his pen and looked across the desk at me.

"Your passport stamp will cost fifteen thousand pesos," he announced.

My mind rapidly converted that sum to U.S. currency, and I was shocked to realize that he was asking for seventy-five dollars. Having crossed many borders in Latin America, I knew this was exorbitant. Most entry stamps at land crossings cost about two dollars. Furthermore, given my shoestring budget, paying such a fee would mean reducing the length of my trip by a week. Clearly, this was not the official cost of an entry stamp; he was simply demanding a good old-fashioned payoff. He was fully aware that Colombian border officials would detain me if I tried to leave the country with a passport that did not contain an entry stamp. Despite my disadvantaged position, I decided that the price was too high.

"I don't have fifteen thousand pesos," I lied. "And besides, the stamp would only have cost me about five hundred pesos at the border."

"But you are not at the border," he said bluntly, and returned to his paperwork.

Aside from the scratching sound emanating from his pen on paper, the room was silent. He refused to look up at me, and I remained determined to call his bluff. I guess you could say that we were engaged in a Colombian standoff. We both stubbornly sat there for what felt like an hour, but was probably more like five minutes, before he looked up again.

"You can get your passport stamped for three thousand pesos," he said.

Fifteen dollars was still an exorbitant sum for an entry stamp, but I decided it was a manageable amount and that I shouldn't push my luck any further.

"Very well," I said as I handed him my passport. I placed three thousand pesos on his desk while he stamped my passport and handed it back to me. I left his office thinking about the two distinctly different sides of Colombia I'd experienced during the previous twenty-four hours: its generosity and its greed.

The next morning, I left Medellín by bus and headed southward along the Andes Mountains to Pasto, a city near the Ecuador border. After getting a room and showering, I made my way to a small café next door to my hotel. I ordered some food and a fruit juice, but when the waitress returned, she placed a cold beer in front of me.

"I didn't order a beer," I pointed out.

"It's from those two men in the corner," she said, pointing to two middle-aged men. I walked over and thanked them for the beer.

"It's the least we can do," they said. "After all, you are a guest in our country."

The next morning I made the short trip to the border. As I crossed into Ecuador, I thought about what a strange and exhilarating place Colombia had turned out to be. In only five days I had experienced smugglers, a corrupt official, wonderful generosity, and breathtaking mountain scenery. Furthermore, all of this had occurred against a backdrop of civil war and drug violence that, thankfully, did not touch me on this visit. The country that I was so reluctant to enter had turned out to be one of the most fascinating places I had ever visited. I promised myself that I'd learn more about Colombia.

As I boarded a bus for the Ecuadorian capital, Quito, a new excitement swept over me. I was only days away from finally experiencing the Amazon rainforest, the one place that I had wanted to visit for as long as I could remember. I had chosen Ecuador as my point of entry because other travelers had told me that in Brazil, the Amazon River is so wide that it is difficult to experience the rainforest intimately by boat. They suggested that I travel on a smaller tributary instead. I spent two days in Quito investigating the different possibilities for traveling to the Amazon region, which in Ecuador is known as El Oriente. I decided on the Napo River due to its accessibility and affordability.

I flew from Quito, which sits over nine thousand feet up in the Andes, down to a small town on the Napo River officially called Francisco de Orellana, but known locally as Coca. It was from this spot that the town's namesake, a Spanish conquistador, set off to become the first European to cross the continent from the Andes to the Atlantic on the Amazon River. And while the Spanish conquistadors were long gone, I would soon learn that a new conquest had recently occurred in that part of the Amazon. This time, instead of Spaniards wielding swords and cannons, the conquistadors were North American corporations that had come armed with oil-drilling equipment.

For the most part, Coca was hot, humid, dusty, and bustling with the energy of a frontier town. It wasn't a particularly pleasant place, and I wanted to escape down the Napo River as soon as possible. After futilely waiting three days for a supply boat that the dockworkers had told me daily would leave *"mañana,"* I decided to find an alternative mode of transportation. I met an indigenous family that was willing to sell me a dugout canoe and paddle for the equivalent of fifteen dollars. I loaded my backpack into my new canoe and set off down the Napo.

While its size pales in comparison to the Amazon River, which it runs into several hundred miles downstream, the Napo is still an impressive waterway measuring about a quarter of a mile across. I spent almost two weeks on the Napo. Aside from a couple of small villages along the river and the occasional single-family dwelling, the scenery was mostly uninhabited rainforest. I had never felt so beyond the laws of society. Alone on that river, completely surrounded by rainforest and battling currents that at one point capsized my canoe, I felt entirely at the mercy of nature. I mused that living in harmony with nature seemed the only way that a human being could survive there. Never before had I felt so insignificant.

During my journey, I stayed with three indigenous families. The most prominent indigenous groups in the Napo region are the Huaorani, Cofan, Secoya, and Quichua, all of whom succeeded in remaining isolated from the outside world until the middle of the twentieth century. By the time of my visit in 1989, many of the indigenous families living along the banks of the Napo had become accustomed to outsiders. But other clans, living deeper in the rainforest, were still relatively isolated. The indigenous people living along the Napo had retained much of their traditional way of life, but one of the families that I stayed with was markedly different from the others. That particular family consisted of a father and daughter whose melancholy and defeated air was truly disturbing. Their village was the second stop on my river journey, on the fifth day after my departure from Coca.

It was late afternoon when I stepped out of my canoe and tied it to a tree. I clambered up the riverbank with my backpack slung over my right shoulder and walked through an eerily deserted village. After a few minutes, I came across a small girl sitting in the dirt in front of a wooden house on stilts. She was five years old, with long black hair, and was dressed in a yellow and white striped shirt and white shorts. She looked up at me and proudly displayed a small green parrot held captive in her hands. A few moments later, the father appeared in the doorway of the house. I introduced myself and inquired whether there was somewhere I could spend the night and whether I could purchase some food. He told me his name was Julio and said, "You're welcome to sleep in the house next door. It is empty, but has a hammock."

There were fifteen or so abandoned houses along the riverbank and, apparently, another dozen houses situated beyond a grassy recreation area. According to Julio, most of those houses were also abandoned, with only a handful of residents remaining.

Julio invited me back to his dwelling for something to eat. To my surprise, he asked if I would like a Coca-Cola with my plate of fish, rice, and beans. His daughter, Liliana, ran over to a hut beside the house, and when she opened the door I saw that it was stocked from floor to ceiling with crates of the soft drink. Naturally curious, I asked Julio how that virtually abandoned village in the middle of the Amazon rainforest had come to be so fully stocked with bottles of Coca-Cola.

"For fifteen years, the oil company was here," Julio said. "They came and promised us jobs that would provide us a better life. And so we abandoned our traditional lifestyle of hunting, fishing, and gathering forest crops. They said that we no longer needed to do those things, because the company would provide us with all the food we needed in return for our labor. They made us believe that it would always be that way."

"What happened?" I asked.

"The oil ran out, and the company left a little more than a year ago." A touch of bitterness crept into his voice.

"And what happened to all the villagers?"

"They also left. They went looking for work elsewhere. Some are in Coca, some in Lago Agrio, and some in Quito. It was difficult to return to our old way of life, because the animals were gone and the oil had polluted the forest and the streams. Also, many of the younger ones had no interest in learning the old ways after experiencing the things that the company had provided, such as alcohol, Coca-Cola, canned food, electricity, and many other things that we had never seen before. My wife was one of those who left. She went to Quito because she didn't like it here anymore."

I sat there astonished.

"So all this Coca-Cola is left from when the company was here?" I asked.

"Yes," Julio replied. "My job was to run the store that sold Coca-Cola and other things that the company brought in on its boats. Now all I have left is the Coca-Cola."

Tragically, Julio's story was not unique. I later learned that U.S.-based multinational oil companies, including Texaco, Occidental, Conoco, Amoco, ARCO, Unocal, and Mobil, had been operating throughout the Napo region since the 1960s, with devastating consequences for the indigenous population and the rainforest.

One famous former oilman who was instrumental in petroleum development in South America was Nelson Rockefeller.

He worked in Venezuela for the family-owned Standard Oil Company before being appointed assistant secretary of state for Latin American affairs by President Harry S. Truman. Rockefeller continued to play an instrumental role in U.S. policy decisions pertaining to the so-called development and modernization of Latin America under the Eisenhower administration. From the perspective of the indigenous Huaorani, however, Rockefeller's influence on a missionary organization called the Summer Institute of Linguistics (SIL) would prove devastating.

SIL sent missionaries to remote areas of the Amazon in order to "civilize" the natives by translating the Bible into indigenous languages. According to Rockefeller biographer Gerard Colby, Latin America's business-friendly rulers—who were often Rockefeller's allies—would hire SIL missionaries to pacify the indigenous peoples in order to ensure that U.S. corporations could safely access valuable natural resources.

After Texaco struck oil in the Ecuadorian Amazon in the 1960s, the company met a lot of resistance from indigenous groups, including the Huaorani. SIL missionaries went ahead of oil company crews to advise the Huaorani to surrender. The Huaorani initially resisted, sometimes violently. In response, SIL used modern technology, including radio transmitters and loudspeakers, to awe the indigenous population into believing that the Christian God was all-powerful. The missionaries ultimately succeeded in subduing several clans. Eventually the oil company gained control of traditional Huaorani lands, and over the next twenty years Texaco's operations in the Ecuadorian Amazon spilled more than one and a half times as much oil as the Exxon Valdez disaster in Alaska.

The repercussions of that conquest were what I was witnessing in that desolate indigenous village, whose only remaining symbol of its "modernization" was countless crates of Coca-Cola.

When I awoke the next morning, I decided to explore the

village. I wandered across the recreational field and past the abandoned buildings that lined one side of it. At the other end of the field was another collection of dwellings similar to those on the riverbank. All but two of the houses were abandoned. Three men and two women were the sole remaining residents in that section of the village.

It was about nine o'clock in the morning when I came across the three men, all of whom appeared to be in their fifties, sitting in front of one of the houses. They greeted me and invited me to join them for a drink. I sat with them but declined the drink they offered, some form of moonshine. I quickly realized that they had either been drinking all night or had started very early that morning, as their words were slurred and they were unsteady on their feet. The women, meanwhile, appeared to be busying themselves with chores inside the house.

The conversation began pleasantly enough as we discussed my journey down the river, but then things began to turn ugly. The drunkest of the three men stood up, grabbed his machete, and launched into a rant against U.S. oil companies.

"Those sons of bitches have ruined us. They came here and ruined our land, our water, and our community. If there were an American here right now, I'd cut his head off," he raged, swirling his machete around recklessly.

Luckily, I had introduced myself as a British citizen and hadn't told them that I actually lived in the United States. As the other two men tried to calm down the inebriated machete wielder, I excused myself and got up to leave. But the angry drunk would have none of it. He had a new audience upon which to vent his anger and resentment, and he was not about to let me slip away. Grabbing the front of my shirt and waving the machete a little too close to my head for comfort, my embittered host continued with his anti-American rant. I again tried to take my leave before he decided that a British head would suffice in the absence of an American one.

Finally his friends got him back into his chair, and I quickly bid them farewell and made my escape. Not wanting to appear panicked, I walked as fast as I could without breaking into a run. As I made my way toward the recreation field, I repeatedly glanced over my shoulder to ensure that I was not being followed. I spent the rest of the day on the riverbank, hoping that the three drunken men would not decide to venture over to that side of the village—and they didn't.

The next morning I said goodbye to Julio and Liliana and resumed my journey down the Napo River. Alone in my canoe, I struggled to come to terms with the devastation visited on that small indigenous community, first by the arrival of the oil company and then by its departure.

The Fourth Hour

1:00 p.m., August 16, 2006

I look across the room at my guard and wonder whether time is passing as slowly for him as it is for me. A break in the monotony arrives with lunch, as the teenage girl hands me a plate of chicken, rice, and beans along with a cup of juice. I suddenly realize how hungry I am and quickly devour the plate's contents. My hosts and my guard are eating outside at the long wooden table next to the kitchen. I carry my empty plate and cup over to them and ask to use the bathroom. The teenage girl points to a small cement-walled structure. It contains two cubicles: one is a toilet and the other a shower. Two giant plastic tubs sitting on top of the corrugated tin roof capture rainwater, which by the force of gravity flows down the pipes that service the toilet and shower. After relieving myself, I return to the kitchen area, and the guard approves my request to walk around outside the house as long as I remain inside the fence.

The light rain that was intermittent during the morning has ended, and the sun is beginning to break through the clouds. I look out beyond the fence at the sun's rays shining on the coca plants growing in the surrounding fields. At the end of one field is a small structure consisting of a corrugated tin roof perched atop several wooden posts. Three men working inside are processing coca leaves into coca paste, the first step in making cocaine. Every so often, other individuals arrive at this lab from beyond the tree line, carrying large sacks of just-harvested coca leaves on their backs. The brown coca paste produced in this lab, and the labs of thousands of other farmers who depend on coca cultivation for their economic survival, is sold to larger jungle labs for processing into cocaine. From those remote labs, drug traffickers ship the finished product to North America and Europe. Despite almost twenty years of waging a war on drugs in Colombia, the U.S. government has failed to stem the flow of cocaine to U.S. cities. In fact, Colombia still produces 90 percent of the cocaine sold in the United States.

With massive support from the United States, the Colombian government successfully dismantled Pablo Escobar's Medellín cartel in the early 1990s and its rival, the Cali cartel, a few years later. While these steps were viewed as major successes in the war on drugs, they did not diminish the amount of cocaine being produced in Colombia. Dozens of smaller cartels, many of them linked to right-wing paramilitary groups, simply filled the void left by the demise of the country's two most infamous drug-trafficking organizations.

Meanwhile, by the late 1990s, the rebel group FARC was profiting, through taxation, from a dramatic increase in the amount of coca being cultivated in areas of southern Colombia under its control, particularly in the departments of Putumayo and Caquetá in the country's Amazon region. The additional revenues had allowed the FARC to better train and equip its fighters and to increase its troop strength from just over three thousand fighters at the end of the 1980s to eighteen thousand a decade later. By the close of the century, the guerrillas were regularly defeating the Colombian army in large battles and even attacking and capturing military bases in southern Colombia.

The U.S. government responded by shifting the target of its drug-war strategy from cocaine traffickers to coca growers in FARC-controlled regions. In January 2000, President Bill Clinton announced a five-year, multibillion-dollar counternarcotics initiative called Plan Colombia. The dramatic increase in funding to Colombia made the country the third-largest recipient of U.S. military aid, behind Israel and Egypt. The principal objective of Plan Colombia was to reduce coca cultivation by 50 percent in five years. More than 70 percent of the U.S. aid was earmarked for the Colombian military so that it could conduct massive aerial fumigation campaigns against coca crops in an attempt to undercut the funding that the guerrillas earned from the coca trade. At the same time, the newly strengthened Colombian military aimed to gain control of the 40 percent of the country controlled by the FARC.

Most coca farmers live in remote regions in southern and eastern Colombia. Many farmers need to grow coca in order to earn a living, because decades of government neglect have failed to provide the necessary infrastructure to make it possible to transport perishable food crops from these remote regions to distant markets. The average coca farmer owns about ten acres of land, lives in a wooden shack with no running water, and perhaps enjoys a few hours of electricity each evening courtesy of a small gasoline generator. Not only do coca farmers earn the least amount of profit among all those engaged in the production, trafficking, and sale of cocaine, but they are also the most vulnerable link in the chain because of their poverty and lack of mobility. Even with the widespread cultivation of coca, 85 percent of rural Colombians live in poverty. And at the close of the twentieth century, those poor farmers became the principal target in the U.S. war on drugs.

During the 1990s, I became a U.S. citizen and visited Latin America on two more occasions, which prompted me to return to school to study international politics and Latin American history. I also married Jacqueline Gentile, a New Yorker I'd met at a friend's New Year's Eve party in Brooklyn. Although she had no background in Latin America, Jacqui was very supportive of my work as an independent journalist during our time together, when I often struggled to earn a living.

When Clinton announced Plan Colombia in January 2000, I was working part-time as an assistant editor for the New York–based magazine *NACLA Report on the Americas.* Within a week I launched an online publication called *Colombia Report*—renamed *Colombia Journal* in 2003—with the goal of informing the U.S. public about its government's escalating role in Colombia's civil conflict. I felt that by investigating the escalating U.S. military intervention in Colombia, I could in some small way make amends for my failure to question the U.S. role in El Salvador after I was released from prison in that country. The title of the first article I penned for *Colombia Report* asked, "Are We 'Salvadorizing' Colombia?"

Because the perspectives of the Colombian government, the military, the U.S. embassy, and business elites dominated mainstream U.S. media coverage of the conflict, and because foreign correspondents for mainstream media outlets reported almost exclusively from the Colombian capital, Bogotá, I decided to conduct almost all of my work in Colombia's rural conflict zones in order to present perspectives that rarely received exposure. In other words, I wanted to go beyond Bogotá's relatively safe confines to investigate how Colombia's conflict was affecting rural Colombians. I wanted to understand the socioeconomic conditions that had led so many Colombian farmers to become dependent on the cultivation of coca. And I sought to probe behind the mainstream media headlines, which mostly reiterated the official line while failing to provide any analysis of the political, social, and economic problems that lay at the root of the conflict.

In June 2000, I arrived in Colombia for my first visit as a

journalist. My objective was to investigate the peace process between the government of Colombian president Andrés Pastrana and the FARC and to elicit feedback about the proposed Plan Colombia. In November 1999, just after assuming office, Pastrana had withdrawn all military and police personnel from a Switzerland-sized area in the department of Caquetá and turned it over to the rebels as a safe haven in which to conduct talks. Negotiators for the two sides were meeting regularly in the safe haven, which was officially called the *zona de despeje*, or "cleared zone," but was unofficially known as Farclandia. Meanwhile, there was no cease-fire agreement between the government and the guerrillas, so the conflict continued to rage throughout the rest of the country.

In addition to the FARC, a much smaller guerrilla group in Colombia was also seeking to overthrow the government. The ELN (Ejército de Liberación Nacional, or National Liberation Army) was formed in 1964 by middle-class intellectuals who were influenced by the Cuban Revolution and by radical Catholic priests who practiced liberation theology. The latter doctrine called for the clergy to prioritize the physical, or "earthly," needs of the poor along with their spiritual needs. As a result of liberation theology, many priests in Latin America began fighting against the social and political injustices that were so prevalent throughout the region. The influence of religion on the ELN was a significant contributing factor to the rebel group's decision not to profit from the drug trade. In contrast to the FARC, which became militarily stronger throughout the 1990s due to revenues generated from taxing large-scale coca production and cocaine processing labs, the ELN struggled to survive on the battlefield.

While the FARC and ELN have been fighting the Colombian military for more than four decades, they have also had to contend with another enemy that emerged in the early 1980s. Drug traffickers, particularly the leaders of the Medellín and Cali cartels, began organizing private paramilitary armies to protect themselves and their families from being kidnapped by guerrillas. But drug traffickers weren't the only ones forming paramilitary groups. The Colombian military, wealthy businesspeople, and the traditional landowning elite also established militias to combat the guerrillas. The ideology of these right-wing death squads was dominated by fanatical anticommunism. Consequently, they sought to rid Colombia of any perceived communist subversion. In the eyes of the paramilitaries, a subversive was any individual or group that sought to achieve social change, including those whose activities were nonviolent. As a result, unionists, community leaders, teachers, students, leftist politicians, human rights workers, peasant and indigenous organizers, and others living in rebel-controlled regions have been victimized by "dirty war" tactics that include murder, forced displacement, disappearances, and kidnapping.

In 1997, paramilitary leader Carlos Castaño formed a new national organization that brought the country's regional militias together under a single command structure. This new paramilitary grouping was called the AUC (Autodefensas Unidas de Colombia, or United Self-Defense Forces of Colombia). A few years later, Castaño himself acknowledged that 70 percent of the AUC's funding came from drug trafficking.

More troubling than the paramilitaries' link to drug trafficking was the violence they perpetrated. During the 1990s, more than forty thousand Colombians were killed in the armed conflict. According to Colombian and international human rights groups and even the U.S. State Department, paramilitaries closely allied with the Colombian military were responsible for 78 percent of the country's human rights abuses, including an overwhelming majority of the massacres. Amazingly, when I arrived in Colombia in June 2000, the FARC and the ELN were on the U.S. State Department's list of foreign terrorist organizations, but the AUC was not. The paramilitary group didn't make it onto the list until September 2001.

In Bogotá, I encountered many Colombians who were critical of both the FARC and the peace process. One conversation with a thirty-eight-year-old upper-middle-class businesswoman named Ana epitomized the attitude of many wealthier Bogotanos. Ana and I were sitting on the patio of a bar overlooking Parque 93, a small park surrounded by upscale cafés in modern and ritzy north Bogotá. Ana told me that all Colombians lived in fear of the guerrillas, and she complained that she could no longer visit her family's country home due to the risk of being kidnapped by the rebels.

"Do you believe that the FARC is fighting to improve life for poor Colombians?" I asked her.

"No. They only want power and money," she replied. "They used to have an ideology many years ago, but now they are just criminals who kidnap and kill innocent people."

I noticed that the right-wing paramilitaries were conspicuously absent from Ana's version of the conflict, and probed further. "But what about the paramilitaries? Human rights groups claim that they are responsible for most of the massacres and other killings of civilians."

"They only exist to defend people from the guerrillas," Ana insisted. Because many Colombians from her sector of society had little to fear from the paramilitaries, most of them were not unduly concerned with the role that the death squads played in the conflict. From the perspective of many in the wealthier classes, the Colombian army and its right-wing paramilitary allies were only defending innocent Colombians like Ana from Marxist guerrillas who sought to kidnap them and steal their wealth and lands.

I flew from Bogotá to San Vicente del Caguán, the de facto capital of Farclandia. After a short taxi ride from the airport, I found myself in the middle of a bustling town with a population of twenty thousand people. San Vicente's streets were no longer patrolled by government soldiers or police, but by a new unarmed civil guard and rifle-toting FARC guerrillas.

Many Colombians in Bogotá had warned me against visiting Farclandia because of the threat of rebel violence and kidnapping. But on the first of my three visits to the rebel zone, I soon discovered that many middle- and upper-class Bogotanos had little understanding of the realities of life in Farclandia—or in most other rural regions, for that matter. The reality in the rebel's safe haven was the exact opposite of what I'd been led to expect from people in Bogotá. Upon talking with local residents in San Vicente, I quickly realized that many among the town's population enjoyed living in the guerrilla zone, not necessarily because they were sympathetic to the FARC, but because the removal of the other armed combatants had led to peace in the safe haven.

When I asked Angela, a mother of three, about life in Farclandia, she declared, "Before the zone, my children could not go out after dark. Now there are no problems."

One local shopkeeper, fully conscious of the ongoing conflict in the rest of the country, concurred. "San Vicente is better under the FARC, because since the army left the region, there have been no killings. The FARC has also paved roads and improved the water. Most Colombians would love to live like this," he explained.

Others told me that they preferred the FARC's system of revolutionary justice to the endemic corruption and inefficiency that plagued Colombia's government-run legal system. In a makeshift courtroom on the outskirts of San Vicente, a FARC judge would listen to both sides of a complaint and make a ruling. Any failure to abide by a judge's ruling would result in expulsion from the rebel-controlled region. For serious crimes such as murder or rape, the FARC would sometimes apply the death penalty. One woman, who had brought a complaint against her husband for spending most of his wages on alcohol and not leaving her with sufficient funds to feed their children, explained why she preferred the FARC's model of justice. "It's better than before because it's easier, faster, and less corrupt. Two parties can present their cases, and there is always a solution. If one party doesn't have the money to pay the fine, then they can make payments over time."

A local taxi driver named Lelo Celis often worked as my driver during my three visits to Farclandia. One evening in San Vicente's central plaza, he voiced the principal concern of the town's residents. Lelo said that the people feared what might occur should the peace process collapse and the army and its paramilitary allies return to the region.

"President Pastrana has to renew the zone; otherwise Carlos Castaño and his paramilitaries will follow the army into San Vicente and target all those believed to have collaborated with the FARC during the past two years," he explained.

Lelo's words would prove tragically prescient. In October 2001, he was killed by paramilitaries.

Not everyone in San Vicente was enamored with the FARC's rule. I visited the church in the central plaza and sat down with the local priest, Father Miguel Serna, to hear his version of life under the guerrillas. While Father Serna admitted that there were no longer any killings in San Vicente and that the FARC did not interfere with the church's activities, he claimed that the rebel group's presence had led to a decline in morals among the town's younger residents.

"The children don't want to work; they'd rather join the FARC," he explained. "Many children have lost their way because they hang out on street corners admiring the guerrillas."

"Do any of the guerrillas ever attend your services?" I asked him.

"No. But I believe that all of the FARC's members are Catholics. The Marxist ideology comes from outside. They are still Catholics; they just don't practice."

"What is your relationship with the FARC's leaders?"

"I don't talk with the leaders of the FARC often, only when necessary. My leader is God. I don't view them as important."

During my first visit to Farclandia, Lelo, the taxi driver, took me and a reporter from the British *Guardian* newspaper named Duncan Campbell out to a small village called Los Pozos, where the peace talks were taking place. We drove along a dirt road that ran through large expanses of pastureland, with the Andes Mountains serving as a majestic backdrop off to our left. Those grasslands had been virgin rainforest until peasants fleeing *La Violencia* arrived to colonize the region in the late 1950s. As he drove, Lelo explained how life had improved in San Vicente since the government handed it over to the FARC.

"The guerrillas have paved many roads and are installing a new water treatment facility," he said, reiterating what I had heard from several people. As Lelo's dilapidated yellow taxi lurched from pothole to muddy pothole, I couldn't help but wonder when the rebels were going to get around to paving that particular road.

"Not only do we have peace," Lelo continued, "but the local economy is booming because of all the journalists and others that are coming here for the peace talks."

The "others" that Lelo referred to were the Colombians participating in public discussions related to the peace process. The FARC was hosting a series of public assemblies in Los Pozos; people from all sectors of society had been invited to attend in order to discuss their concerns with rebel leaders. As a result, San Vicente was frequently overrun with busloads and planeloads of businesspeople, students, community leaders, union representatives, and any other Colombians who were not too afraid of the guerrillas to journey to the remote region to add their two cents' worth to the process.

After the hour-long bumpy ride, we finally arrived in Los Pozos and came to a halt in front of a spacious compound surrounded by wire fencing. We told the young guerrilla guard at the gate that we were there to interview FARC commander Simón Trinidad, whose real name was Ricardo Palmera. The guard instructed Lelo to wait for us in the village and then led Duncan and me inside the compound to a small open-sided structure covered with a thatched roof. Commander Trinidad

was in a meeting, but we were told to sit and wait for him—
he would join us as soon as possible. A young male guerrilla
dressed in camouflage combat fatigues and toting an AK-47
assault rifle served us traditional Colombian coffee, known as
tinto, in white china cups. The scene was a little surreal, to say
the least.

After about thirty minutes, Simón Trinidad walked out of a
nearby building and strolled over to greet us. He invited us to
sit back down and, after laying his AK-47 on the table, seated
himself. The FARC commander was dressed in camouflage
combat fatigues and black rubber boots. Hanging from his
left hip was a machete encased in a decorative leather sheath.
Trinidad was one of the FARC's negotiators in the peace
process, a far cry from his days as a banker and university professor in the northern Colombian city of Valledupar in the department of Cesar.

Although the rebel group's original leaders, including
Supreme Commander Manuel "Sureshot" Marulanda, were
peasants, a second generation of FARC commanders consisted
primarily of urban intellectuals who had taken up arms in the
1980s. Trinidad epitomized the latter faction; he'd grown up in
a wealthy landowning family and obtained a university degree
in economics. After a short stint working in a bank, he began
teaching accounting at the University of Cesar. In the early
1980s, he and several other professors at the university became
active in a fledgling political party called Common Cause.
Trinidad and his associates worked with the poor in Valledupar's barrios until the army arrested the group and accused
them of being guerrillas. According to Trinidad, he and the others were interrogated and tortured for five days before being
released.

In 1984, the FARC signed a cease-fire accord with the government of President Belisario Betancur. At the same time that
the guerrillas were engaged in peace talks with the government,
various sectors of Colombia's civil society formed a political

party called the Patriotic Union (Unión Patriótica, or UP) in order to participate in elections. Trinidad and many other left-leaning intellectuals joined the UP. So did many members of the FARC. It was at this time, according to Trinidad, that he first made contact with the rebel group. The UP won twelve seats in the 1986 congressional elections; two of the victorious candidates were FARC members.

The electoral successes of the UP concerned Colombia's conservative elites, and the paramilitaries initiated a dirty war against the party. Over the next five years, more than two thousand UP members, including two presidential candidates and four elected congressmen, were assassinated. Finally, in 1990, the cease-fire and peace process collapsed when the Colombian army launched a surprise attack against the FARC's headquarters at Casa Verde in the mountains of southern Colombia. During the paramilitaries' dirty war against the UP, many members of the party fled to the jungle to join the FARC—partly to avoid assassination, but also because they had concluded that achieving social justice through democratic channels was not possible in Colombia. In 1987, Trinidad joined the exodus of UP members when he abandoned life in Valledupar and became a FARC guerrilla.

I asked Trinidad why he thought the objective of Plan Colombia was to primarily target peasant coca growers and the FARC instead of drug traffickers and the paramilitaries.

"We are fighting for a change in the Colombian economic model and for a new state to provide a better life and social justice for Colombians," the rebel commander explained. "Who are the people that are opposed to these social, economic, and political changes? They are the people who monopolize the riches and resources in Colombia. For these reasons, we are the principal target in the war against narco-traffickers. But we aren't narco-traffickers, and the peasants aren't narco-traffickers. They are using it as an excuse to fight against us."

"While the FARC might not be narco-traffickers, it does

allow farmers to cultivate coca in the regions under its control," I pointed out.

"They are obligated to cultivate illicit crops because of a government that has neglected them for many years. We have made it clear that we will not take food out of the mouth of the poor peasant. We will not leave them without jobs. The economic model of the Colombian state has caused this problem, and it is the state that has to fix the problem. We are the state's enemy, not their antinarcotics police. The state has to offer people employment, honest work, and social justice to improve their lives."

When Duncan asked why the FARC had abducted and killed three U.S. human rights activists who were working with the indigenous U'wa in northern Colombia in 1999, Trinidad simply shook his head and declared, "That was a grave mistake, a grave mistake."

After speaking with Trinidad for an hour and a half, it was evident to me that he was intelligent, personable, and very adept at handling journalists, all undoubtedly reasons for his assignment as a rebel negotiator. It was also clear that he was a passionate man. Trinidad was one of the rebel commanders who appeared to be motivated by the political struggle more than the military one. For him, guerrilla warfare was not an end in itself, but a means to achieve a more just society.

Four years after our interview, in 2004, Trinidad was arrested in Ecuador while seeking a meeting with United Nations officials to arrange a prisoner exchange between the Colombian government and the FARC. Ecuadorian authorities handed him over to the Colombian government, which later extradited him to the United States to stand trial on charges of terrorism, kidnapping, and drug trafficking.

On a subsequent visit to Los Pozos to again meet with Trinidad, I interviewed a female guerrilla guard to learn more about what it was like to be a woman in the FARC. Women constituted an estimated 30 percent of the rebel group's fighters, and many female guerrillas were present in Farclandia. The guard at the FARC compound in Los Pozos had long black hair and was dressed in plain green combat fatigues. She carried an AK-47 and a white-handled Colt 45 semiautomatic pistol, which protruded from a holster on her left hip. She was shy when I first approached her and reluctant to respond to my inquiries about why she had decided to enlist in the FARC. Nevertheless, I persisted, and slowly she began to reveal a little of her story. She told me that her name was Erika, adding that it was a nom de guerre.

"How long have you been in the FARC?" I asked her.

"Two years."

"How old were you when you joined?"

"Sixteen," she replied, making it clear that I was going to have to work hard to get anything out of her.

I persevered with my questions, and Erika eventually explained that she had fled her home in the southern department of Huila after witnessing a paramilitary massacre. But instead of joining the ranks of Colombia's internally displaced population, as so many people in that situation had done, she decided instead to join the FARC.

"It's a difficult life being a guerrilla," she explained. "There is a lot of sacrifice, like always being away from family."

"What does your family think about you being a guerrilla?"

"Mostly they agree with it, because they know why we are fighting. But it's hard for my father to accept my being in the FARC, because I'm so young."

"Do you have a boyfriend?"

"Yes, I have a boyfriend. He's twenty years old and is also a guerrilla. We have been together for the past year." A slight smile invaded her stoic expression. I sensed that a good-natured teenage girl still lurked somewhere inside that uniform.

"Do you miss doing the things that many others your age are doing, such as dressing up and going out dancing?"

"Fashion doesn't matter to me. We are focused internally, ideologically. Material objects don't interest us." And then, with another hint of a smile, she added, "But sometimes in the evenings we dance to music on Radio Resistencia."

I found it difficult to fathom a sixteen-year-old girl leaving home to live the hard life of a guerrilla in the jungle. But Erika was not an anomaly; there were thousands of young Colombian women who had chosen the same path.

In another conversation, I asked Trinidad how the FARC justified allowing children to join its ranks. He claimed that the rebel group did not allow anyone under fifteen years of age to enlist, citing Article 38 of the UN Convention on the Rights of the Child as the legal basis for the FARC's decision. And in reference to those teenagers that were old enough to join, he noted, "Many of these children don't have parents, because they were killed by the military or the paramilitaries, and so they ask the guerrillas to let them join. It sounds beautiful when you say that children shouldn't be guerrillas, but many children end up in the streets of the cities doing drugs and inhaling gasoline and glue. In the guerrillas they have dignity and respect, and we provide them with clothes, food, and education."

While Trinidad might believe that a homeless child is better off in the FARC than living in the streets, many Colombian and international human rights organizations have criticized the rebel group for its enlistment of boys and girls under the age of eighteen.

During one of my visits to Farclandia, I left the safe haven by road to interview Colombian soldiers stationed just beyond the perimeter of the rebel-controlled zone. On the outskirts of the town of Doncello, I ran into an armored unit that had turned a small farm into a temporary base. The road was lined with tanks and armored cars. Another tank was parked in the shade of a large tree in the farmyard. Two soldiers clad in green T-shirts and camouflage pants were repairing something on top of the gun turret. Another couple of soldiers were relaxing in hammocks on the porch of the farmhouse, while several more played cards nearby. They were part of a three-thousand-strong troop deployment that was awaiting orders to invade the rebel's safe haven should the peace process collapse.

As soon as the soldiers learned that I'd just come from Farclandia, they immediately became inquisitive about the guerrillas in San Vicente. To be more precise, they were curious about the female guerrillas.

"Are they beautiful?" one of them asked, as a small crowd of soldiers in their late teens and early twenties gathered around me.

"Some of them are very beautiful," I replied, eliciting hoots and whistles from my suddenly attentive audience. No doubt my response affirmed some of the fantasies that these bored young soldiers had entertained about beautiful uniformed women with guns. It soon became evident that these troops were chomping at the bit to invade Farclandia, although I never did determine whether their bravado was motivated by a thirst for blood, a wish to escape the monotony of their daily routine, or a desire to get their hands on attractive female guerrillas.

My driver and I began our return trip to Farclandia in the late afternoon, making our way through the final military checkpoint and then, a few miles down the road, stopping at the rebel roadblock just inside the safe haven. The pothole-filled paved road ran from Florencia, the capital of Caquetá, to San Vicente and represented the most significant highway in the entire Colombian Amazon region. Consequently, almost everyone entering Farclandia by road traveled along that route, including many journalists and participants in the public assemblies hosted by the FARC. To my knowledge, there were no incidents at rebel checkpoints along that road during the two and a half years that the safe haven was in existence. In fact, it was probably one of the safest stretches of highway in all of

Colombia, because the FARC was consciously trying to foster a good image for the international community.

Given that I had freely passed through that particular checkpoint unhindered on numerous trips in and out of Far-clandia, I was shocked to see the melodramatics exhibited by U.S. journalist Geraldo Rivera during his one-hour tele-vised special report titled "Colombia's Enduring Drug Wars." Rivera's special, which was broadcast on the NBC news-magazine show *Dateline* on August 31, 2001, represented one of the rare occasions when Colombia's conflict received prime-time coverage on a U.S. broadcast network.

Watching the show in my apartment in New York, I cringed when Rivera approached the rebel checkpoint at the border of Farclandia. He was sitting in the front passenger seat of the car, being filmed by a camera operator in the backseat. As the vehi-cle slowed down, Rivera turned around and began whispering into the camera, explaining that they were approaching the rebel checkpoint and that it was very dangerous to enter the FARC-controlled zone. The entire scene was focused on how brave he was to encounter the guerrillas in the jungles of Colombia; he must have known that his audience would never realize that he was actually on one of the safest sections of road in the country. Rivera's sensationalized portrayal of the conflict also reinforced the Western perception of the allegedly danger-ous and unpredictable nature of the guerrillas.

During the entire one-hour special, Rivera never once made mention of the right-wing paramilitaries, despite the fact that they were far more deeply involved in drug trafficking than the FARC and were the principal perpetrators of violence in Colombia. In fact, in the months leading up to Rivera's visit, the number of massacres perpetrated by the paramilitaries in-creased dramatically. In one month alone, according to human rights groups, paramilitaries were responsible for twenty-six massacres that resulted in the deaths of 180 civilians. And yet in Rivera's version of Colombia's conflict, the paramilitaries did not exist. Viewers of his special report were left with the distinct impression that it was simply a war being fought over drugs between the U.S.-backed Colombian government and "narco-guerrillas." This distortion and oversimplification of Colombia's conflict was not unique; it represented the norm for most mainstream U.S. media outlets.

Less than two weeks after Rivera's television special, the terror-ist attacks against the World Trade Center and the Pentagon put an end to the increased media attention that U.S. policy in Colombia had received since the implementation of Plan Colombia. Following 9/11, the Farclandia safe zone existed for only five more months, because the U.S. and Colombian gov-ernments branded the guerrillas as terrorists. At midnight on February 20, 2002, sensing the growing public frustration with the oft-stalled negotiations and following the FARC's kidnap-ping—outside the safe haven—of a Colombian senator, Presi-dent Pastrana ended the fledgling peace process by ordering the military to invade Farclandia. Government officials in Wash-ington and Bogotá, as well as the mainstream media in both countries, immediately blamed the FARC for the failure of the peace process, because the rebel group had refused to agree to a cease-fire. For its part, the FARC repeatedly stated during ne-gotiations that it would not sign a cease-fire agreement until the government dismantled the paramilitaries. The guerrilla group was not about to make the same mistake it had made in the 1980s when paramilitaries virtually eradicated the Patriotic Union Party.

When I left Farclandia at the end of my first visit in June 2000, there was still an air of optimism in Colombia regarding the peace process. I had gained some insight into the FARC's per-spective on the armed conflict and the escalating U.S. military intervention under Plan Colombia. But that was only one side of a multifaceted situation. My next trip to Colombia would allow me to witness the consequences of Plan Colombia's initial aerial fumigation campaign and to get a glimpse of the conflict through the eyes of the paramilitaries.

The Fifth Hour
2:00 p.m., August 16, 2006

Through the fence, I watch the hired coca pickers make their way toward the house. The five men and two women enter the compound, wash their hands, and sit around the wooden table situated next to the kitchen. They are talking and laughing among themselves as they eat their lunch. After thirty minutes, they exit the compound and return to work. Observing these basic activities helps me break the monotony of my captivity.

Ten minutes later, the tedium is again broken as a dark blue mud-spattered SUV pulls up to the farmhouse. I watch four uniformed guerrillas pour out of it and enter the compound. Each one shakes my hand before sitting down at the table to eat lunch.

One of the rebels invites me to sit with them while they eat. He introduces himself as Hector, and I can't help but notice that he is very fair-skinned for a Colombian. It's clear that Hector is the leader of the group and that he fancies himself as some sort of comedian or practical joker. He points to one of the two capybaras—giant South American rodents—that have been wandering around the compound all day and are currently scavenging for food scraps under the table.

"Are you hungry?" he asks me with a chuckle.

"No, thank you. I've eaten already."

"But have you ever eaten one of those?" He nods his head in the direction of the giant rodents.

"No." I'm wondering where this discussion is going.

"They're delicious," Hector says, smiling.

I just smile back, unsure whether he is serious. I feel relieved when the conversation shifts back to more familiar ground.

"So you are a journalist?" Hector asks as he gets up from the table and beckons me to follow him. We head out of the compound toward the SUV, his three comrades and their rifles following closely behind. He opens the door on the driver's side, reaches in, and pulls out my digital camera.

"How does it work?" he asks, his tone making it sound more like an order than a question.

I reach out, flick the switch that turns the camera on, and adjust a second knob to illuminate the LCD screen.

"Now just point it and press the button," I tell him.

Hector orders me to step back and then takes a photo of me.

"How do I look at the photo?" he asks.

I show him as the other rebels gather around to check out their leader's photographic prowess. I casually toss out the question that I have been waiting to ask.

"When will I be able to investigate the fumigations in this region?"

"I don't know," Hector responds. "It's not my decision. They are checking you out."

I nod my head and assume that "they" are higher-ranking members of the FARC.

Hector then asks, "How do you feel about being kidnapped?"

"I'm not crazy about the idea," I respond.

He just nods his head and smiles. Needless to say, he is not putting my mind at ease.

Hector shakes my hand one more time and then orders the others to get into the SUV. He jumps in behind the wheel and starts the engine, and they speed away as I reenter the compound under the watchful eye of my guard.

I return to my white plastic chair in the house and tell myself that Hector doesn't know anything about my fate yet; the kidnapping question was his way of playing mind games with me. But I remain concerned about what lies ahead. I hope that they take my request to work in the region up to the highest ranks of the FARC, as I'm relatively confident that one of the top commanders will be familiar with both my name and my work. Even if they don't know my work, I'm hopeful that they'll decide against harming a foreign journalist. I'm also holding out hope that the rebel commanders will approve my request to investigate the aerial fumigations, since much of my writing has questioned Washington's decision to emphasize military solutions to coca cultivation and the country's violence rather than to address the social and economic causes. My greatest fear is that my request won't make it very far up the chain of command and that a local or regional rebel leader who has no idea who I am will make some rash decision regarding my fate.

Again I try to suppress my rising anxiety. I force my thoughts back to the first time that I investigated the aerial fumigation of coca crops almost six years ago. It was also the first time that I encountered the paramilitaries.

I arrived in the town of Puerto Asís in the southern department of Putumayo two weeks after Plan Colombia's initial spraying operation had ended. I took a taxi from the small airport to the Hotel Chilimaco in the center of town. After checking in, I sat at a table in the open-air restaurant on the second floor, which overlooked the town's main intersection. I drank a refreshing guanabana juice while watching the traffic below, which was dominated by a seemingly endless stream of small motorcycles. As in San Vicente and other similar towns in the Colombian Amazon, motorcycles are the favorite mode of transportation for many locals because they are relatively cheap. It's not unusual to see a family of three piled onto a small 125cc bike.

But I wasn't in Puerto Asís to analyze the transportation habits of the local population; I was there because it was ground zero for Plan Colombia. On December 19, 2000, U.S.-piloted spray planes, supported by U.S.-supplied Black Hawk helicopter gunships, swooped down over the coca fields of Putumayo. The spraying operation lasted six weeks and, according to the Clinton administration, successfully destroyed 62,000 acres of coca.

The morning after my arrival, I found a taxi to take me thirty minutes outside of Puerto Asís to a military base that housed soldiers from the Colombian army's 24th Brigade. On the way to the base, I asked my driver about the armed groups operating in the area. He said that the guerrillas dominated in the countryside, while the army controlled the towns.

"What about the paramilitaries?" I asked.

"The paramilitaries and the army are the same. They work together to kill the guerrillas," he replied—a statement I would hear repeatedly over the years from local residents of towns throughout Colombia.

"Which group has the most support in Puerto Asís?"

"People here don't like the guerrillas, because the taxes they charge businesses are too high. The paras charge much less."

Paramilitaries belonging to the national AUC organization had arrived in Putumayo in 1998. They immediately made their presence felt through a series of massacres that left more than one hundred people dead. The paramilitaries worked closely with the army in their war against the guerrillas and suspected rebel sympathizers. It was this collusion that led my driver to state that the two were basically the same military force.

In September 2001, Human Rights Watch published a report documenting the ties between the army's 24th Brigade in Putumayo and the paramilitaries. In the report, a former bookkeeper for the AUC detailed how payments were made to soldiers in the 24th Brigade based on rank: "Each captain received between US$2,000 and US$3,000 per month. Majors got US$2,500. A lieutenant receives US$1,500. The colonels also got paid, but not directly. They would send intermediaries to pick up the cash."

The bookkeeper claimed that the AUC's budget in Putumayo amounted to $650,000 a month, and asserted that most of the revenues were generated by taxes imposed on cocaine processing labs in the areas under paramilitary control.

My driver and I arrived at the army base, which was located in the center of the small town of Santa Ana. I stepped out of the taxi, showed my press card to the guards at the gate, and told them I'd like to interview their commanding officer. I waited at the gate while one of the guards disappeared inside the base. He returned about five minutes later and, after writing my name and passport number into a logbook, asked me to follow him into the base. He led me to a bench outside a mustard-colored single-story building.

While I was waiting for my interview, a helicopter arrived, landing less than a hundred yards from me. Several uniformed Colombian soldiers climbed out of it, followed by two *gringos* in civilian clothes. I got up from the bench and started to wander toward the helicopter to get a better look, but one of several soldiers who were standing guard around the landing zone yelled at me to stop and ordered me back to my bench. Most likely, the *gringos* were either U.S. intelligence officers or military personnel.

Not long afterward, a short, stocky Colombian army officer wearing wire-rimmed spectacles exited the building and walked over to me. He stuck out his hand and introduced himself as Colonel Blas Ortíz. After some small talk, I asked Colonel Ortíz about the aerial fumigations that had just been conducted. He explained that the spraying had targeted only industrial-sized coca farms of more than twenty-five acres. The colonel admitted that some food crops had been sprayed, but they didn't belong to peasants.

"One of the techniques used by the big coca growers is to grow two acres of yucca or bananas in the middle of one hundred and twenty-five acres of coca," he explained. "These two acres don't belong to the peasants; they belong to the big coca grower. They use this strategy to avoid being fumigated."

I had already heard from several locals that most of the coca in the region was cultivated by peasants on small farms that averaged about ten acres in size, and so I was skeptical of the colonel's claims.

Back in Puerto Asís, I visited the office of the National Plan for Alternative Development (Plan Nacional de Desarrollo Alternativo, or PLANTE), the government agency in charge of the alternative crop program. I was immediately led into the office of Dr. Ruben Dario Pinzón, the head of the agency's operation in Putumayo. The large floor fan near the open window sent a relatively refreshing breeze in my direction—a welcome relief from the heat and humidity outside. Dr. Pinzón told me that, under Plan Colombia, farmers could sign social pacts that called for them to voluntarily uproot their coca plants in return for a thousand dollars in materials, technical assistance, and a promise that their alternative crops would not be fumigated. PLANTE was responsible for providing the aid to those farmers who signed the social pacts. But although some peasants in Putumayo had signed social pacts, many others remained distrustful of a government that had repeatedly failed to deliver on past promises.

As one local resident told me, "Historically, the government has never helped anyone here. People helped themselves, and with coca the economy became good. Now the government wants to help, but people are afraid it will ruin the economy."

Dr. Pinzón's account of the fumigations, which was very different from the one I had heard from Colonel Ortíz an hour earlier, appeared to validate the fear of government intervention. "Peasants financed by PLANTE have been fumigated because they are in a small area in the middle of coca growers," Dr. Pinzón told me. "It is impossible to protect them, because the pilots can't control exactly where they fumigate, so they fumigate the whole area."

As so often happens in Colombia, particularly where politics and the conflict are concerned, I had heard two distinctly different takes on the aerial fumigation campaign. Furthermore, government representatives had provided both views. Clearly, the only way to determine the consequences of the spraying would be to visit coca-growing areas myself.

I walked back to my hotel and, after showering and changing into clean clothes, headed to the restaurant to rendezvous with Eros Hoagland, a photojournalist I had met in Farclandia a week earlier. We had arranged to meet at the Hotel Chilimaco before traveling together to the Guamuez Valley, the principal region targeted by the fumigations. Eros, from California, is the son of war photographer John Hoagland, who was killed by the Salvadoran army in 1984 while covering that country's civil conflict.

The next day, Eros and I set off by car on the ninety-minute drive to the town of La Hormiga. The number of coca fields alongside the road increased dramatically as we got closer to our destination. Most of the coca bushes were covered with green leaves and clearly had not been affected by the fumigations. We also passed numerous burned-out vehicles; they had been set ablaze by FARC guerrillas because their drivers had ignored an armed blockade implemented by the rebels a few months earlier to protest Plan Colombia. Signs of rebel activity were also evident where the oil pipeline that ran parallel to the road had been bombed, blackening the surrounding earth and the dirt road. We were clearly in a conflict zone.

Soon after pulling into La Hormiga, we learned that fifteen peasants had been massacred the previous day in the nearby hamlet of Los Angeles. Eros and I made our way to the local army base to find more information. There we met with Major Silva, the commander of the three hundred soldiers from the 24th Brigade that were stationed in La Hormiga. He said there were reports that fifteen people had been killed in a massacre and another 250 had been displaced.

"Who committed the massacre?" I asked.

"The guerrillas," he replied without hesitation.

I later came to realize that the Colombian army's modus operandi was to immediately blame the guerrillas for any killings that occurred in rural regions, unless there was clear evidence to the contrary. In some cases, the army's rush to judgment proved valid; but in many instances, evidence later emerged implicating the paramilitaries, or sometimes even the military itself, in the atrocity.

Major Silva told us that six of the dead bodies had been taken to the nearby village of El Placer. Eros and I found a taxi driver willing to take us to the village, which was only fifteen minutes away and under the control of the paramilitaries. On the drive to El Placer, we saw our first evidence of the aerial fumigations. Numerous fields along the road were full of dead cornstalks and yucca plants. Directly across the road from one fumigated cornfield were hundreds of green coca bushes, apparently untouched by the spraying.

Just outside El Placer, we stopped at a paramilitary checkpoint. Four partly uniformed, heavily armed men asked for our identification and then wanted to know what we were doing there.

"We heard that some of the bodies from the massacre are at the cemetery, and we would like to see them," Eros explained.

The paramilitaries allowed us to pass, and we quickly located the cemetery.

It was late in the afternoon when we walked into the cemetery, passing rows of graves until we reached a building. An old man sat in a chair in the middle of the structure; several other people hung around, whispering quietly to each other. None of them appeared to be mourning. The corpses of two men and one woman were lying on the cement floor, waiting to be claimed by loved ones; relatives had already retrieved the other three bodies.

The corpse nearest the front of the building was that of a shirtless, skinny, middle-aged man dressed in baggy beige trousers. He'd been shot in the side of the face. Next to him was the body of a short woman, dressed in a blue T-shirt, with a bullet hole in her cheek. Most disturbing, however, was her rounded belly pushing out against the dirty blue shirt. I turned to one of the women nearby to confirm the obvious.

"Was she pregnant?" I asked.

"Yes," the woman replied. "Eight months."

"Do you know her?"

"Not really," she said. Pointing to the shirtless corpse, she explained, "They are a couple. They are from Ecuador and work as coca pickers. I don't think they have any family here."

"What will happen to their bodies if nobody comes to collect them?" I asked.

"They will be buried in the ground at the rear of the cemetery."

I walked over to the third corpse, that of a large man dressed in a bright orange T-shirt and blue jeans. His hands were tied together at the wrists with a white plastic bag, and his face had been pummeled beyond recognition—caved in by repeated blows from a hammer, a large stone, or some other blunt object. I turned to the old man and asked whether he knew who had committed the massacre. He just shrugged his shoulders as if to say, "Who knows?"

"We heard that fifteen people were killed. Where are the other bodies?" I asked.

"They haven't found them yet," he replied.

After taking several photos of the bodies, Eros and I made our way back to the car. I had never before seen corpses that were the result of violent deaths. I'd anticipated feeling nauseated, at the very least; but looking at the three bodies in the cemetery, I didn't feel anything. I felt as if I should have felt something, but I didn't.

Back in La Hormiga, Eros and I dropped off our gear in our respective rooms and met in the restaurant across the street for dinner. We didn't talk much as we ate, and while I couldn't stop visualizing those three dead bodies, I was surprised to find that it didn't disrupt my appetite.

Later I realized that my emotional reaction, or lack thereof, was related to my father's death, which had occurred only five weeks earlier. He was sixty-seven years old when he died from a heart attack on Christmas Eve in 2000. I'd stayed with my mother for three weeks after the funeral to offer her support and to help her organize his affairs. During this time I had unknowingly suppressed many emotions related to my father's death. In fact, I was still in a state of emotional shock when I arrived in Colombia and saw the bodies of the massacre victims.

It wasn't until I was back home in New York more than a month later that my emotions finally came to the surface. There were days when I would find myself sitting on the couch in my living room, crying. At first I didn't understand why I was crying; the tears just seemed to come out of nowhere. But then I realized that thoughts of my father would always enter my mind during these emotional outbursts. I was finally grieving the loss of my father. For the first time, the full impact of his death, of the fact that I would never see his face again or hear his voice again, overwhelmed me. Suddenly I was feeling an enormous emptiness, and there was nothing I could do about it but cry.

Following dinner in that La Hormiga restaurant, Eros and I prepared for an interview that we were scheduled to conduct at seven o'clock that evening with the AUC's top commander in Putumayo. The meeting had been arranged by a contact of

Eros's. It was to take place at a restaurant located on the second floor of a building on the town's main street, only a hundred yards or so from the army base.

We arrived a little before seven o'clock, but the door at street level was locked and there were no lights on inside the restaurant. We stood there on the sidewalk and waited, not sure what was happening. Perhaps the meeting had been cancelled, we thought. But just then a white pickup truck, with two men in the cab and two more standing in the rear, pulled up next to us. The two large men in the back of the truck jumped down to the sidewalk, and the man in the passenger seat emerged. He was the AUC commander. His body was chiseled, but not overly large, and he was neatly attired in a T-shirt and jeans, with gold jewelry adorning his neck, wrists, and fingers. His head was shaved, making him look a bit like a young, darker-skinned Yul Brynner.

The door to the restaurant was suddenly opened from the inside; the restaurant had apparently been closed for the specific purpose of hosting our meeting, giving the whole scene a very clandestine feel. We all made our way to a long table surrounded by eight chairs. The commander sat at the head of the table and introduced himself as Luis Enrique, alias "the Cobra." He was twenty-eight years old and commanded six hundred AUC fighters in Putumayo. The Cobra's demeanor wasn't particularly friendly, although he was courteous. I'm not sure whether the tension I felt actually stemmed from the atmosphere in that room or just from the fact that I was fully conscious of what this man was capable of doing. After all, he had ordered several brutal massacres, some of which had been carried out using machetes and chainsaws.

The Cobra explained that the AUC had arrived in Putumayo two years earlier, but he personally had arrived from Urabá only a year ago.

"What is the mission of the Self-Defense Forces here in Putumayo?" I asked.

"We have to provide security for the population. We didn't come to Putumayo because there is coca here. We came because the guerrillas are here. I don't want you to think that we are narco-traffickers just because we ask for taxes from coca growers in order to maintain my men," he explained.

"Why did you join the paramilitaries?" I asked, and immediately realized that I had used the wrong term.

"We are not paramilitaries! Paramilitaries are people sent by the government. We are the Self-Defense Forces of Colombia!" he declared, clearly irritated by my choice of words. He went on, "I joined because the government wasn't able to protect our rights. The Self-Defense Forces were not created because the guerrillas existed; they were created because the government couldn't defend the people's rights."

Treading carefully after my verbal blunder, I asked him about the massacre that had occurred in the hamlet of Los Angeles the previous day.

"The guerrillas killed fifteen peasants. They were just peasants, not members of the Self-Defense Forces. The massacre was committed by the FARC's 48th Front, and they killed them with stone hammers and guns."

I then raised the question I was most nervous about asking. "Why do human rights organizations claim that the Self-Defense Forces are responsible for the majority of the human rights violations in Colombia?"

"It is very simple," he replied, apparently unperturbed. "It is not a secret that the NGOs [nongovernmental organizations] are managed by guerrillas. NGOs are giving money to certain people so they'll make claims against army generals. We are just working to defend our rights, to defend the peasants, and to defend the people here. The NGOs are managed by the subversives."

The Cobra's answer was the AUC's official line, claiming that those who work for NGOs, particularly human rights groups, are guerrillas. It is this assumption that lies at the root of the paramilitaries' justification for waging a dirty war against anyone who works to address issues related to social justice.

I plowed ahead with another sensitive question, asking the Cobra whether he worked with members of the Colombian military in Putumayo. He denied any collusion between his men and the military, and then went so far as to claim that the government was more focused on targeting the Self-Defense Forces than the guerrillas.

We thanked the Cobra for meeting with us, and Eros asked whether it would be possible to photograph some of his uniformed fighters. He told us to go to the small town of La Dorada the next day, ask for Commander Guillermo, and tell him that Commander Enrique had sent us. With that we all shook hands, and Eros and I left the restaurant and made our way back to the hotel.

The next morning we found a driver to take us across the border into Ecuador to search for Colombians who had been displaced by the fumigations and by violence. On the way back we planned to stop in La Dorada to photograph the paramilitaries. It was a forty-minute drive from La Hormiga to the small village of San Miguel on the Colombian side of the border, and along the way we witnessed more devastation wrought by the spraying of not only coca bushes but also food crops. Several families who had abandoned their lands after they were fumigated weeks earlier were now living in run-down wooden shacks in San Miguel.

I spoke with a middle-aged woman named Cecilia who was cooking and serving food in a small roadside stall near the bridge that linked Colombia to Ecuador. Cecilia told me that she, along with her husband and three children, had abandoned their farm in La Dorada a month earlier after it had been fumigated.

"Why did you have to leave?" I asked.

"Everything was killed—our corn, yucca, everything."

Cecilia explained how the members of her family were now dependent on the small amount of money they earned selling home-cooked food to travelers crossing the border. I purchased a few *arepas,* Colombian-style corn tortillas, and wished her luck.

Back in the car, we headed across the bridge into Ecuador and drove another forty minutes through the rainforest to the town of Lago Agrio. There were no border guards at the bridge or at any point along the road to the Ecuadorian Amazon's principal oil town, which had become a prime destination for Colombian refugees. Lago Agrio had the air of a wild frontier town; Colombians constituted a significant percentage of the population, although refugees were not the only ones who crossed the border. Colombian guerrillas and paramilitaries, dressed in civilian clothes, routinely visited Lago Agrio to purchase supplies and to obtain some respite from the conflict. That respite was not always easy to come by, and the presence of so many armed Colombians had contributed significantly to the remote Amazon outpost's having the highest number of murders per capita in Ecuador.

Eros and I located the church building that contained the office of the local coordinator for Colombian refugees. A middle-aged woman sitting at a desk listened to our request to speak with the coordinator and then introduced us to Father Edgar Piños, a priest who oversaw the church's operations to aid the refugees. I asked Father Piños how many Colombian refugees had arrived in Lago Agrio since the start of the fumigations two months earlier.

"We have 698 documented refugees here in four centers," he replied. "But there are more than two thousand here in total. Many are too afraid to officially register."

"What kind of aid are they receiving?"

"The church tries to help them address their psychological traumas and with filing for asylum. Meanwhile, Doctors Without Borders provides health care, and the Red Cross donates food."

"What kinds of traumas are the refugees suffering from?"

"They are afraid and feel insecure because they are no longer in their own country," Father Piños explained. "They don't know when they will be able to return home, or worse, whether they will be forced to return home before it's safe."

Father Piños refused our request to speak with some of the refugees, maintaining that they felt vulnerable and he didn't want to add to their anxiety. Eighteen months later, the United Nations High Commissioner for Refugees would report that the number of Colombian refugees that had filed for asylum in Ecuador had surpassed five thousand, while thousands more who were too afraid to file had also fled across the border— most to Lago Agrio.

It was early afternoon when we left Lago Agrio and headed back to Colombia. By the time we crossed the border, the heat and humidity were causing both Eros and I to doze off in the car. I was sitting in the back, and Eros was in the passenger seat directly in front of me. I awoke as the car came to a halt and tapped Eros on the shoulder to wake him up. He opened his eyes just as the barrel of an AK-47 assault rifle came through the open window, pointing directly at his head.

"Who are you and what are you doing here?" demanded the man at the other end of the rifle.

He was a fully uniformed AUC fighter. We showed him our passports and explained that we were journalists looking for Commander Guillermo. He handed our passports to a paramilitary fighter standing next to him, who looked at them and then spoke into a two-way radio. A couple of minutes later, he handed the passports back to us and told us to wait, at which point we got out of the car and stood in the shade.

When Commander Guillermo arrived in a white pickup truck, we told him that Commander Enrique had given us permission to photograph his fighters. After communicating through his own handheld radio, he asked us to get back into our car and to follow him.

We drove to a field on the edge of La Dorada. The grass was knee-high, and there were numerous trees scattered throughout the field, but basically it had good sight lines from the edge of the village to the beginning of the rainforest two hundred yards or so away. A small encampment with a black plastic tentlike shelter was situated in the shade of a very large tree, and about a dozen or so uniformed paramilitary fighters were in the camp. Some wore black AUC armbands, and all but two insisted on covering their faces with bandanas or scarves when we began taking photos. The only one who didn't carry an AK-47 assault rifle was armed with an M60 heavy machine gun instead. The heavy machine gunner was the most sinister looking of the bunch. He wore a red beret and was one of the two not concerned with concealing his identity.

While we looked on and took photographs, Guillermo put his fighters through some military exercise. We didn't know it at the time, but we were standing in the midst of several mass graves containing victims of paramilitary massacres. Five years after our visit, prosecutors would unearth the remains of fifty-eight people murdered by the very same paramilitaries that we were photographing. More than two hundred more bodies would be discovered in mass graves in surrounding villages. When we were finished, we thanked Guillermo, climbed back into our car, and returned to La Hormiga.

The next morning I left the hotel alone to conduct some research on the fumigations. My first stop was the local health clinic, where I asked Doctor Edgar Perea about children who had allegedly become sick from the chemicals used in the spraying.

"I have treated people with skin rashes, stomachaches, and diarrhea caused by the fumigation," he said. "And I have treated five children affected by the fumigation in the past twenty-five days. I don't know how many the other doctors have treated."

Given that most sick children in the more remote rural regions probably never made the trip to La Hormiga to see a doctor, it was safe to assume that Doctor Perea and his colleagues had treated only a small fraction of those affected by the fumigations. From the extensive destruction of crops that I had seen throughout the Guamuez Valley and the illnesses described by Doctor Perea, it appeared that more than a common herbicide was being used in the fumigation campaign.

The U.S. government had repeatedly pointed out that glyphosate, the chemical used in the fumigations, was the most widely used herbicide in the world. In 2000, the U.S. State Department even claimed that glyphosate was no more toxic than "common salt, aspirin, caffeine, nicotine and even Vitamin A." But scientists in the United States, Europe, and Colombia have suggested that such statements were little more than misinformation that sought to hide the true nature of the chemical concoction being used in Colombia. I thought back to a comment that FARC Commander Iván Ríos had made when I interviewed him in Farclandia prior to going to Putumayo. Ríos had told me, "They are fumigating with glyphosate mixed with a special ingredient that sticks to the leaves and is more harmful to the people." I had originally dismissed the remark as likely rebel propaganda. But when I later looked into Ríos's claim, I found that Plan Colombia was not using the conventional glyphosate manufactured by Monsanto under the brand name Roundup, but rather was using a stronger version called Roundup Ultra.

I also discovered that there was indeed a "special ingredient" being added to the glyphosate. The special ingredient was Cosmo-Flux 411F, which "makes the glyphosate heavier and stickier, making it adhere better to the coca plants," according to Ricardo Vargas, a researcher for Acción Andina, an organization studying drug policy in the Andes. Additionally, Doctor

Elsa Nivia, Colombia's regional director of the Pesticide Action Network, claimed Cosmo-Flux does more than just make glyphosate adhere better to plants. She said it "substantially increases the biological activity of the agrochemicals, allowing better results with smaller doses." However, the fumigation campaign in Colombia was not using smaller doses of glyphosate in order to make more efficient use of the herbicide; Cosmo-Flux was being added to a dosage that was five times greater than that recommended by the manufacturer. Furthermore, it was a chemical concoction that had never been approved for use in the United States.

Several years later, the harmful effects of the chemicals were revealed in a study conducted by the Human Molecular Genetics Unit at the Catholic University of Ecuador. Blood samples showed that Ecuadorians who lived along the border and had been sprayed by fumigations intended to target Colombian coca farms suffered 800 percent more chromosome damage than Ecuadorians living more than fifty miles from the border. Those affected reported intestinal problems, vomiting, diarrhea, headaches, skin and eye infections, dizziness, blurred vision, respiratory problems, and other maladies. But it was the chromosome damage that most troubled researcher César Paz because, as he pointed out, "the damage found in the genetic material of those analyzed can develop into cancer and miscarriages."

Shortly after I left the health clinic in La Hormiga, I heard the distinctive sound of helicopters. A moment later, I saw a U.S.-supplied Huey helicopter descending toward the army base a little further along the street. Close behind it came another helicopter, and then another, while a couple more circled overhead.

I made my way to the base and easily gained access, since I had been there two days earlier. General Antonio Ladron de Guevara, the commander of the 24th Brigade, had arrived from the departmental capital, Mocoa, to direct one thousand counterinsurgency troops in an operation to retrieve the remaining bodies from the massacre site in the hamlet of Los Angeles.

I stood next to the tall, slender general and watched wave after wave of helicopters touch down to pick up squads of soldiers in order to transport them to Los Angeles. I asked the general whether I could accompany the troops on one of the helicopters, but he refused, saying that I could fly in with him once the area had been secured. I inquired about the army's relations with peasants in remote communities like Los Angeles.

"We have a situation where there is much disinformation, making it difficult for us to gain the confidence of the people in these areas," the general explained.

He went on to describe how the rebels and the peasants are sometimes the same people. "It is difficult because the guerrillas kill four or five people and then change into civilian clothes and act like they don't know anything about what happened."

Growing restless, I sought out Eros, and we found a driver willing to take us to Los Angeles. The road to the hamlet was a narrow dirt road that cut through the rainforest. As we neared the first house in the hamlet, a group of soldiers ordered our driver to stop. We told them that we were journalists wishing to accompany the operation. With surprising ease, we obtained permission to observe the house-to-house search for bodies. The army patrol that we were accompanying was searching for massacre victims in the hamlet, while other soldiers were situated in the rainforest perimeter to defend against a guerrilla ambush.

The homes in Los Angeles were not particularly close together—each was surrounded by land used for grazing animals and cultivating crops—and the hamlet was eerily deserted. Other than our patrol, there were no signs of life inside or outside the simple wooden houses spaced along the dirt road. There weren't even any animals left in the hamlet. Several houses had "AUC" spray-painted on the walls. It was difficult to imagine that only days earlier there had been more than 250 men, women, and children going about their daily lives there, cultivating their crops and caring for their animals. But now the hamlet was a ghost town.

As we walked along the dirt road, a faint but unpleasant odor began to penetrate my nostrils. I tried to ignore it. We continued moving forward into the breeze that was carrying the increasingly powerful and pungent smell. A group of soldiers was standing off to the left side of the road in front of a small, unpainted wooden house, and one of them told us that a body had been discovered at the side of the structure. As Eros and I made our way around the corner, the stench became almost unbearable. It was by far the foulest and most disturbing odor I have ever experienced—it seemed to penetrate not only my nose, but every inch of my being. I suddenly realized that the oppressive stench was emanating from the decomposing corpse, which had been rotting in the tropical heat for more than three days.

Four soldiers holding bandanas over their noses were standing over the lower half of a body. When I first saw only two legs clad in jeans and sneakers, I thought that the corpse had been cut in half. But as I drew closer, I realized that it had been shoved into a hole in the side of a hill and only the lower half was visible. The body was that of a heavyset man, and the soldiers appeared to be in no hurry to remove it from the hole. Eros and I took several photos before moving upwind to try to escape the stench as best we could.

We returned to the corpse when a red pickup truck carrying four teenage boys arrived on the scene. The army had called them in to retrieve the body and take it to the cemetery in El Placer. After getting out of the truck, the boys covered their faces with their shirts in an attempt to defend themselves from the oppressive stench. Two of them grabbed the legs of the dead body and pulled it out of the hole. The face was one of the most horrific sights I had ever seen, and for a moment I wondered whether I'd be sick. The lips were massively swollen, and the eyes bulged so much that I couldn't help but wonder what was preventing them from popping out of their sockets—they were reminiscent of the exaggerated features of a ghoulish cartoon figure. The skin on the face, as well as that on the hands and arms, was a sickly white color and hanging loose as though it were two sizes too big. I surmised that the disfigurations resulted from a combination of the water and the heat. It wasn't immediately apparent how the man had died, and the overbearing stench kept me from conducting a further inspection of the body. The four boys picked up the corpse, carried it out to the road, and laid it in the bed of the pickup truck.

After the body had been removed from the hamlet, we continued with the patrol. Even though we were now upwind of where the corpse had been found, the smell still lingered in my nostrils. We spent the next hour patrolling with the soldiers but didn't discover any more bodies. We learned from one soldier that many of the displaced villagers were in El Placer, so we decided to head there to get their story.

After locating our driver, who had been lingering at the rear of the patrol, we made our way to El Placer. We told our driver our objective, and almost immediately after entering the village he pulled over to a group of men in civilian clothes. One of them was carrying an AK-47, and two others had revolvers tucked into their waistbands. They were obviously paramilitaries.

When we asked the men where we could find the peasants who had been displaced from Los Angeles, they had a quick word among themselves, and then the one with the AK-47 jumped into the back of the car with us and directed our driver to a nearby two-story cement building. The paramilitary fighter led Eros and I upstairs to the second floor, where we found more than a dozen people who had set up camp in two rooms. The fighter refused to leave and stood guard over us, or perhaps over the displaced villagers, as we introduced ourselves to them and began asking questions about their ordeal. Most of the villagers remained silent, and the couple of men who were willing to speak did so hesitantly. It quickly became apparent that they were too afraid to provide us with any details of either the massacre or their displacement. After five minutes of futilely attempting to gather information, Eros looked over at me and said, "Let's get out of here." With a nod of his head in the direction of the paramilitary fighter, he added, "They're not going to tell us anything as long as he is here." We descended the stairs, found our driver, and returned to our hotel in La Hormiga.

The next day we drove back to Puerto Asís. While dining and sleeping that night in the Hotel Chilimaco, far removed from the massacre site, I repeatedly caught whiffs of that foul stench. It would return to haunt me on and off for the next several days. That smell was not the only aspect of the massacre that haunted me; I also could not rid myself of the horrific image of that dead body in the hole. In fact, I still remember it vividly from time to time.

The Sixth Hour
3:00 p.m., August 16, 2006

Time is still passing interminably slowly. I try not to keep looking at my watch, as that seems to further slow the passage of the minutes and hours. My guard is back in his plastic chair, listening to Radio Resistencia. I ask him why he joined the FARC, but he just looks at me and shakes his head slowly from side to side. Perhaps he had family members killed by the army or paramilitaries, I speculate to myself. Perhaps he is old enough to remember the repression of *La Violencia* and ever since then has believed that armed struggle is the only way to defend himself and his family. It could simply be that he prefers the life of a guerrilla to that of a farmer. Or perhaps he is both a guerrilla and a farmer.

I think of the many ways that the conflict has affected rural Colombians. Over the past twenty years, the armed combatants have forcibly displaced more than three million people from their homes and land, resulting in Colombia having the third largest internally displaced population in the world, after the Sudan and Iraq. Displaced people from the countryside often head to urban areas in search of safety, only to find that they have no means to support themselves and that the local authorities and their new neighbors suspect them of being guerrillas. Likewise, organizations that attempt to help the displaced or any other disadvantaged sector of the population often find themselves labeled "guerrillas" or "subversives."

Such was the case in the city of Barrancabermeja, known locally as Barranca, when I visited it in February 2001. Barranca is situated on the banks of the Magdalena River and is home to Colombia's largest oil refinery. When I was there, it also hosted a significant displaced population—in fact, more than thirty thousand of the city's two hundred thousand residents had been displaced from the surrounding countryside. For decades, ELN guerrillas controlled most of the city's poor barrios and much of the black market in gasoline. But in early 2000, AUC leader Carlos Castaño announced that he wanted Barranca cleansed of guerrillas. By the middle of the following year, the paramilitaries had mostly succeeded in seizing control of the city's barrios through a campaign of terror.

Upon my arrival, I found the heat and humidity to be more oppressive in Barranca than anywhere else I had been in Colombia. I also soon discovered that Barranca was the hottest urban war zone in the country. My first stop was the office of CREDHOS, known in English as the Regional Corporation for the Defense of Human Rights, a leading human rights group that documents abuses in the region. For half an hour I waited in the outer room of the CREDHOS office, which was sweltering despite the best efforts of an oscillating fan. Eventually I was invited into the office of Régulo Madero, the local president of CREDHOS.

"How bad is the violence in Barranca?" I asked Madero.

"Over the past decade, Barranca has averaged 330 murders a year," he replied. "But in the past year there were 567 selective homicides for political reasons."

Madero went on to point out that paramilitaries were responsible for the overwhelming majority of the murders. When paramilitary fighters entered guerrilla-controlled neighborhoods, they would kill any civilian they suspected of being a rebel sympathizer. In the eyes of the paramilitaries, he explained, a rebel sympathizer was anyone in Barranca who was engaged in social work. If poor people attempted to improve their living conditions, then the paramilitaries immediately considered them to be guerrillas. Members of the Popular Women's Organization (Organización Femenina Popular, or OFP), for example, organized soup kitchens in the city's poor barrios and courageously fought for women's rights. As a result, they had repeatedly been accused of being guerrillas by the paramilitaries. Over the years, the organization's leader, Yolanda Becerra, had received numerous death threats, as had other members. And several members had been assassinated by the paramilitaries.

"Are the paramilitaries receiving any support from the army and police in their dirty war here in Barranca?" I asked.

"The complicity between the institution of the government, the public forces, and the paramilitaries is a fact," Madero responded. "This generates an anarchic situation, and the first victims are human rights and the dignity of the people."

Madero had not been immune from the dirty war—he'd received several death threats himself. As a result, international accompaniers from Peace Brigades International remained with him at all times in an attempt to provide him with some protection.

I left the CREDHOS office inspired by the bravery of Madero's unwavering commitment to work on behalf of innocent Colombians who had been victims of human rights abuses. Astoundingly, in a nationally televised speech in September 2003, Colombian president Alvaro Uribe called the country's human rights defenders "terrorists," accusing them of being spokespersons for the guerrillas. In reality, all they had done was criticize his government's security policies. I found it impossible—and ludicrous—to think of Madero as a terrorist.

Through my work in Colombia, I have met many people like Madero whose daily nonviolent struggles for social justice, often in the face of death, have continually inspired me. Sometimes when I return home from Colombia, people ask me, "Don't you find the violence, poverty, and suffering depressing?" At such times I think of people like Madero, my friend and union leader Francisco Ramírez, and the many other courageous human rights workers and union, indigenous, and community leaders I have met whose names I don't dare to mention for their own security. And I think of all the Colombians who get up each morning and don't have the option of just walking away from it all. And I answer, "Sometimes I get depressed, but mostly I feel inspired by these Colombians who struggle against such overwhelming odds and with such dignity to achieve the rights that so many of us take for granted."

I have struggled with guilt, as have many others whose work involves dealing with violence and poverty in countries like Colombia. Often when I return home to the comforts of life in North America, part of me feels that I don't have a right to feel depressed or sad. After all, who am I to feel down, given my relatively privileged position in life? And although my rational mind knows that someone who does the work I do cannot help but be affected by some of the traumatic experiences, it's still difficult to convince myself that I actually have every right to respond emotionally.

Following my meeting with Madero, I decided to meet with some of Barranca's displaced population. Several blocks from the CREDHOS office was the Casa Campesinos, a community center near the market that had become the temporary home for 130 villagers who had been forcibly displaced three months earlier. It was an old building with peeling yellow paint and red tiled floors. There were only a dozen or so people milling around in the front room when I entered, and I walked over to a middle-aged man and introduced myself. He shook my hand and said his name was Luis. As we talked, Luis told me it was a struggle to feed his wife and four children because the government provided very little help.

"Mostly we depend on Red Cross food parcels," he explained.

"Where were you displaced from?" I asked.

"La Ciénega, which is forty-five minutes from Barranca by boat. Our entire village is here living in this building. We are not used to the city. We don't know what's going to happen to us here."

"Who forced you to leave your village?"

"The paramilitaries killed two friends, so we had to come here to escape."

"Have you been threatened since you arrived here?" I asked, recalling that Madero had told me that many among the displaced population were being displaced again, this time from Barranca to other cities.

"Our leaders have been threatened by the paramilitaries, and one of them had to leave town because they were following him all the time," Luis replied.

The paramilitaries usually displace rural communities for one of two reasons. Either they believe that members of the community are guerrilla sympathizers, or they realize that the village is situated on resource-rich lands. In the latter case, the forced displacement becomes a violent form of land speculation in which the paramilitaries seize the properties and sell them to Colombia's business elites or multinational companies. The typical method of displacement involves paramilitary fighters entering a village and gathering the people into the central plaza, then massacring a handful of people in front of their fellow villagers, often using chainsaws or machetes. The remaining villagers are then given twenty-four hours to flee the region or meet the same fate. Over the years it has proven to be a very effective way for the paramilitaries to gain control over territory.

Luis introduced me to a sixteen-year-old girl named Yamile, who was also from La Ciénega. She had medium-length brown hair tied back in a ponytail and was dressed in a blue T-shirt and a light brown knee-length skirt. I sat down with Yamile and thought about how much she looked like an average teenage girl from back home. But Yamile's biggest worries had nothing to do with boys or clothes or homework or any typical adolescent concerns. Instead, she described how she had to bear much of the responsibility for caring for her five younger siblings while her parents went out into the streets each day in a desperate search for food and other basic essentials for the family. She said that there was no school for her to attend and that it was difficult to adjust to life in such an unfamiliar urban environment.

"It's difficult here because I am used to living on our land," she explained. "I miss attending school in the days and dancing to *vallenato* music in the evenings."

"What are your hopes for the future?" I asked her.

"Peace, love, and calm," she quietly stated.

While Colombia's displaced rural population often endures a life of poverty, hardship, and exclusion in the cities, many of those peasants who remain in the countryside fare no better. In March 2002 I flew from Bogotá to Medellín, where I transferred to a small twin-propeller plane for the short flight to the town of El Bagre, situated on the banks of the Nechí River in the department of Antioquia. From El Bagre, I took a launch down the river to Zaragoza. Along the way we passed peasants panning for gold in the shallow waters along the riverbank. That part of Antioquia is one of Colombia's principal gold-mining regions, and thousands of peasants spend their days in the rivers desperately searching for meager amounts of the treasured commodity. But it wasn't gold mining that had taken me to the region; I was there to investigate how land-mines planted by the armed groups were affecting the rural population.

Two days earlier I had interviewed Diana Roa of the Colombian Campaign Against Landmines (Campaña Colombiana Contra Minas, or CCCM) in the organization's offices in northern Bogotá. At that time, Colombia had the third-highest number of annual landmine casualties in the world. Three years later, it would achieve the ignominious position as the global leader in landmine casualties. When I met with Roa, she was clearly unhappy with the Colombian government's recent announcement that it would not meet its obligations under the Ottawa Treaty to remove all landmines currently in use and to destroy all stockpiles by 2010.

"There are no legal repercussions according to the treaty," she pointed out. "We can only hope that other signatory nations will apply pressure."

She told me that landmines were known to be present in 168 municipalities in 24 of Colombia's 32 departments, and she complained that the Colombian government was engaged only in military demining intended to protect soldiers during operations. The CCCM was pushing for the government to also implement humanitarian demining that met the needs of affected communities, such as ensuring that the areas around schools were mine-free. According to Roa, 52 percent of landmine victims were civilians.

"Who is responsible for planting most of the mines?" I asked.

"The illegal armed groups are responsible for the majority. The FARC is first, then the ELN, and then the AUC," she replied.

Roa went on to explain that most of the mines planted by the armed groups were homemade and that when the CCCM raised the issue with the FARC, "the rebels said that landmines are a weapon of the poor and when the government stops using bombs, planes, and satellites, they will stop using mines."

I asked Roa whether there was a mine-affected community that I could visit. She suggested the town of Zaragoza and gave me the contact information for Martina Murillo, a local CCCM volunteer there.

Upon my arrival in Zaragoza, I met with Martina. She told me that the town had a population of sixteen thousand, while an equal number lived in the outlying rural part of the municipality where most of the landmines were located. She explained that her job was to help prevent accidents through mine-risk education and to let people know what to do when a person has stepped on a landmine. She also helped victims with their rehabilitation.

"Who planted the mines in this region?" I asked Martina.

"The ELN, the AUC, the FARC, and the army," she replied. "Most of them have been planted by the illegal groups, except the ones around the army base."

According to Martina, there had been eleven known victims of landmines in the municipality of Zaragoza in the previous four years. Three of the victims were children between ten and sixteen years of age.

It is difficult for locals to detect landmines because the illegal armed groups use many different types of homemade devices. Many of them are pressure-activated mines that are either chemically or electronically detonated. A canister, often an empty food can, is filled with shrapnel and an explosive compound. A plastic syringe is inserted into the top of the can, and the whole device is then buried in the ground with only the small top of the syringe's plunger left exposed. When a victim steps on the plunger, sulfuric acid is injected into the detonator if it is a chemical device, or a connection is made to a small battery if it is electronic, and the mine explodes. The locals call landmines *quiebrapatas,* which translates as "leg breakers," because an overwhelming number of victims lose a leg.

Twenty minutes outside of town, Martina and I visited the site of two landmine accidents that had occurred less than a year earlier. We stopped in front of a small, basic wooden house, where Martina introduced me to a middle-aged farmer named Ariano Morales. Ariano, Martina, and I left the car on the dirt road and walked up a muddy path over two small hills. As we neared the crest of a third hill, I was observing the spectacular vista—there was forest only an arm's length away to our left and a panoramic view of a river valley and farmland to our right—when Ariano stopped.

He pointed to the ground and said, "This is where it happened."

"This is where his brother Gregorio stepped on the landmine," Martina elaborated.

"Gregorio's accident occurred at five in the afternoon," Ariano said. "We heard the explosion and then carried him five kilometers in a hammock to the local hospital. It took one and a half hours."

"What was he doing up here that day?" I asked.

"He used to walk two hours each way to take his crops to market," Ariano replied, staring down at the spot on the ground. "Now he lives with his wife and four kids in Zaragoza."

Martina explained that forty-year-old Gregorio had lost his left leg below the knee. She pointed to a small clearing in the trees and said that a ten-year-old girl named Irma Restrepo had stepped on a landmine on that spot three days later. Irma, who lost her entire left leg, had been collecting palm leaves with her father. She and her family fled to Medellín afterward, where they became part of the city's growing displaced population.

We made our way back down to the car, where Martina and I bid farewell to Ariano, and returned to Zaragoza. We pulled up in front of Gregorio's home, a run-down two-room wooden shack that he shared with his wife and their four children, all of whom were under eight years old. Gregorio's home was situated in a small shantytown populated by displaced people, and although it had electricity, it lacked running water and sewage drains. Martina led me to the open front door and, leaning inside, explained to someone in the house that a journalist from the United States was visiting and would like to speak with Gregorio. I heard a woman's voice inviting us in, and Martina introduced me to Gregorio's wife.

We stood in a small room with a dirt floor; the only furniture consisted of four plastic chairs evenly spaced around a wooden table. Each chair was occupied by one of Gregorio's children, all busily coloring pieces of paper. The room was dark and musty, in serious need of airing out.

Gregorio's wife and Martina led me through another doorway into the only other room in the house. This room was even darker than the front room, and the smell even more pungent. In the darkness I could make out a figure lying on one of the two double beds that almost filled the room. As we entered, the figure slowly rose up and with great effort slid down to the foot of the bed and into what little light shone through the door. I was horrified by the image I encountered. The man was dressed only in shorts, and most of his face, chest, arms, and legs were covered in raw-looking red sores, some of which were bleeding. His left leg ended just below the knee. Martina introduced me to Gregorio, and as I shook his hand and looked at his face, I found it difficult to believe that this man was only forty years old.

It appeared to require great effort for Gregorio to speak. He mumbled something about not feeling well, so I decided, rather than peppering him with questions, to simply ask whether there was anything he would like to tell me about his ordeal.

He weakly whispered, "No."

I thanked him and, not knowing what else to say, just wished him well.

Martina and I said goodbye to Gregorio's wife. As we exited the house, I felt shaken by one of the most disturbing and depressing encounters I had ever experienced. That house reeked of death, even though nobody in it was actually dying, at least not in the physical sense. Martina told me that Gregorio had given up. He refused to get out of bed and engage in rehabilitation. The family had no income and was entirely dependent on the charity of others. Meanwhile, said Martina, Gregorio's wife wasn't sure how much longer she could endure the situation. She was particularly worried about the children.

Of all my experiences in rural Colombia, where the civilian population has been caught in the middle of the armed conflict, none have been as gut-wrenching and heartbreaking as witnessing the plight of Gregorio and his family. Gregorio represented more vividly than most the fact that civilians are the principal victims of the conflict, both physically and psychologically. But more than anything, he symbolized the complete loss of hope that befalls some of these people. And that seemed to me to be a fate worse than death.

Several months after visiting Gregorio and his family, I decided to return to Putumayo to try to determine the impact of one and a half years of Plan Colombia on the civilian population. I flew from Bogotá to the city of Pasto, high in the Andes in the southern department of Nariño. I'd decided to travel by land into Putumayo—traversing a dirt road that wound its way from Pasto down the eastern flank of the Andes to Puerto Asís in the Amazon—to experience the transportation infrastructure for myself.

Several hours into the journey, my driver and I stopped behind a long line of vehicles. A landslide had blocked the road, and my driver told me that it would likely be at least two days before it was cleared. We got out of the car and strolled past the parked vehicles, most of which were dilapidated buses and trucks. When we reached the site of the landslide, my driver told me to wait while he clambered over the large pile of mud and rocks. Ten minutes later he returned with another driver and his passenger, who had been traveling in the opposite direction. The two drivers agreed to trade passengers, allowing them both to turn around and head back to their points of origin. I climbed over the rubble with my new driver, and after he had managed to turn his car around on the edge of a steep precipice, we began our descent toward the Amazon. The entire trip took more than twelve hours and provided me with a much more vivid understanding of the infrastructure problems that Putumayan farmers repeatedly complained about. Landslides frequently shut down that road, making it virtually impossible for peasants to transport perishable crops to the country's major cities.

When I finally arrived in Puerto Asís, I immediately set about investigating how Plan Colombia was affecting farmers. I met with several local officials, all of whom stated unequivocally that the spraying continued to kill food crops, cause illnesses, and force people to abandon their lands. When I spoke with Jair Giovani Ruiz, an agro-industrial engineer with the Ministry of the Environment, he hinted at the corruption that existed in the disbursement of Plan Colombia funds. Ruiz told me that peasants had received little of the alternative crop funding.

"Maybe a cow or three chickens, but the farmers can't live off of these. Maybe the money got lost on the way, or maybe the government contracted a lot of experts to supply a cow," he suggested. The bottom line, said Ruiz, was that "Plan Colombia's resources have been poorly managed."

I hired a driver named Miguel to take me into the countryside to visit a farm that had been fumigated a week earlier. About thirty minutes outside Puerto Asís, we turned onto a dirt road and made our way through the rainforest. We pulled up in front of a small wooden farmhouse, and a man who appeared to be in his mid thirties came out to meet us. His name was Victoriano, and he lived as many coca farmers lived—in poverty. His home had electricity, but no running water, and only three small rooms for him, his wife, and their four children. Coca farmers like Victoriano earn the least amount of profit among those involved in the drug trade; while most farmers earn just enough to keep their families out of extreme poverty, the co-caine traffickers garner incredible riches. And yet it was coca farmers like Victoriano that were the principal target of Plan Colombia.

As Victoriano and I walked across a field, I noticed that there were no coca bushes. Victoriano told me that after having his coca crops sprayed twice during the first year of Plan Colombia, he decided to accept the government's offer to sign a social pact. Under the pact he had signed four months earlier, Victoriano uprooted his coca bushes and replaced them with lulo plants, which produce a fruit used to make juice drinks. In return, the government gave Victoriano material aid, technical advice, and a promise that his farm would not be fumigated again.

"What material aid did the government give you?" I asked.

"A cow and barbed wire," he replied.

"And you got fumigated again last week?" I asked, repeating what my driver Miguel had told me on the journey out.

Victoriano nodded in affirmation. He pointed to a plant in the ground just in front of us. "This is what the fumigation did to my lulo plants," he said. Pointing to the rest of the field, he declared, "They are all dead."

I suddenly realized that the vegetation surrounding us, which I had taken to be just wild plants or large weeds, was actually Victoriano's crop. These small, withered plants were the young lulo seedlings that had represented future income for Victoriano and his family.

"What will you do now?" I asked.

"Grow coca again," he replied.

As I said goodbye to Victoriano, I felt angry that we were waging a war on peasants like him, who would gladly quit growing coca if provided with a viable alternative. It was becoming increasingly clear to me, after one and a half years of Plan Colombia, that the war on drugs could not be won militarily.

• • •

That afternoon, back in Puerto Asís, I ran into a photojournalist I knew named Scott Dalton. Scott had worked for the Associated Press in Colombia for several years before becoming a freelance photographer and would later coproduce a documentary film called *La Sierra,* which looked at the lives of paramilitaries in the barrios of Medellín. He was in Putumayo with a documentary film crew that was doing a report on Colombia's conflict.

The next morning Scott, the film crew, and I headed out of town to visit a cocaine processing lab in the jungle. Just past the town of Santa Ana, about thirty minutes outside of Puerto Asís, we turned off the main road onto a bumpy dirt road that could be traversed only by a four-wheel-drive vehicle. Every so often we passed small clearings in the rainforest where the trees had been felled and a small farm established.

Finally we pulled off the road and parked in front of a wooden house. Three women were sitting outside on chairs while four small children played nearby. Our driver spoke to one of the women, who then disappeared around the side of the house. The children eyed the five *gringos* with suspicion and curiosity. I pulled some colorful pens out of my pocket and asked the women whether I could give them to the children—when working in rural conflict zones, I had found that befriending the children helped the parents to relax and open up. With the women's consent, the children immediately came over to me to lay claim to their gifts, and the mood of the women and children quickly shifted from wariness to festiveness as we all began to talk and laugh.

The first woman reappeared from behind the house with a man who looked to be in his mid twenties. He spoke with our driver for a minute, introduced himself to us as Fernando, and beckoned us to follow him as he turned to walk back around the side of the house.

Attached to the rear of the house, surrounded by jungle on three sides, was a small open-sided structure with a slanting wooden roof: the cocaine processing lab. A large pile of coca leaves sat on the cement floor in one corner. Along the far side of the lab were several fifty-five-gallon drums of chemicals used in the processing. On a platform at the end of the lab sat a two-ring kerosene burner, a small scale, and several plastic buckets and aluminum cooking pots. Fernando did not own the lab, which was located in paramilitary-controlled territory; he was simply an employee who processed coca paste into cocaine base.

Fernando spent the next two hours showing us, step by step, the process of turning coca paste into cocaine base. We observed his every move, asking questions and taking photographs.

There are three principal stages in the processing of coca leaves into cocaine. The first stage involves harvesting and crushing the leaves, then mixing them with sodium bicarbonate, gasoline, and other additives to form a brown coca paste, which is approximately 40 percent pure cocaine. Often the coca growers do this first step of processing themselves before selling the paste to drug labs, where the next stage in the process occurs. However, the processing lab I visited in Putumayo would occasionally buy raw coca leaves and perform both of the first two stages of processing. The second stage involves mixing the brown coca paste with sulfuric acid, potassium permanganate, and other chemicals. The mixture is then drained and heated until it dries into a solid white compound, which is then broken up into small white rocks. The resulting cocaine base is 90 percent pure cocaine. The third and final stage, which usually takes place in large remote jungle labs, involves processing the cocaine base into cocaine hydrochloride, or powder cocaine, which is 99 percent pure cocaine. Traffickers then ship the cocaine hydrochloride to drug dealers in North America and Europe.

At one point during the demonstration, we heard the sound

of helicopters in the distance, and Fernando said that they were likely supporting spray planes conducting fumigations in the area. I listened as the sound grew louder, thinking to myself how unfortunate it would be if a counternarcotics operation being undertaken by the Colombian military were to target this specific lab while we were all present. After all, they might come in with their guns blasting. I walked over to the edge of the lab and looked up through small gaps in the rainforest canopy at the helicopters that by now were almost overhead. A couple of minutes later they passed us by, and the noise began to fade into the distance.

When Fernando finished making the cocaine base, he began spooning it into clear plastic bags, which he placed on the scale. He noted down in a book the weight of each of the six bags. The plastic bags were then wrapped in brown packing tape and stacked neatly in a pile. The finished quantity amounted to four kilograms, or kilos, of cocaine base. I was staring at six brick-sized packages of cocaine that, when sold wholesale by the kilo in the United States, would be worth approximately one hundred thousand dollars. The total retail value of that cocaine when sold by the gram in the United States would be about four hundred thousand dollars.

A financial breakdown of the cocaine trade clearly illustrates how Plan Colombia is targeting the weakest and poorest link in the production and trafficking chain. It takes one hundred kilos of coca leaves to make one kilo of coca paste, and the average coca farm can produce two thousand kilos of coca leaves a year if it is not fumigated. Therefore, given that a kilo of coca paste sells for about six hundred dollars, the average small farmer earns, at most, a thousand dollars a month. Out of this money he has to purchase pesticides and the chemicals for processing the leaves into paste, pay coca pickers to harvest and process the leaves, and pay taxes to the paramilitaries if they control that particular region—leaving him a couple of hundred dollars, if he is lucky.

Meanwhile, the cocaine processors, who are often the drug-trafficking cartels, purchase the coca paste from the farmers for six hundred dollars a kilo and then sell the processed cocaine to drug-dealing organizations in the United States for twenty-three thousand dollars a kilo. The U.S. drug dealers break down each kilo into grams and sell them for approximately one hundred dollars each, for total earnings of one hundred thousand dollars per kilo. In actuality, the dealers earn even more than this amount because they cut the cocaine with cornstarch, talcum powder, or other similar products in order to increase the number of grams they can sell.

At the end of the day, the farmer's profits amount to several hundred dollars per kilo of coca paste. In contrast, Colombia's drug traffickers pocket over ten thousand dollars for each kilo of cocaine sold, while the profits of U.S. dealers are in the tens of thousands of dollars for each kilo. Clearly, the overwhelming majority of the profits go to Colombia's drug trafficking cartels and U.S. dealers, yet our war on drugs focuses on destroying the livelihood of impoverished Colombian farmers, particularly those living in FARC-controlled regions.

It was midafternoon when we returned from the cocaine lab to Puerto Asís, where I separated from Scott and the film crew. I caught a taxi to the local port on the Putumayo River, about three miles upstream from the town. Calling it a port might be a bit of an exaggeration, as it amounted to little more than a collection of canoes, small boats, and a few wooden shacks on the muddy banks of the river. Ironically, the port was named Hong Kong. My objective in going there was to find someone willing to transport me across the river to FARC-controlled territory to interview the guerrillas about Plan Colombia.

Approaching the clearing in the rainforest that contained the port, my taxi passed through an army patrol of fifteen soldiers walking along either side of the dirt road. The emblems on their uniforms identified them as members of the Colombian army's counternarcotics brigade, which was created, trained, and armed by U.S. Army Special Forces.

The Plan Colombia aid bill had included a requirement that some of the funding be used to create a counternarcotics brigade that would function independently from the Colombian army's counterinsurgency troops. The purpose of creating the new brigade was to appease members of the U.S. Congress concerned with aid going to Colombian army units that routinely collaborated with right-wing paramilitaries in the country's dirty war. Following 9/11, however, many of the conditions limiting U.S. military aid to counternarcotics operations were lifted, allowing the U.S.-trained troops and U.S.-supplied helicopters to be used against the FARC as part of Washington's global war on terror.

In the port area, several men of varying ages were sitting and talking to each other in front of one of the wooden shacks. I got out of the taxi, walked over to them, and identified myself as a journalist.

"Is there someone who would be able take me to a village on the other side of the river tomorrow morning?" I asked, speaking to no one in particular.

"Why do you want to go over there?" one of the men responded.

"I would like to interview people about the fumigations."

At that moment, all of the men looked away from me and suddenly fell silent. One of them stood up and began walking to the water's edge. Again I asked whether anyone would be able to take me across the river. They all remained silent, ignoring me, and I stood there confused. Then one of them subtly nodded his head in the direction behind me. I turned around and saw a white pickup truck pulling to a halt about ten yards away. Four partly uniformed paramilitaries jumped down from the back of the truck and approached the boatman who had just walked down to the river. Two were carrying AK-47 assault rifles, and one had a two-way radio with a long antenna. I glanced in the direction of the road and saw that the Colombian army patrol I had passed on the way to the port was no more than fifty yards from where I was standing. Not only were the paramilitaries in plain view of the soldiers, but they also had to have passed right through the middle of the patrol to enter the port area.

I stood there watching the soldiers watch the paramilitaries, who were openly wielding their rifles as they arranged transportation down the river. There was no reaction from the troops; they were completely unconcerned with the presence of the paramilitaries. This incident made clear why so many Colombians claim that there is no difference between the army and the paramilitaries and that they work together to combat the guerrillas. I also found it intriguing that the soldiers appeared to be untroubled by the fact that a foreign journalist was openly observing their collusion with the paramilitaries, given that they were members of the Plan Colombia counternarcotics brigade. I watched the four paramilitaries, who completely ignored my presence, climb into a motorized canoe with the boatman and head off downriver in the direction of Puerto Asís. I then decided that it was too risky to try to arrange a trip across the river now that I had become so highly visible to both the army and the paramilitaries. I thanked the boatmen and returned to Puerto Asís.

Two hours later, I was sitting in the hotel restaurant with Scott when a hotel employee told us that there had been a massacre an hour earlier and that the bodies of the victims were at the morgue. Scott, the film crew, and I headed out to investigate the situation.

When we arrived at the morgue, about fifteen women and children were hanging around outside in the conflict zone version of rubbernecking at a traffic accident. While we were waiting for the coroner to speak with us, I asked a couple of the women whether they knew what had happened. Both of them told me that paramilitaries had killed three suspected guerrilla sympathizers. I thought back to the paramilitaries I had just seen at the port and wondered whether they could have been the killers. Probably not, as the paramilitaries operating in the town would likely have been dressed in civilian clothes and carrying revolvers rather than assault rifles. Nevertheless, within an hour of the collusion I'd witnessed between the army and paramilitaries, three people were killed in a paramilitary massacre.

The coroner invited us into the morgue and then led us into the room that contained the bodies of the victims, all men who appeared to be in their twenties. Two of them were lying on the white tile floor, one without a shirt. They both had bullet holes in their foreheads. I stared down at the shirtless man, whose eyes were open and staring blankly into space. A pool of blood was forming on the floor underneath his head, leaking from the exit wound in the rear of his skull. The third victim was on a table on the opposite side of the room, his torso cut open, perhaps by a machete, from the base of the neck to below the belly button. The entire scene was disturbing, to say the least.

There was little else to do at the morgue, so we headed back to the hotel. I sat in the restaurant drinking a cold beer and wondered whether U.S. aid to a military closely allied with paramilitary death squads was only further fueling Colombia's dirty war. With four thousand people killed annually by political violence, more than a quarter of a million forcibly displaced every year, over a thousand kidnapped, and Colombia leading the world in the number of unionists, human rights defenders, teachers, and community leaders assassinated, it was clear that the civilian population was bearing the brunt of the country's violence.

The prevalence of paramilitary violence in Puerto Asís had led the town to become known locally as Muerto Asís. The nickname replaced the Spanish word "puerto," which means "port," with "muerto," which means "dead." I decided to visit the town's cemetery to look at the graves of the victims of the violence.

A large concrete arch dominated the entrance to the cemetery. Emblazoned across the top of it were the words "Aquí todos somos iguales," which translates as "Here we are all equal." It is one of the cruel ironies of Colombia's conflict that only in death can poor people achieve a measure of equality with the country's rich elites.

As I walked among the newest-looking headstones, I was immediately struck by the ages of those interred there. The majority of those buried over the previous few years had died in their teens and twenties, supporting claims made by locals that violence was the leading cause of death in Puerto Asís. I looked down at one headstone and read the inscription:

Luis Dario Coro
Born March 16, 1973
Died Sept. 17, 1999

To walk past grave after grave of people who had died so young was unsettling.

That graveyard encapsulated the true tragedy of Colombia's violence. The country's impoverished youth were the ones who were doing both the killing and the dying. Even more tragically, most of those who had been killed did not die in combat. Most of the victims were neither armed nor engaged in acts of violence when they were killed. It all seemed so senseless.

The Seventh Hour

4:00 p.m., August 16, 2006

The teenage girl brings me a drink of juice in a plastic cup. After I down it, I take the empty cup over to the kitchen and hand it back to her. The sky is beginning to cloud over as I once again stroll around the inside of the perimeter fence. I stand staring through the wire, wishing that the FARC would make their decision and put an end to this interminable boredom. I look across the coca field at the hired help still working in the coca paste lab. There is little other activity besides the occasional bird flying overhead. It is difficult to believe that I am in the middle of one of the strongholds of the Bush administration's principal non–Middle Eastern enemy in the war on terror.

I think back to that fateful day that led to the Bush administration launching its global war on terror. I was packing clothes into a bag in my lower Manhattan apartment on the morning of September 11, 2001, preparing for an afternoon flight to Colombia. I heard the newscaster on the television announce that a plane had just crashed into one of the twin towers at the

World Trade Center. After the news revealed that a second plane had struck the other tower, it became evident that it was no accident, and so I set aside my packing to watch the television coverage. Shortly after the first tower collapsed, a neighbor knocked on the door and said that people were going up to the roof to watch what was happening. People had gathered on the rooftops of buildings throughout the Lower East Side, staring at the smoke billowing from the lone remaining tower a little more than a mile to the south. Suddenly a huge cloud of dust began to rise up from the base of the tower, enveloping and obscuring the entire structure. Despite the distance, I could hear a deep rumble. As the giant cloud of dust began to dissipate, a collective gasp could be heard from across the neighborhood. The second tower had vanished. It was as though a magician had just removed his handkerchief and the object of focus had disappeared before the audience's eyes. As the world soon found out, this act of terrorism was perpetrated by the Islamic fundamentalist group al-Qaeda.

My flight to Colombia was cancelled, of course, as all aircraft were grounded for the next several days. Desperately wanting to find a way to help in this time of crisis, my wife Jacqui and I spent the next day trying to donate blood, but the donor centers were already overstocked. We purchased groceries and donated them to the rescue and aid stations. Yearning to do more, the following day I made my way down to Ground Zero, the site of the collapsed towers, and volunteered in the search for survivors.

The scene was one of utter devastation. Two piles of rubble standing about six stories high were all that remained of the two towers, each of which had stood 110 stories tall. Two of the world's most identifiable architectural landmarks had been reduced to a mangled mess of concrete, steel, and dust. Among the debris were thousands of pieces of paper and occasionally a recognizable item, such as a computer monitor, that had miraculously survived the collapse. More disturbingly, I also came across people's personal effects, including a child's backpack and torn pieces of photographs of victims' loved ones.

For the next twelve hours, I worked on one of the many human chains that wound their way over the mounds of rubble from where the firefighters were burrowing into the debris in search of survivors back to the perimeter of the disaster zone. We found no survivors that day. We also didn't find any bodies, only parts of bodies.

At nine o'clock that evening, I made my way out of Ground Zero and headed uptown to rendezvous with Jacqui at her brother's apartment near Bellevue Hospital, which was one of the two trauma centers where survivors were to be taken. An hour later, as we walked out onto First Avenue to make our way home, half a dozen Latinos called out to us and ran in our direction. My clothes were still covered in the white dust that permeated everything at the disaster site.

"Have you been down at Ground Zero?" one of them asked me.

"Yes," I replied.

"Did you find any survivors?"

The one asking the questions was a young man who appeared to be in his mid twenties. Beside him stood a woman about the same age and several other men and women who looked to be in their late teens. Clearly, they were hanging around Bellevue Hospital hoping to hear news of a loved one who had been in the World Trade Center that fateful morning two days earlier. Their facial expressions exhibited a seemingly contradictory blend of hope and despair. And then I realized that I was the source of that hope.

"The rescue line that I was working on didn't find any survivors," I answered. "But there were many other lines working down there, and I don't know if they found anyone or not."

In my heart I knew there were no more survivors, but I didn't have it in me to tell them that. I didn't know what to say to those people who were grasping at any straw. And then the man who had asked the questions suddenly felt compelled to tell me the story of their missing loved ones.

"My brother works with his fiancé in the restaurant on the 106th floor," he began. "He moved here from Mexico a year ago. They are planning to get married in the spring."

I couldn't help but notice that he told the story using the present tense, as though the full reality of the nightmare had not yet registered. No doubt speaking in the present tense helped keep their loved ones alive. I uttered the only words I could think of at that moment.

"There are a lot of people down at Ground Zero working incredibly hard," I mumbled inanely. "If there are any survivors, I'm sure they will find them."

I wished them luck, turned, and walked away, feeling both physically and emotionally drained. All I could think about was the suffering that those people were enduring and the cruel reality that they were not going to achieve any sense of closure in the near future, if ever.

Nine days after the 9/11 attacks, President Bush announced to Congress and the nation that the United States was launching a global war on terror. He claimed that the United States was attacked because the terrorists hated American values.

"They hate our freedoms—our freedom of religion, our freedom of speech, our freedom to vote and assemble and disagree with each other," he declared.

But based on my experiences in Latin America over the years, I felt that Bush was misleading the American people. It wasn't the freedoms enjoyed by Americans that critics of the United States hated; it was the policies of the U.S. government and U.S. corporations around the world that were the most significant contributing factor to anti-American attitudes. Salvadorans during the 1980s had nothing against the way of life of the average U.S. citizen living in Iowa, Texas, or any other state. They did, however, have serious grievances against the

United States for supporting a Salvadoran government and military that brutally repressed them.

The indigenous people I had met in the Ecuadorian Amazon knew absolutely nothing about the freedoms enjoyed by the American people. However, they were seething at the actions of U.S. oil companies operating in their traditional lands. There was also plenty of anti-American sentiment in Colombia, particularly in the rural regions targeted by Plan Colombia's fumigations. Again, this anger wasn't rooted in a hatred for U.S. freedoms; it resulted from U.S. government policies that destroyed the livelihoods of Colombian peasants without offering them any viable alternatives. I couldn't help but feel that, although those Latin Americans who disliked U.S. policies were unlikely to retaliate in the manner of the fanatics who committed those unjustifiable acts of violence on 9/11, their dislike and distrust of the United States was both understandable and shared by many people around the world.

In his speech, President Bush made it clear that it was not only Islamic terrorists that the United States would target in its new war.

"Our war on terror begins with al-Qaeda, but it does not end there," Bush declared. "It will not end until every terrorist group of global reach has been found, stopped, and defeated."

It soon became apparent that Washington's principal non-Islamic target in its global war on terror would be the FARC, despite the fact that the rebel group's military operations were conducted within the geographic borders of Colombia and posed no security threat whatsoever to the United States.

Less than three weeks after the 9/11 attacks, Senator Bob Graham of Florida, a Democrat and chair of the Senate Select Committee on Intelligence, launched a campaign to portray the FARC as a major international terrorist threat.

"The FARC are doing the same thing as global-level terrorists; that is, organizing in small cells that don't have contact with each other and depend on a central command to organize attacks, in terms of logistics and finance. It is the same style of operation as Bin Laden," Graham claimed.

In October, the State Department's top counterterrorism official, Francis Taylor, declared that Washington's strategy for fighting terrorism in the Western Hemisphere would include, "where appropriate, as we are doing in Afghanistan, the use of military power."

Taylor left little doubt about the "appropriate" target when he stated that the FARC "is the most dangerous international terrorist group based in this hemisphere."

Meanwhile, Taylor's boss, U.S. Secretary of State Colin Powell, told the Senate Foreign Relations Committee that the FARC belonged in the same category as al-Qaeda: "There is no difficulty in identifying [Osama bin Laden] as a terrorist and getting everybody to rally against him. Now, there are other organizations that probably meet a similar standard. The FARC in Colombia comes to mind."

And in the last week of October, Senator Graham ramped up his accusations by declaring that Colombia should be the principal battlefield in the global war on terror. According to the Florida senator, there were almost five hundred incidents of terrorism committed worldwide against U.S. citizens and interests in 2000, and "of those almost five hundred incidents, forty-four percent were in one country. Was that country Egypt? No. Israel? No. Afghanistan? Hardly a tick. Forty-four percent were in Colombia. That's where the terrorist war has been raging."

What Graham failed to mention was that the overwhelming majority of the so-called terrorist attacks against the United States by Colombian guerrillas consisted of bombing the oil pipelines of U.S. companies. In other words, they were designed to hurt corporate profit margins, not U.S. civilians. In fact, the Florida senator neglected to point out that rebel attacks in Colombia did not kill a single U.S. citizen in 2000, the year to which Graham was referring. Nevertheless, the propaganda campaign vilifying the FARC successfully laid the groundwork for the U.S. ambassador to Colombia, Anne Patterson, to announce at the end of October that the United States would provide counterterrorism aid to Colombia as part of Washington's global war on terror.

In July 2002, the U.S. Congress approved $128 million in counterterrorism aid in addition to the funding for Plan Colombia. More important than the additional funds, however, was the fact that the new aid bill also eliminated the conditions restricting U.S. drug war funding to counternarcotics operations. This change allowed Plan Colombia's military aid, including the three thousand soldiers in the counternarcotics brigade and more than sixty helicopters, to be used for counterinsurgency operations under the war on terror. In effect, the Bush administration had made the war on drugs and the war on terror the same war.

As part of its new war on terror, the Bush administration announced its plans to deploy seventy U.S. Army Special Forces soldiers to the department of Arauca in eastern Colombia. There was no coca cultivation in Arauca, nor any cocaine processing labs. There was, however, plenty of oil, and the most prominent company operating in the region was Los Angeles–based Occidental Petroleum. Occidental partly owned and operated a pipeline that ran from its Caño Limón oil field to the Caribbean coast. The pipeline was bombed a record 170 times in 2001, shutting it down for 240 days that year and costing the company one hundred million dollars in lost earnings. The mission of the U.S. Army Special Forces troops would be to provide counterinsurgency training to the Colombian Army's 18th Brigade, whose primary mission was to defend Occidental's oil field and pipeline against guerrilla attacks.

I made my first visit to Arauca in August 2002, a month after the announcement that U.S. troops would be deployed there. In the departmental capital, Arauca City, I interviewed Brigadier General Carlos Lemus, the commander of the Colombian army's 18th Brigade. The insignia of the 18th Brigade features an oil derrick, and General Lemus directed operations from a large, comfortable office inundated with souvenirs bearing the name of the company whose oil it was his mission to protect. Occidental Petroleum contributed both money and logistical support to the Colombian military to assist with the protection of the Caño Limón pipeline. I learned the extent of the company's influence over the army when I requested permission to accompany an army patrol responding to a rebel attack on the pipeline; General Lemus told me that such a request would have to be approved by Occidental officials. When I asked the general about the planned U.S. military aid and training under the war on terror, not surprisingly, he said he welcomed it.

"We need some of these things to help protect the pipeline and to provide troop mobility, training, and more intelligence capacity to allow our troops to be able to respond to attacks more efficiently and faster," he explained.

After leaving the 18th Brigade's headquarters, I decided to try to arrange an interview with an ELN rebel commander. All my attempts over the previous three years to meet with the ELN had failed. Given the rebel group's prominence in Arauca, I thought I would try again. I visited a local community radio station and met with a reporter whose name had been given to me by a colleague in Bogotá. The reporter said that he had developed contacts with the various armed groups, but could not arrange a meeting with the ELN for me at that time. But he did give me the name of a person in a small village about one hour outside Arauca City who might be able to help me.

The next morning I found a taxi driver willing to take me to the village, and we set off on a two-lane paved highway across Los Llanos. Most of Arauca is situated in this vast area of grasslands, which covers thousands of square miles and is intersected by countless rivers. During the rainy season, much of the territory becomes flooded and many of the roads impassable.

When we reached the village, I began asking around for my contact, only to find that he was nowhere to be found. After an hour it became apparent that I was not going to locate him, and so I decided to head back to Arauca City.

About halfway back to Arauca City, we passed two cement buildings beside the road. The walls were covered with AUC graffiti, and the buildings appeared to be abandoned. I asked my driver to stop so I could take a photograph. The road was deserted as I got out of the taxi—in fact, we had seen few vehicles on our journey to and from the village. I walked behind the car, and as I began snapping photos of the graffiti-covered buildings, a man's voice called out from behind me.

"What are you doing here?" the voice asked sternly.

I turned and saw a uniformed fighter, armed with an AK-47 and carrying a handheld radio, walking along the road toward me. Several more uniformed men carrying AK-47s emerged from the trees and bushes that lined each side of the road. The black armbands on their sleeves identified them as members of the Self-Defense Groups of Córdoba and Urabá (Autodefensas Campesinas de Córdoba y Urabá, or ACCU), the country's most powerful paramilitary group. At the time, it was headed by Carlos Castaño and was the dominant member of the AUC. My heart began to race as six paramilitaries approached me.

As he drew near, the one holding the two-way radio repeated his question. "What are you doing here?"

I knew I couldn't tell him that I had been seeking a meeting with the guerrillas, because that might lead him to suspect me of being a rebel collaborator.

"I am looking for you," I responded. "I am a journalist from the United States, and I would like to interview your commander, if that's possible."

"Why were you taking photographs?" he asked, ignoring my request.

I told him that I was just taking pictures of the graffiti on the buildings. Again I asked whether I could meet with his commander, hoping that he would believe my excuse for being in the middle of nowhere in a region mostly controlled by the guerrillas. I also hoped that my driver did not tell them where we had been, which was also in his best interests, since they might suspect him of being a rebel sympathizer.

The paramilitary fighter asked to see my identification and then, with my press card in hand, turned and spoke into the two-way radio. A minute later, he turned back around and beckoned me to follow him. We walked two hundred yards along the road and stopped where a narrow dirt road intersected the main paved one. The leader again communicated through the handheld radio before turning to face me.

"You have to wait here," he stated.

"Do I get to speak with your commander?" I asked.

"We wait here," he said again, ignoring my question.

Ten minutes later a white SUV approached us on the dirt road. When it pulled up, I saw that there were four fully uniformed paramilitaries inside. I was told to climb into the backseat, then the SUV turned around and we took off in the direction from which it had come. My driver remained behind with the paramilitaries that had initially detained us.

None of the paramilitaries in the SUV would answer my question about whether we were going to meet their commander. After about ten minutes, we stopped in the middle of nowhere, with nary a building or a person in sight. I was ordered out of the vehicle, and all four paramilitaries followed. It suddenly crossed my mind that they might be about to execute me, but nothing happened—we all just stood there in silence.

A few minutes later, a white pickup truck appeared from further along the same dirt road. The paramilitaries who'd been riding in the back jumped down as the one in the passenger seat waved me over. My intuition told me that he was the commander, so I approached him and requested an interview. He ignored my request and instead began questioning me from inside the vehicle while the others encircled me.

"Why are you in Arauca?" he asked.

"To investigate the security situation," I replied.

"Do you have a gun?" he asked, simultaneously signaling to one of the other paramilitaries to frisk me. "Why do you want to speak with us?"

"To get your view on the conflict here in Arauca and your opinion about the planned arrival of the U.S. soldiers," I answered. Hoping to alleviate his suspicions, I nervously added, "I have interviewed commanders of the Self-Defense Forces in other parts of Colombia."

"Where have you met with the Self-Defense Forces?" he asked.

"In Putumayo, eighteen months ago."

The next question did not come from the commander sitting in the vehicle, but from one of the fighters standing beside me.

"Who did you speak with in Putumayo?"

"Commander Enrique," I replied without hesitation.

"What does he look like?" he asked, obviously testing me.

"He had a shaved head and wore lots of gold jewelry. We met in a second floor restaurant on the main street in La Hormiga."

The paramilitary who had asked the last couple of questions turned to the commander and nodded his head in approval.

"Do you know Commander Enrique?" I asked the fighter beside me.

"I was stationed in Putumayo until a year ago," he said.

I would never have imagined that one of those paramilitaries had been in Putumayo, given that it was six hundred miles south of Arauca. It drove home the fact that the AUC was indeed a national organization. It also made me realize how easy it would be to get caught in a lie, and I reminded myself to stick to the truth as much as possible.

The commander ordered me into the back of the pickup truck with the other paramilitaries. We drove down the dirt road and across a field, finally arriving at a fenced-in compound amid a cluster of trees that surrounded a small farmhouse. Everyone poured out of the vehicle, and the commander ordered me to sit in a chair under a tree. A paramilitary who was holding a cell phone in his hand climbed a ladder that was propped against the same tree. Apparently that was the only place he could get a signal for his phone. From above me, I heard him ask the person on the other end of the phone, "We have a *gringo* journalist here. What do you want us to do with him?"

A shudder ran down my spine. I couldn't hear the rest of the short conversation, but I assumed that he had given my name to the party on the other end of the line—probably a higher-ranking paramilitary who could have been anywhere in Colombia, perhaps even in Carlos Castaño's camp.

Suddenly the thought occurred to me that they might investigate my work on the Internet. Most of my writings had been critical of U.S. policy in Colombia, particularly the provision of military aid to an army allied with right-wing paramilitary death squads. And since I saw my responsibility as a U.S. journalist to be providing information to the American people about the policies of their government and about what their tax dollars were funding, my articles were much more focused on the role of the Colombian military and the paramilitaries in the country's armed conflict than on the role of the guerrillas. In other words, many of my articles had been extremely critical of the paramilitaries. As a result, I had received many unpleasant e-mails over the years accusing me of being a guerrilla. Some e-mails were threatening, including occasionally wishing me dead. One in particular said the "paramilitaries will take care of you next time you are in Colombia." I feared that whoever was on the receiving end of the phone call would begin to investigate my work and decide to fulfill that threat.

The paramilitary fighter climbed back down from the tree without an answer to his question. Every thirty minutes or so, he would climb back up and make a call to see whether a decision about my fate had been reached. Meanwhile, an elderly woman emerged from the farmhouse with cups of coffee for everyone. The commander sat down next to me, and I discovered that his name, or at least his nom de guerre, was Freddy. Our interaction shifted back and forth between interrogation and conversation.

"Have you met with the guerrillas?" he asked me at one point.

"No, I have not," I responded, thankful that I had failed to hook up with the ELN and could answer truthfully.

"What about the army?"

"I met with General Lemus yesterday," I answered honestly, realizing that paramilitary informers might already be aware of that fact.

"What did he say about us?" Commander Freddy asked.

I purposely responded vaguely, explaining that the general had only acknowledged that both the guerrillas and the Self-Defense Forces were active in the region. I didn't want my actions to be perceived as "informing" on the army to the paramilitaries, just in case any of those fighters in the farmyard also proved to be an informant for the Colombian military—but I didn't want to annoy my paramilitary hosts by refusing to answer. It felt like I was walking a tightrope.

We continued to wait, and my fear and anxiety came and went in waves. I'd seen in Puerto Asís what the paramilitaries were capable of doing with machetes, chainsaws, or any other instrument of death they might choose to use on me should they receive the order. Castaño's ACCU fighters were the most brutal and feared paramilitaries in the country. I already knew that this particular unit, known as the Arauca Vanquishers Block, was believed to have been responsible for 70 percent of the more than 420 political killings that had occurred in the vicinity of Arauca City during the previous year. But I also knew that the worst thing I could do would be to show fear. In

Colombia, the armed groups interpret fear as a sign that a person has something to hide. It doesn't seem to cross their mind that simply being held at gunpoint by a bunch of men who've probably killed before is more than ample reason for the average person to be terrified.

At one point, Commander Freddy asked me if I was nervous.

"A little," I replied.

"Why?"

"Because all of you have guns and I don't," I joked.

Thankfully, he just chuckled and changed the subject.

"Does your government think we are terrorists?" he asked, obviously aware of the Bush administration's new war on terror in Colombia.

"The U.S. government considers the AUC, FARC, and ELN to be terrorists," I answered, assuming that he was already aware of that fact and just wanted to see how I would respond.

"What do you think of the Self-Defense Forces?" he asked.

I knew my answer needed to be tactful and neutral, so I responded, "I understand that the Colombian state is weak and some sectors of society feel the need to organize to defend themselves against the guerrillas." This was basically stating the AUC's own justification for its existence. Then he asked, "What do you think of the guerrillas?"

His line of questioning was making me increasingly nervous.

"I think some of their tactics, like kidnapping and mortar attacks that kill civilians, only turn the Colombian people against them," I replied.

To my relief, he seemed satisfied with my response.

Almost four hours after I was initially detained, the paramilitary fighter with the cell phone again descended from the tree. This time, however, he had received an answer. He whispered something to Commander Freddy, who then sat down opposite me. I nervously awaited the verdict.

"I am not permitted to give you an interview," he explained. "But I can give you a statement about the role of the Self-Defense Forces here in Arauca."

I did my best not to let him see the overwhelming sense of relief that washed over me—a decision to give me a statement meant that they were going to let me go. I pulled my tape recorder out of my pocket, and Commander Freddy gave a two-minute statement, the core of which was, "The Self-Defense Forces came to Arauca to liberate the people from the guerrillas. We are living in a state of war with the guerrillas; we are not here to combat the state."

Afterward I asked the commander whether I could take some photos of him and his fighters. He agreed, and after donning bandanas to conceal their identities, several of them began posing. We then all piled into the vehicles and returned to the road where my driver was still waiting.

I climbed into the taxi and let out a deep breath as we pulled away from the paramilitaries, telling myself that I would never again try to contact the armed groups. Never again! It was something that I had told myself on several previous occasions following close calls, but I would inevitably deal with them again in the future. I checked with my driver to make sure that he was okay; thirty minutes later, we arrived safely in Arauca City.

In early February 2003, six months after being detained by the paramilitaries, I met up with British photojournalist Jason Howe in Bogotá. Jason is six feet tall, slender, in his early thirties, and most of the time sports a five o'clock shadow. He had worked extensively in Colombia during the previous two years and would later cover the wars in Iraq and Afghanistan. Jason and I decided to fly to the town of Saravena in Arauca, which was situated less than three miles from the Caño Limón oil pipeline and was where forty U.S. Army Special Forces troops had recently been deployed as part of the Bush administration's war on terror in Colombia. I wanted to determine the objective of the U.S. military deployment to Arauca.

We descended the steps of the small twin-propeller plane onto the runway at Saravena's airport—or more accurately, the remains of Saravena's airport. Several months earlier, the FARC had launched nine homemade mortars against the airport in an attack that left twelve civilians and six soldiers wounded.

Along with the other passengers, we walked to the remains of the small terminal building. The roof was gone, and the bright sunlight shone down on the rubble strewn about the inside of the structure. There was no glass left in the windows, and shrapnel had torn chunks of concrete from the outside walls.

After leaving the terminal, we were about to climb into a taxi when a soldier approached us and asked why we were in Saravena. I told him that we were journalists investigating the security situation in the region.

"Do you have permission to come to Saravena?" he asked.

"We do not need permission to come here," I responded.

Although Jason and I knew that the soldier didn't have the legal authority to prevent us from visiting Saravena, that didn't necessarily mean he wouldn't try to stop us. The soldier told us to wait while he radioed his commander. Several minutes later he said, "You will have to sign a document stating that the Colombian army is not responsible for anything that happens to you while you are here."

After signing the document, we caught a taxi into the town of thirty thousand people, which was known locally as "Little Sarajevo." The reason for the nickname became apparent when we reached the center of town and saw almost a dozen bombed-out buildings, including the town hall and the municipal building, within a two-block radius of the central plaza. As with the airport terminal, most of the roofs had collapsed, the windows had been blown out, and the interiors were full of rubble. Saravena more closely resembled a conventional war zone than any other town I had visited in Colombia. As we later learned, substantial popular support in the town's poor barrios had allowed the rebels to attack the center of Saravena with bombs, mortars, grenades, or gunfire on eighty different days during the previous year. Many of the shops and offices that had not been destroyed had been abandoned for fear of attack. As a result, the eerie quiet and desolation of Saravena's central plaza stood in stark contrast to the hustle and bustle commonly found in most Colombian towns. The principal target of the rebel mortar attacks had been the police station, which, ironically, was the only building on that side of the plaza that remained relatively unscathed.

After checking into a hotel half a block away from the bombed-out central plaza, Jason and I walked over to the heavily fortified police station. The roads surrounding the station had been permanently closed to traffic, and barricades prevented the guerrillas from using car bombs against the building. Sandbagged walls surrounded the police station, and each corner contained a watchtower, inside which officers stood guard armed with M16 semiautomatic assault rifles.

Jason and I approached an officer at the entrance to the police station and identified ourselves as journalists. The officer responded to our request to interview his commander by inviting us to follow him through the sandbagged wall into the building. Within minutes a short, rather heavyset man in his mid forties, smartly dressed in green combat fatigues and oozing a confidence that bordered on cockiness, emerged from his office to meet us. He introduced himself as Major Joaquin Aldana, commander of the National Police detachment in Saravena. I asked him which armed groups were active in Saravena.

"There are two terrorist groups: the ELN and the FARC. Both of them commit terrorist acts," he replied.

"How much of the town is controlled by the police?" I asked.

"We have complete control of the center of town where the commercial area is; that is, around the police station. And we make patrols through the other neighborhoods."

"Do many people here in Saravena support the guerrillas?"

"There has been a lot of subversive influence on people's political thinking in this town. The terrorists say that they have implemented a lot of public works in the town and that they have created social organizations. There are people who have benefited because the terrorists helped build houses. But people now see that was in the past."

Aldana claimed that the guerrillas no longer had a social project and were focused only on destroying the town. I couldn't help but notice that, like many of Colombia's politically savvy police and army officials following 9/11, Major Aldana consciously and repeatedly used the word "terrorists" when referring to the guerrillas. It seemed to be an attempt to delegitimize the rebels and to appeal to Washington's desire to wage a war on terror.

The commander then told us that he had recently received a detachment of 120 Carabineros (militarized police) who had been specially trained under a program run by the U.S. Army's 7th Special Forces Group in Tolemaida in Central Colombia. The National Police in Colombia are markedly different from police in North America and Europe. Colombia's police fall under the jurisdiction of the Ministry of Defense. As part of the Colombian military, they wear combat fatigues, carry assault rifles and heavy machine guns, and receive military training to fight the guerrillas. Major Aldana boasted that, since the arrival of the Carabineros, "we have started to defeat the terrorists who hide behind the fear they instill in the people."

Over the next several days, I discovered a divide in the people's attitudes. The merchants and wealthier residents who lived and worked in the town center were appreciative of the increased security provided by the police and thought that the situation had improved over the previous six months. In the surrounding barrios, residents felt differently; they believed that the police and army had used the security measures implemented under newly elected president Alvaro Uribe to justify escalating the repression against social activists and the poor. Only two months earlier, the army had rounded up more than two thousand residents of the town's barrios and taken them to the local sports stadium, where they were interrogated. Many of those detained were union leaders, human rights defenders, community leaders, and others who were engaged in the struggle for social justice and were critical of the government's policies. The arrests had been made under President Uribe's Democratic Defense and Security Strategy, which was intended to strengthen state control over the country's conflict zones. President Uribe's security policies had succeeded in reducing kidnapping and criminal violence in urban areas, but those gains had been achieved in part through the state security forces becoming more directly engaged in human rights abuses such as the mass arrests in Saravena, the "disappearance" of so-called subversives, and even extrajudicial executions. Although the government's militaristic policies had increased security for urban Colombians, little had changed for rural residents in the country's conflict zones. Meanwhile, the United Nations, as well as Colombian and international human rights groups, repeatedly condemned the repressive security policies being implemented by the Uribe government.

One morning Jason and I observed a Colombian army psychological operations unit in its attempt to win over the "hearts and minds" of residents in an ELN-controlled barrio. One soldier sat in the back of an army truck voicing anti-rebel propaganda over a loudspeaker system. We walked around the streets observing the reactions of residents. While some locals eyed the soldiers warily and a few others went about their business as usual, most residents remained behind closed doors. But there was no escaping the propaganda blitzkrieg. In a bizarre scene that could have been lifted straight out of a Fellini movie, two soldiers dressed in colorful red and yellow clown outfits, accompanied by uniformed troops, went door to door handing out leaflets offering rewards to residents willing to provide information about rebel activities. Armed with a large bag of candy, the clowns also befriended any children they encountered, as nervous parents looked on. While this military circus was taking place, several soldiers were busying themselves painting a colorful mural of a sunset over ELN graffiti on a nearby wall. In the end, this military presence proved to be only a temporary hindrance to the guerrillas, who simply melted into the fabric of the community during the few hours that the army was in the barrio.

In the midst of the operation, I approached an elderly man standing just inside the gateway to an alley that ran between two houses. When I asked him about the security situation in Saravena, he beckoned me to follow him down the alleyway to a courtyard behind one of the houses, where several men and women were sitting. I introduced myself as a journalist and again asked about the security situation. The residents were hesitant to speak to me at length, which was not surprising given that their neighborhood was crawling with soldiers, but they did claim that harassment by the army and police had intensified during the previous six months. We'd been talking for less than five minutes when two soldiers appeared in the courtyard, causing everyone to fall silent. The soldiers ordered me to return to the street. They clearly did not want me to converse with people whom they most likely considered to be guerrillas or guerrilla sympathizers.

Later that day I met with Saravena's mayor, José Trinidad, to hear his take on the increased militarization of the town under the war on terror. I found him working in the living room of his home, which had been converted into an office following a rebel mortar attack that destroyed the municipal building. Inviting me to sit opposite him, he apologized for the unprofessional environment. Trinidad said that he welcomed the increased military and police presence in the town, but was critical of the national government's failure to address the region's social and economic ills.

"The inhabitants of Saravena have been asking the government for social investment," he explained. "We believe that the public order problem is not going to be solved with the presence of the public forces. It must be complemented with social investment. We have asked the national government to help us generate employment. And we also require investment in education and health."

Trinidad noted that the Uribe government had recently announced that the department of Arauca would no longer receive its share of the nation's oil revenues because the president believed that too much of the money went to the rebels through extortion and sympathetic local politicians.

"Do the guerrillas receive much support from people in Saravena's barrios?" I asked.

"There are people who sympathize with the groups on the margin of the law. Lately there have been a lot of people who have been arrested and accused of helping the guerrillas," he replied, apparently referring to the many arbitrary mass arrests that had taken place in Saravena over the previous six months. "But the state has not been able to prove these things."

"Have you been threatened by the guerrillas?"

"Yes. Last year the ELN kidnapped two councilmen and me for eight days, and then, after we were set free, the FARC tried to kidnap us again, but we managed to avoid it. We have also received threats from paramilitary groups based in Arauca City."

Following my interview with the mayor, I met Jason at the police station, since Major Aldana had given us permission to accompany one of his police patrols through the rebel-controlled barrios. It was four o'clock in the afternoon when the patrol, consisting of forty heavily armed Carabineros, departed the police station on foot. Jason and I accompanied the police officers as they made their way out of the town center and onto the dirt streets of a neighborhood controlled by the FARC's 45th Front.

The jovial demeanor that the officers had exhibited during roll call at the police station and through the streets of the commercial district quickly evaporated when we entered rebel-controlled territory. The atmosphere was tense, and I found myself constantly anticipating a sudden burst of gunfire or an explosion. The Carabineros patrolled in two columns, one down each side of the street, with each police officer maintaining a twenty-yard distance from the one ahead of him—thus ensuring that a single hand grenade wouldn't kill more than one of them. Each time an officer decided to investigate a vehicle, building, or individual, the entire patrol, which sometimes encompassed four or five blocks, came to a halt. While the patrol remained stationary, all the officers would take cover behind trees or beside nearby buildings in order to guard against a possible ambush.

We passed into another barrio, where many of the houses were adorned with graffiti announcing that the FARC's 10th Front held sway in that particular part of Saravena. People standing in their doorways or leering over fences eyed the Carabineros suspiciously, never offering any verbal greeting to the armed intruders. In a barrio close to the commercial center, one that was controlled by the ELN's Domingo Lain Front, the patrol commander stopped to question several indigenous men who were shooting billiards in a local pool hall. Everyone in the vicinity of the patrol felt the tension when a little girl wandered over to one of the Carabineros standing guard across the street from the pool hall. She stood at his feet, peering expectantly up at the stern face of the officer, who was focusing his rifle sights on passersby. The child's mother nervously ran over and grabbed the bewildered youngster, and the two of them quickly disappeared into a nearby house.

Soon the patrol was on the move again, much to the relief of the young Carabineros, who clearly wanted nothing more than to return to the relatively safe confines of the heavily fortified police station. By the end of the patrol, it was evident to me that the state's security forces had a long way to go to win over the trust of the residents of Saravena's barrios.

On the afternoon of our first day in town, Jason and I had visited the army base on the outskirts of Saravena. We had conducted an interview with the local army commander, Major William Bautista, who gave us permission to photograph his troops as long as we agreed not to approach the U.S. Army Special Forces soldiers stationed at the base. Somehow the access we enjoyed that first day evolved into our being allowed to come and go at will. Every time we showed up at the base, the guards at the gate would simply allow us to enter and roam about freely.

After photographing Colombian soldiers engaged in training exercises one morning, Jason and I made our way to the base café to temporarily escape the oppressive heat. To our amazement, while we were sitting there downing our refreshing fruit juices, three U.S. soldiers dressed in white T-shirts and blue shorts, with M16 assault rifles slung over their shoulders, entered the café. They ordered their own fruit juices and sat down next to Jason and me.

"What are you guys doing here?" one of them asked us in a friendly tone, apparently surprised to see two *gringos* in that remote corner of Colombia.

"We're journalists covering the security situation here in Arauca," I explained before asking where they had been stationed previously.

"We were in Afghanistan before they sent us here," the same soldier responded.

"What do you think about the situation here in Colombia?"

"I don't like these half-ass wars. If we're going to get involved, we should just throw it down like we've done in Afghanistan," he said, apparently referring to their role as military advisors rather than as combatants.

"What do you think about the fact that paramilitaries often enter villages and massacre suspected guerrilla sympathizers?" I asked.

"Sometimes that's what you have to do, I guess," he answered without hesitation and with a nonchalant shrug of his shoulders. I did my best to conceal my surprise, astounded by his response. The three of them shook our hands and left.

The next morning, Jason and I returned to the army base, ready to observe a psychological operations program that we had heard about. The program, called Soldier for a Day, targeted children between three and seventeen years of age who were brought to the army base every Thursday, basically to play soldier. When we arrived at the base, eighteen children, ages four and up, were engaged in a variety of activities with soldiers who wore camouflage combat fatigues. Some of the soldiers were part of the psychological operations unit we had previously observed in town; several others were army psychologists. We watched a couple of the psychologists apply camouflage makeup to the faces of several children. The image of such young children being dressed as soldiers in a country at peace would have been unsettling enough, but witnessing it in a country that was in the midst of an armed conflict was truly disturbing. Meanwhile, two soldiers attired in clown suits provided entertainment. Some of the children appeared to enjoy the charade, while others looked bewildered. Throughout the program, the "little soldiers" were continuously bombarded with pro-army and anti-rebel propaganda, although they also got to play games and enjoy a dip in the camp's swimming pool.

While the children were in the pool, I sat down with a twenty-three-year-old female army psychologist named Paola

Alzate and asked her to explain the purpose of the Soldier for a Day program.

"In Saravena, children have it very difficult," she said. "At six years of age they are talking about cylinder bombs, tanks, militias, and they know how bombs are made. These children have traumas, and what they want to do when they grow up is join the army because they believe that it is the only way to solve the situation. They are dreaming of learning how to handle guns to kill the bad guy in the neighborhood. They dream of learning how to drive a tank to be able to destroy the home-made mortars."

"Are the parents of some of these children in the guerrilla militias?" I asked.

"Yes, we have some cases where the children are the sons or nephews of militia members. In some cases when we put camouflage headbands on them, they say that they can't take them home because their fathers will yell at them. When those kinds of things happen, we try to talk to them to find out what is happening at home. In many cases, they are children whose parents are in the militias, and those children become conflicted about what's right and what's wrong."

The grand finale of the program involved the children—with Jason and me in tow—climbing on top of an armored personnel carrier, fully equipped with a .50-caliber machine gun, for a ride around the base. As we motored around on that vehicle, I couldn't help but feel there was something seriously misguided about using the military as a tool to try to help children who have been traumatized by the conflict. Clearly, the army's disturbing ulterior motive was to use the children as a means to obtain information about what was happening not only in Saravena's barrios but also inside their homes.

That evening, Jason and I were relaxing in our hotel when we heard an explosion. We had become accustomed to these attacks—there were rebel grenade, mortar, and gunfire attacks against the police on three of the four nights that we spent in Saravena—and quickly made our way to the police station to investigate.

While Major Aldana was explaining to us how a grenade had wounded two policemen, a handful of officers arrived at the station with the injured parties. One of them had received only scratches, but the other had suffered serious leg wounds. The police officer who'd been badly wounded was laid on the floor to wait for a vehicle to take him to the army base for treatment, and I approached him to ask what had happened.

"We were patrolling the sector when we felt the grenade at our feet, and we turned to run away. I was running when I felt the pain in my legs. I did not feel it immediately; I felt it a few minutes after the explosion." He grimaced in pain.

Jason and I left and walked at a brisk pace down the silent street toward the site of the attack—a mere four blocks from the police station, in the opposite direction from our hotel. It was dark; the streets surrounding the police station were not illuminated. We were midway along the third block when the silence was shattered by the sound of automatic weapons fire, which seemed to be coming from the intersection directly ahead of us. Unsure who was firing at whom and in what direction, we both reflexively leaped for cover. As I jumped up onto the curb and into a recessed doorway, I saw Jason go crashing headfirst into the metal door ahead of me. Strangely, the idea that he might have been shot never entered my mind. Instead, I was thinking that his evasive maneuver was a bit melodramatic, like John Wayne diving for cover in one of his war movies.

And then I heard him yell out in his distinct British accent, "Fuck!"

"Are you okay?" I asked.

"Yes." He sounded a little disgruntled.

"What happened?"

"I tripped over the curb and smashed my head into the door.

It's bleeding. And I've broken my fuckin' camera lens and flash."

After a couple of minutes, the gunfire stopped. We waited several more minutes to make sure it didn't flare up again before continuing down the road, staying close to the walls of the buildings and in the shadows to avoid being illuminated by the moonlight. As we approached the intersection, we could see police officers lying in the prone position with their rifles aimed off into the darkness.

"Journalists! Journalists!" we whispered to them as we approached, not wanting to be mistaken for guerrillas.

As we crouched down on the street corner, a scene unfolded that I would never have believed had I not seen it with my own eyes. Even though the shooting had ceased only minutes earlier, a man was cycling casually down the middle of the street and through the intersection. Shaking our heads in disbelief, we raced across the intersection to the scene of the original grenade attack. But since there were no witnesses and Jason had broken his camera lens and flash, there was nothing much to do there, so we decided to return to the police station.

Less than a block later, gunfire again erupted all around us. Once more we took cover against the walls of the buildings that lined the street. This time the shooting didn't let up, but we decided to make our way to the police station, moving slowly and carefully and keeping as close to the buildings as possible.

When we arrived at the station, Major Aldana told us that the guerrillas had launched a large-scale attack against the town and that he was calling in reinforcements from the army base. Given that the police station would be the likely target of any potential rebel mortar fire, Jason and I decided to retreat quickly. We left the police station and crossed the central plaza to the hotel. Almost instantly after we were inside, automatic weapons fire broke out at the intersection half a block away— the same intersection that we had just walked through a minute earlier. Thankful that we had made it back safely, we cracked open a couple of beers, placed a wet compress on Jason's head, and rode out the remainder of the ninety-minute battle in the hotel lobby. The fighting eventually ended when the army's tanks rolled into town and the guerrillas melted back into the barrios.

Interestingly, I hadn't felt any fear while Jason and I were on the street during the fighting. It wasn't until I was safely in the hotel that the realization of what had just happened hit me, and I thought to myself, "Wow! That was intense." But it was a different type of intensity than I had experienced during my detention by the paramilitaries six months earlier. Clearly, having four hours to reflect on my predicament during the detention had contributed to my feeling terrified. In contrast, during the street battle there was little time to reflect on what was happening, which meant that I did not experience the same feeling of impotence that had so tormented me when I was held at gunpoint by the paramilitaries.

Later that evening, Jason and I received confirmation that the ELN guerrillas had agreed to meet with us in the mountains and that someone would pick us up at our hotel the next morning. We had been trying to arrange the meeting since our arrival in Saravena, but were no longer sure that we wanted to go through with it. Only weeks earlier the ELN had kidnapped two foreign journalists in Arauca. The journalists—American photographer Scott Dalton, whom I'd worked with in Putumayo, and British writer Ruth Morris—had been working together on assignment for the *Los Angeles Times*. Until this incident, foreign reporters covering Colombia's civil conflict had enjoyed immunity from rebel kidnappings. Initial statements by the ELN declared that the two reporters would not be released until the "political and military situation merited," which appeared to be a call for the withdrawal of U.S. troops. However, in the face of international condemnation, the ELN revised its position and freed the journalists after eleven days.

Jason and I were having second thoughts about meeting with the guerrillas, not only because of the recent kidnapping, but also because most of our work in Saravena had been with the army and police. The guerrillas were undoubtedly aware of this fact and might consider us informers. It's always risky to contact opposing combatants in the same region because it increases the possibility that one of the sides will assume you are working for the enemy. Finally, after much discussion, we decided against meeting with the rebels. Instead, we'd try to participate in the U.S. embassy–sponsored press junket to the army base scheduled for the following day. Apparently the guerrillas had intended their attack on the town to serve as a military statement on the eve of the press junket, which was designed to promote the war-on-terror mission of the U.S. Army Special Forces troops.

I had contacted the U.S. embassy a week earlier to request permission to participate in the junket but hadn't received a response. Over the years, the embassy's media relations officers had always failed to accommodate my requests to interview embassy officials and to accompany fumigation operations and raids against cocaine processing labs. I knew that reporters working for mainstream media outlets regularly received such access, but not journalists who, like me, worked for smaller media outlets and were critical of U.S. policies. During one phone call, after introducing myself as an independent journalist but without mentioning my online publication, the embassy's media relations official immediately asked whether what I learned from an interview would be published in *Colombia Journal*.

"You're familiar with *Colombia Journal?*" I asked, surprised.

"Oh yes, we are familiar with your work," he replied, a hint of accusation in his tone.

It quickly became clear that the embassy was determined to do all it could to deny me access to U.S. officials and counternarcotics operations. Such censorship based on a journalist's or media outlet's political point of view is a blatant attempt to restrict the flow of information to the American people in order to ensure that only the government's perspective is presented to the public.

Fortunately, being blacklisted by the embassy didn't mean that I lacked access to all U.S. officials; it just meant that the access I did have was off the record. During my trips to Bogotá, I would sometimes meet in private with a counternarcotics official from the U.S. embassy who had many years of experience working in Colombia. I met with that official on several occasions over the years, and he represented my only contact with the U.S. embassy. Our talks were always off the record, and we never discussed particulars related to the work either of us was doing. He would provide me with interesting background information about how counternarcotics programs functioned, but without specific details about individual operations. Likewise, I would provide him with insights into life in rural Colombia—where no U.S. official would ever visit—without mentioning names of specific people or places. In a way, these conversations provided us both with insights into worlds that neither of us could access.

I never once got the impression from my contact that he saw his job as simply the furthering of U.S. interests at the expense of poor Colombians; he seemed to genuinely care for the Colombian people and thought that the work he did was helping them. In our conversations we would express differing views about how to improve life for Colombians. He maintained a mainstream view that military aid was essential in order to establish security for the Colombian people so that they could then benefit from neoliberal economic reforms intended to incorporate Colombia into the new world economic order. In contrast, I believed that providing aid to a military allied with paramilitary death squads only fueled the country's conflict—and that the conflict wouldn't end until a social and economic model was established that truly served the interests of most Colombians. In my view, the dominant neoliberal— free-market—model mostly benefited multinational corporations, not the majority of Colombians; I felt that U.S. military aid had done little to improve the lives of rural Colombians and that often, particularly in the coca-growing regions, Plan Colombia had made their lives worse. Ultimately, we basically agreed to disagree.

The morning following the street battle in Saravena, Jason and I left a note at the hotel desk for our rebel contact, apologizing for not being able to meet with him. We then headed out of town to the army base, arriving just as the plane carrying the embassy officials and foreign press correspondents was landing at the adjoining airport. On that morning we were not granted instant access to the base. We insisted that the guards at the gate contact the U.S. embassy officials to let them know that a U.S. journalist was waiting to participate in the proceedings. As it turned out, the embassy media relations officer I had spoken with a week earlier was traveling with the press corps and, not wanting to refuse participation to us in front of Colombian troops and other reporters, decided to allow Jason and me to enter and participate.

The press junket typified how most foreign correspondents covered the rural conflict in Colombia. Official press junkets, regularly organized by the Colombian military and the U.S. embassy, are a convenient way for correspondents based in Bogotá to visit remote rural regions affected by the civil conflict. The problem with this arrangement, however, is that the journalists are flown to a specific destination chosen by the authorities, where they spend a few hours with officials and get presented with a prepackaged story. Inevitably, the official line dominates the published account.

The Colombian government and the U.S. embassy are fully aware of the mainstream media's overreliance on official sources. They regularly hold press conferences or dispatch officials to public events such as the opening of a new factory or the launching of a new military operation, realizing that the media will obediently cover these events because they provide convenient stories for reporters working under tight deadlines. The foreign correspondents based in Colombia tend to all attend the same events and press junkets because none of them wants to be the only one not covering a particular "story." Consequently, several almost identical versions of the same article are frequently published the following day by various U.S. media outlets. Government officials know that if they keep the media occupied daily with prepackaged stories that portray government policy in a positive light, then reporters may be too busy to conduct deeper investigative journalism. With the notable exception of *Washington Post* reporter Scott Wilson, who during his time in the country occasionally ventured out into rural conflict zones and presented alternative perspectives on the political situation, mainstream media correspondents in Colombia appear to view their journalistic responsibility in much the same way that *New York Times* reporter Judith Miller did in the lead-up to the war in Iraq. When asked why her articles seldom included the views of experts skeptical of the Bush administration's claims of weapons of mass destruction, Miller replied, "My job isn't to assess the government's information and be an independent intelligence analyst myself. My job is to tell readers of the *New York Times* what the government thought of Iraq's arsenal."

In its coverage of Colombia's conflict, the mainstream media have tended to reflect the perspective of the dominant political and economic sectors of Colombian society. For example, the issue of kidnapping has received widespread media coverage because leftist guerrillas are the principal perpetrators and the victims are primarily politicians, members of the state security forces, and civilians from the urban middle and upper classes. Although kidnapped Colombians are clearly victims of the country's violence and their plight deserves attention, their numbers pale in comparison to the number of peasants who have been massacred and forcibly displaced by right-wing para-militaries. At the outset of Plan Colombia, approximately three thousand Colombians were being kidnapped annually. Meanwhile, more than a quarter of a million peasants were being forcibly displaced from their homes and land every year. And yet most people were oblivious to the fact that Colombia had one of the largest internally displaced populations in the world. The mainstream media have mostly ignored the plight of poor rural Colombians.

As usual, correspondents from the largest daily newspapers in the United States, along with reporters from large international outlets, participated in the press junket to Saravena. We all sat there and listened to the commander of the U.S. Army Special Forces troops explain how they were training units of the 18th Brigade in counterinsurgency to help defend the civilian population from the terrorists. Then we watched as Colombian troops put on an exhibition of the combat skills they had recently learned from their U.S. advisors.

Less than two hours after touching down in Saravena, the reporters and embassy officials were back on the plane, returning to the relatively safe confines of Bogotá. The reporters never left the base during their brief stay and didn't speak with anyone other than U.S. government and army officials. As I'd anticipated, many U.S. media outlets carried almost identical articles the next day describing the difficult but important job that U.S. soldiers were performing in Colombia to combat terrorism. The Associated Press article differed slightly from the rest in that it mentioned the rebel attack in Saravena that had occurred the night before the press junket—but only because I'd described the attack to the AP reporter while he was at the army base and he'd decided to include it in his story. All in all, the Saravena stories were not the sort of frontline investigative reporting that we'd like to believe is routinely conducted by the U.S. mainstream media.

• • •

Jason and I flew back to Bogotá the day after the press junket, and I obtained an interview with an Occidental Petroleum representative to discuss the company's operations in Arauca. The representative refused to go on the record, telling me that I could use the information only for background and therefore couldn't quote him. Nevertheless, he did admit that the company provided logistical support to Colombian army units that protected the oil pipeline. Essentially, Occidental was providing logistical support, and U.S. military advisors were providing counterinsurgency training, to Colombian army units that were deeply involved in gross violations of human rights.

Over the next eighteen months, while the U.S. soldiers were based in Arauca, there was a significant drop in the number of rebel attacks against Occidental's Caño Limón oil pipeline. At the same time, however, not only was the 18th Brigade using its newly acquired counterinsurgency skills against the guerrillas, it was also targeting civilians critical of the Uribe government's policies. In May 2003, paramilitaries and soldiers from the 18th Brigade entered the indigenous reserve at Betoyes in Arauca, where they raped and killed a pregnant sixteen-year-old indigenous girl and then cut the fetus out of her stomach before disposing of her body in a river. Two other indigenous people were also killed, and more than eight hundred were forcibly displaced.

On August 21, soldiers from the army base in Saravena raided homes and arrested forty-two trade unionists, social activists, and human rights defenders who were accused of being terrorists. Several months later, soldiers from various units of the 18th Brigade rounded up more than twenty-five opposition politicians in Arauca less than a week before local elections. Among those arrested for suspected ties to guerrillas were the mayor of Arauca City, the president of the regional assembly, a candidate for governor, and five mayoral candidates. Amnesty International accused the Uribe administration of politicizing human rights, claiming, "A lot of it has to do with silencing those who campaign for human and socioeconomic rights." The timing of the arrests, only days before local elections, also led an Amnesty spokesperson to declare, "It is part of a strategy to undermine the opposition's credibility."

In August 2004, Colombian soldiers from the same base housing the U.S. military advisors again ventured out into Saravena's barrios. This time the soldiers dragged three union leaders out of their beds in the middle of the night and executed them in cold blood. The Colombian army initially claimed that the three unionists were armed guerrillas killed in battle, but an investigation conducted by local and international human rights groups ultimately pressured the Colombian attorney general's office into launching its own probe. Deputy Attorney General Luis Alberto Santana later announced, "The evidence shows that a homicide was committed. We have ruled out that there was combat." In a rare case of justice being carried out in Colombia's dirty war, one army officer and two Colombian soldiers were arrested and charged with the murder of the three union leaders.

Given the atrocities that were being perpetrated by Colombian soldiers trained by U.S. military advisors in Arauca, I couldn't help but think that U.S. military aid was being used as much to wage a war of terror as to fight a war against terror. At best, it appeared to be funding a selective war on terror—one that targeted civilians seen as suspected leftist terrorists, yet supported a military responsible for perpetrating state terrorism and maintaining close ties to right-wing terrorists. And thanks in part to the mainstream media's failure to seriously question the legitimacy of the U.S. war on terror in Colombia, the Bush administration was able to implement its policies virtually unchallenged.

The Eighth Hour
5:00 p.m., August 16, 2006

I try to doze off in my white plastic chair, thinking that sleep might serve as an escape from the monotony. My eyes keep opening, and I realize that this is an exercise in futility because I'm not really tired.

The maroon SUV that brought me here pulls up to the farmhouse, and the same partially uniformed driver gets out. He enters the house with two young male guerrillas in tow. He greets me with a handshake and asks whether everything is okay. I resist the urge to yell out, "No, everything is not fucking okay! I have been held at gunpoint all day, and I am bored out of my fucking mind. But mostly I am fucking scared!" Instead, I calmly tell him that everything is fine. He and the two young guerrillas stand their AK-47 assault rifles in the corner before taking off their ammunition pouches and hanging them over the railing at the front of the house. I realize that this is his house and that the young guerrillas, who appear to be in their late teens, are his sons. Apparently my host is both a farmer and a guerrilla.

From past experiences in different parts of Colombia, I have learned that relations between the local population and the FARC differ greatly depending on the history of the region. There are three principal scenarios. In areas where the guerrillas have maintained a presence for decades—as in much of Caquetá, Meta, Guaviare, and Putumayo, as well as parts of Huila and Nariño—the peasants and the rebels are often organically linked; many local peasants are guerrillas and vice versa. By contrast, in rural regions in which the FARC has established its presence primarily in the past fifteen years, the local peasants often view the rebels with a certain amount of distrust because the guerrillas are not historically or organically linked to the local peasant population. Furthermore, in those regions the guerrillas' operations are often primarily military in nature, and there is usually an army and paramilitary presence as well, which often results in the civilian population becoming caught in the middle of the conflict between the armed groups. This is especially true in many parts of northern Colombia. The third scenario involves larger towns and cities where the state has historically dominated. Although the FARC may have some support in the poor barrios and even among certain progressive sectors of the middle class, for the most part the population in these areas tends to view the guerrillas as the principal problem.

Given that the FARC has existed in the Macarena region since it was first colonized forty years ago, this area falls under the first scenario: many of the peasants are either guerrillas themselves or supportive of the guerrillas, and they are intensely distrustful of a national government that has persecuted them for decades. Without a doubt, the most dangerous of the aforementioned scenarios for the rural civilian population is the second one, in which all the armed factions are present in a particular region and none is organically linked to the local peasantry. Such is the case in the western department of the Chocó, Colombia's poorest region.

In June 2003, I flew from Medellín to Quibdó, the capital of the Chocó. I was traveling with Terry Gibbs, who later became my wife. At the time, she was director of the North American Congress on Latin America (NACLA), a New York–based non-profit organization that provides analysis of U.S. policy in Latin America.

Terry and I had met a couple of times the previous year at NACLA-related events in New York, but we didn't really begin to get to know each other until the World Social Forum in Porto Alegre, Brazil, in January 2003. I was speaking on a panel addressing race issues in Latin America, and Terry was the moderator. The forum took place during a difficult time in my life. My marriage to Jacqui was falling apart; I had become emotionally detached, not only from my wife but also from others who were close to me. Although I didn't fully realize it at the time, the trauma resulting from some of my more stressful Colombia experiences and the death of my father had made me withdrawn and insulated.

But things changed in Porto Alegre. Following our panel, Terry and I hung out together and stayed up all night in the hotel bar, talking about our personal lives and our work in great detail. I couldn't believe that I was having such an intimate conversation with someone who was a virtual stranger, yet felt like my oldest friend. We discovered that we shared the same mixed cultural background, having both lived almost half of our lives in Britain and much of the rest in North America. But most importantly for me, we realized that we shared the same passion for working in Latin America. Like me, Terry had experienced many political and cultural aspects of the region, having lived and worked in Nicaragua and in postconflict El Salvador during the 1990s. We connected in an intense and powerful way, both emotionally and intellectually. Our conversation finally concluded at six o'clock in the morning because I had to leave for the airport to catch a flight to Colombia. Terry and I parted as the sun began to rise, and I knew then that I was in love with her. Shortly after my return to New York, we began living together.

Five months after the World Social Forum, Terry and I were working together in Colombia for the first time, despite my reservations about the potential risks. Normally I preferred to work alone, although I would occasionally work with experienced journalists I felt I could trust should the going get rough. But although Terry had never previously worked as a journalist in a conflict zone, she had a lot of experience conducting research in Latin America and spoke Spanish. Any reservations I held soon dissipated as Terry immediately adapted to working in the challenging psychological and physical conditions of rural Colombia's conflict zones.

As our twin-propeller plane began its descent into Quibdó, we could see the many shades of green that constituted the canopy of the rainforest that spread out in every direction below. The Chocó is a long stretch of territory that runs more than half the length of Colombia along the Pacific coast. It's almost entirely covered in rainforest and contains a small coastal mountain range and a section of the western range of the Andes. The principal mode of transportation is by boat on the Chocó's intricate network of rivers. The Atrato River is the department's largest waterway and the region's gateway to the Caribbean Sea. There's only one road of any significance in the entire department, a rough, unpaved highway that winds its way down the western flank of the Andes and through the rainforest to Quibdó.

The region is almost as remote from central Colombia socioculturally as it is geographically. The overwhelming majority of the population consists of Afro-Colombians, many of whom are descendents of escaped slaves who established communities in the region. Much of the remainder of the population is made up of indigenous groups living as they have done for thousands of years in remote rainforest villages. Almost 80 percent of

Chocoanos live in extreme poverty, and 70 percent—three times the national average—are illiterate. The region has historically been neglected by the national government in every way except for militarily.

Before leaving for the Chocó, I'd visited the Bogotá office of CODHES, the Consultancy for Human Rights and Displacement—a Colombian nongovernmental organization that focuses on Colombia's displacement problem—and met with the organization's director, Harvey Suarez, to learn about forced displacement in the region. According to Suarez, the Chocó has one of the highest rates of forced displacement in the country, which has resulted in Afro-Colombians being disproportionately affected.

"We're talking about the systematic expulsion of Afro-Colombian communities that are involved in a legal process to gain collective title to their lands," Suarez explained. "People in the Chocó try not to leave the territory, because they know that no one receives a title to their land if they are not in the territory."

He went on to point out that displacement in the Chocó had been driven in part by a violent form of land speculation, perpetrated primarily by paramilitary groups. The speculation process took off in 1996 after President Ernesto Samper first mentioned the possibility of building a canal through the northern part of the Chocó to link the Atlantic and Pacific oceans. More recently, the development of the lumber industry and plantations of African palm have led to forced displacements by paramilitaries interested in gaining control of economically valuable territory.

"Displacement isn't a collateral effect of the war, it's a central strategy of the war. It is entirely functional," Suarez explained.

He also noted that the Colombian army had contributed to the hardships endured by the people of the Chocó through the implementation of economic blockades.

"There's a lot of pressure on the communities from the army, including fuel, medicines, and resource control," he pointed out. "There are some places where the confinement, the siege of communities, has created a humanitarian crisis."

After arriving in the Chocó and before exploring the transportation options down the Atrato River from Quibdó, Terry and I decided to meet with Luis Moreno. A native Chocoano, Luis was the regional coordinator of the government's Social Solidarity Network, an agency that addresses social welfare issues, including the provision of aid to internally displaced people. The Social Solidarity Network's office in Quibdó was sparsely furnished and appeared to serve as a warehouse, with sacks of basic food items such as rice and sugar stacked in one corner. Luis invited us into his office, which was similarly furnished and stocked, and explained that since 1999 there had been an average of one entire community forcibly displaced every six months along the Atrato River. His agency was able to provide emergency aid to a displaced family for only three months; after that family members had to fend for themselves.

The 350-mile-long Atrato was an important transportation corridor not only for commercial trade, but also for drugs and weapons, which was why control of the river was so crucial. Luis explained, "For the people, the Atrato is the essence of life because all of us owe ourselves to the river. Most of the population of the Chocó lives on the banks of the river, because the river for us is the fountain of life. It serves us for communication, water supply, fishing, food, for everything. The Atrato provides all of that."

After saying goodbye to Luis, we made our way through the hustle and bustle of Quibdó's streets to the river. The town was full of life, especially on the waterfront, where old riverboats were moored and fruit and vegetable carts were filled to overflowing. We began asking around for a boat that could take us almost one hundred miles down the Atrato to the small town of Bellavista. A boatman told us it was too late to leave that day, so we went in search of a hotel, intent on returning to the docks first thing the next morning. We ate dinner in our *residencia*—a type of inexpensive no-frills hotel—and then sat on the open deck overlooking the Atrato River discussing the next day's river trip, including the dangers that lay ahead.

The next morning, we paid for two fares on a motorboat that was taking passengers to Bellavista. The motorboat, we were told, would get us there in four hours, whereas the more traditional long canoe powered by an outboard motor would take at least six hours. At almost midday, with eight passengers and the driver crammed into the small boat, we departed the dock and headed out into the brown waters of the Atrato. As we sped down the river, we passed several small villages consisting of wooden houses on stilts, but mostly we were surrounded by rainforest.

The boat made one scheduled stop, two and a half hours into the journey, at a small village that contained an army checkpoint. Soldiers inspected the identification documents of each passenger and logged the information in a book, keeping track of who was traveling on the river.

Thirty minutes further downriver, we made an unscheduled stop. We were cruising down the middle of the wide waterway when a small motorized canoe approached us from the bank to our left. One person was operating the outboard motor, and a man dressed in camouflage combat fatigues, holding an AK-47 assault rifle, was standing in the front of the canoe. The armed man waved his rifle from side to side, ordering our driver to slow down and follow him to the shore. We could see four uniformed and heavily armed fighters on the bank and several more standing guard in the trees around the perimeter of a small clearing. My anxiety increased as we neared the shore, because checkpoints such as this one can be unpredictable. Although I had always been allowed to continue on my way in the past, for Colombians these encounters often led to detention, kidnapping, or even death. Also, this was Terry's first encounter with one of the armed groups, and I knew that she was nervous.

Once we had moored, two of the fighters asked for everyone's identification, which we passed to them. They asked each of us where we were from and where we were going. After a couple of minutes, the fighters returned all the documents except for one. Evidently that person was not from the region, and so they were checking up on him through their two-way radio. The purpose of the checkpoint was evidently to control the movement of people by questioning anyone who did not live in the region to determine why they were there. Surprisingly, the armed men were not particularly curious about Terry's or my presence on the Atrato. If they were paramilitaries, the soldiers at the army checkpoint we had stopped at thirty minutes earlier might have forewarned them.

While we waited, I tried to figure out whether the men belonged to the paramilitaries or the FARC—there were no markings on their uniforms, and fighters from both groups carry AK-47 assault rifles and wear camouflage fatigues and rubber boots. I guessed that they were paramilitaries because they were all men who appeared to be in their late twenties, whereas FARC units often include women and their members tend to be younger, usually in their late teens or early twenties.

I asked whether Terry and I could interview the commander of the group. The commander agreed to my request, and so we clambered out of the boat onto the muddy riverbank. We introduced ourselves and then began one of the most futile interviews I have ever engaged in.

"What is your name and rank?" I asked.

The commander responded by shaking his head, unwilling to divulge that information.

"What group do you belong to?"

Again he shook his head slowly from side to side.

"What is the purpose of this checkpoint?"

He shook his head again.

"Has there been any conflict in this region recently?" I asked, becoming frustrated.

He shook his head again and this time managed to utter a few words. "I can't tell you that."

I turned off my tape recorder and told Terry that this was a waste of time. We thanked the commander, and as we climbed back into the boat, I wondered why on earth he had agreed to do an interview in the first place. Meanwhile, the other passenger's identification had been returned to him, and everyone was ready to resume the journey. After we left the shore, I asked the man seated next to me whether he knew what group the armed men belonged to. He just shook his head. Either he genuinely didn't know or he was unwilling to discuss the issue with me— a perfectly understandable response from someone forced to live among the armed groups.

An hour later, we arrived at Bellavista. Dugout canoes laden with bananas, pineapples, sugarcane, and miscellaneous packages vied for space near the dirt embankment as lively exchanges took place between people calling instructions back and forth. A large poster, which had been placed strategically on the riverbank by the army, was the only outward sign of the tragedy that had occurred there just over a year earlier. It read: "On May 2, 2002, the FARC assassinated 119 people here. We will never forget." The larger-than-life face of a boy peered out from beside the words. Almost one year after Bellavista's residents had returned to the homes they had abandoned following the tragedy, community members were still trying to process what had happened on that fateful day.

The trouble had begun in mid-April 2002, when four hundred right-wing paramilitaries made their way up the Atrato River to Bellavista and neighboring Vigía del Fuerte, passing unhindered through an army checkpoint in Ríosucio just a few hours downriver from their destinations in guerrilla-controlled territory. When the paramilitaries arrived in Bellavista on April

21, the acting mayor and a local priest immediately notified the regional and national authorities about the imminent danger faced by the community. Their pleas for help fell on deaf ears. Fighting began ten days later, on May 1, when FARC guerrillas attempted to drive the paramilitaries out of Bellavista and Vigía del Fuerte in an offensive that lasted throughout the night and into the next day.

In an attempt to avoid getting caught in the crossfire, hundreds of Bellavista residents fled from a northern barrio to seek refuge in a small church in the town center. Shortly before noon, a FARC mortar—aimed at paramilitaries who had set up camp next to the church—missed its intended target. The stray projectile struck the church and, after crashing through the roof, tore through the bodies of those who had taken refuge inside. One hundred and nineteen people were killed in the attack, most of them women and children. In the ensuing days, most of the town's fourteen hundred residents fled to Quibdó; only six hundred returned four months later to try to rebuild their lives.

Terry and I disembarked from our motorboat and were immediately approached by a police officer, who requested to see our identification and then logged the required information in a book. We shortly learned that there were no *residencias* in Bellavista and that we would have to cross the river to Vigía del Fuerte to find a room. We located a man who was willing to run us across the Atrato in his small canoe. In Vigía we found a *residencia* called Media Luna, the Half Moon. Although our hotel's name sounded very romantic, our room amounted to little more than four barely painted, rough-hewn wooden walls, a lumpy bed under mosquito netting, and a bathroom containing a fifty-five gallon plastic drum full of rainwater to be used for both bathing and flushing the toilet. To top it all off, we shared the room for the next week with a giant black spider that measured at least five inches across and liked to hang out on the ceiling directly above our bed. The mosquito netting constituted our only defense were he to lose his grip and fall during the night. Terry affectionately named him Henry.

Vigía del Fuerte was virtually a mirror image of Bellavista. There was a paved walkway along the riverfront and another one a block in from the river. Beyond that, the walkways were made of wooden planks on stilts, linking together rustic wooden houses situated over stagnant waters that served as perfect breeding grounds for mosquitoes. Two army boats were moored on the riverbank, and soldiers patrolled the walkways in pairs. There were no streets in Vigía because there were no vehicles, and nobody owned vehicles because there were no roads in and out of the town. There was also no electricity, although several homes and small businesses had their own gasoline generators.

The police station, which was one of only a handful of concrete buildings, lay in ruins—it had been destroyed several years earlier by a FARC mortar attack that killed twenty-four police officers. Following that attack, the national government withdrew the police from both Vigía and Bellavista. The two towns then fell under the de facto jurisdiction of the FARC until the paramilitaries arrived in April 2002. Following the ensuing battle between the FARC and the paramilitaries, the national government deployed the army to the two towns.

The next morning, we crossed the river and sought out the mayor of Bellavista. When we entered the municipal building, we were told that the mayor was in Quibdó, but we were welcome to meet with Manuel Corrales, the secretary general of Bojayá municipality and acting mayor of Bellavista. Corrales explained that life in the region had been particularly difficult in recent years, in part because of forced displacements resulting from the conflict.

"The situation facing the entire municipality, which consists of twenty-two indigenous communities and twenty black, is precarious because there is a lack of everything. Ten years ago there were a lot of bananas, cacao, and yucca being produced along the Bojayá River and the Opogodó River, but this has changed because so many communities have been displaced. So there is a general context of insecurity and uncertainty."

"Is the national government providing any social and economic assistance?" Terry asked.

"When we arrived in 2001, there hadn't been a doctor in the municipality for two years; there wasn't even a nurse. During our administration, we have had two doctors, but there hasn't been one for the past month or two. But since the May second attack, this municipality has received a lot more attention."

Unfortunately, said Corrales, the military presence in the town constituted most of that attention. His view corresponded with something that CODHES investigator Laura Zapata had told me back in Bogotá: "The response from the state has been restricted to the militarization of the zone. So the people keep thinking that the state only sends military troops, that it doesn't send any help in terms of education and health."

We asked Corrales to describe what happened when the paramilitaries arrived prior to the May 2 killings.

"They said they weren't here to attack us, that they weren't going to kill anyone like they did before when they chopped off heads and cut open torsos; that they were here to confront the guerrillas and to get them out of the community."

Corrales explained that government troops didn't arrive in Bellavista until six days after the fighting had ended, despite the fact that the army's 12th Infantry Battalion was based in Quibdó, only four hours upriver by motorboat. And the paramilitaries remained in the town for almost two weeks after the army had arrived. Although Corrales was critical of the army's lack of response, he held the FARC primarily responsible for the tragedy.

"It's clear that those mortars are not accurate. They knew

that they were putting the population in danger," he told us. "The people are convinced that the guerrillas knew those people were in the church."

Terry and I thanked Corrales for his time and then walked over to the church where the tragedy had occurred. A new roof had been installed and a fresh coat of paint applied to its walls. It was hard to believe that the pristine church standing before us was the site of such horror only a year earlier.

Outside the church, we met Carlos Rojas, a psychologist from Medellín who had spent the previous eleven months helping survivors come to terms with their ordeal. Carlos was a gentle man who emitted a degree of compassion and warmth that I had rarely experienced, and he was clearly passionate about helping the people of Bellavista cope with their trauma. He took us inside the church and showed us a glass case containing the remnants of a statue of Jesus Christ that had been blown to bits by the mortar blast. We also gazed at a painting that hauntingly captured the horror of that day, when nearly 10 percent of the town's population perished. It showed three women wailing on their knees with the flaming church behind them. In front of the women was a pile of dead children, with a chalice lying on its side next to the stacked corpses. With the painting serving as a disturbing backdrop, Terry and I sat down in a pew to talk with Carlos.

Carlos described some of the horrific details of what occurred in the church that day, including the death of a pregnant woman. Apparently the force of the mortar's explosion had ripped her apart and splattered her fetus all over the wall. He explained how it had not been easy for survivors to live with the memory of such gruesome images. Many men in the community had lost their entire family in the tragedy, and as a result, some had turned to alcohol in an attempt to dull their pain.

"When they get drunk they discover their feelings," Carlos explained. "A man has lost his wife and six kids, so he gets drunk, and in the same moment he weeps, laughs, and dances."

Carlos said that he had witnessed a number of pathologies in the survivors. Many suffered from posttraumatic stress disorder, anxiety, and fear; some endured sleep disorders, and several women had difficulty having orgasms. Others had experienced a loss of desire to live, and four survivors had committed suicide.

"Where do you get the strength to do this type of work?" Terry asked him.

"Well, I go to Medellín every month. I go to see a psychologist, someone I can talk to. And I also have a passion for people."

Carlos invited us to meet one of the survivors he'd been working with. We walked to the outskirts of the town center, crossed a small bridge, and entered a neighborhood called Pueblo Nuevo. Stopping at a simple wooden house on the riverbank, Carlos asked the children playing out front whether Macaria was home. One of the children ran inside and returned in a moment with an Afro-Colombian woman who appeared to be in her mid thirties. Carlos introduced us to Macaria and asked whether she'd be willing to discuss her ordeal with us.

She said that the fighting had started on May 1 and that armed men were running all over the neighborhood. In the afternoon, the local authorities advised the residents of Pueblo Nuevo to go to the church for their own safety.

"So we stayed there all afternoon and overnight," Macaria explained. "The night was peaceful, and nothing happened. But after ten thirty the next morning, the shooting started again. Later there was a loud noise. I was with my little girl. When we heard the blast, I threw myself to the floor and covered my little girl and stayed there. When I tried to get up, I felt like I was suffocating. I looked around, and there was the smell of sulfur; it was sickening. Everything was dark and full of smoke. When I could finally see, there were just pieces of human flesh left. Those who survived had run away from the scene. I was left disabled on the floor. Something had entered my back and gotten stuck; it messed up my leg and damaged all of the tendons.

So I wasn't able to walk, and my daughter had also hurt her leg. I kept losing consciousness. I woke up the next morning among the dead and the injured children, who were asking for help. But I couldn't help them, because I was in worse condition than them."

"How did you begin to cope with the ordeal afterwards?" Terry asked her.

"Afterwards, I became very sick as a result of what had happened. It really has been very difficult. I have been able to overcome this crisis, thanks to Carlos, who has been my doctor. He has always been there for me, and he is always helping—always."

"How did you find the strength to survive in the church?" Terry asked.

"There were moments when I lost consciousness. I would go away and stay in the void. But I had an internal force that ordered me not to pass away. I always had that faith and that hope in something. So when I would regain consciousness, I would cry a lot. I pleaded to God. I would say the prayers that they teach to everyone. I would say a prayer and ask God for help. After that day, I would try to be in a good mood, but there were moments when I couldn't be. At times the negative feelings would overwhelm me, so then I'd go to Carlos. It was through him that I started to understand many things; he's the one who always helps me out."

"And the other families that were in the church, have you had the opportunity to speak with them and to help each other?" asked Terry.

"Those of us that are left, yes. We speak a lot about the topic. We received therapy with Carlos and the diocese, and so it has been very positive because we like to mutually help each other out. The dialogue and therapy that some of us do helps us improve, but let me tell you that one does become scarred for life. There is something that is always there; it's like a ghost. It's always there in the mind. There are moments that it goes away, but then there are moments when it comes back alive. So it's here with me. I have tried to overcome it. When that ghost comes to me, that's when I seek out someone to speak to. I don't like solitude, because solitude prompts that ghost back into my mind. But I love my family very much. I'm fighting for my family; I think it's worth it. That's why I'm fighting against this ghost."

Carlos explained that Macaria was his best patient and had made excellent progress during the previous year, but that there were still things going on in Bellavista that tormented her and the other survivors. For example, the army's soldiers sometimes fired their weapons into the air at night to intimidate any fighters from armed groups that might be lurking outside the town. The problem with that tactic was that it also terrorized the civilian population. Carlos had spoken with the army commander to request an end to the nighttime shootings, but to no avail.

After we said goodbye to Macaria and were walking back to the center of town, Carlos explained that Macaria had accepted that she is scarred for life and knows it will not be easy.

He then asked, "How should one feel when one wakes up from a nightmare to find three hundred and something pieces of body parts stuck all over the place—on the wall, on the ceiling, and on top of you?"

Back in Vigía, Terry and I found a man named Costeño who was willing to take us in his motorized canoe thirty minutes up the Atrato to the Afro-Colombian village of San Miguel. The breeze on the river was a welcome relief from the suffocating heat and humidity in town. It was also a welcome relief from the intensity of our conversations with Carlos and Macaria. After leaving Carlos, neither Terry nor I had much to say to each other. Listening to Macaria's story had been almost too much to bear. I couldn't even begin to conceive of having to endure such an ordeal or of having to live with it afterward. And yet Macaria proved to be a truly inspiring person.

Our canoe pulled up to the shore in San Miguel beside two women who were washing clothes in the river next to a wooden outhouse built on stilts over the water. Terry and I clambered up the muddy bank and stood facing a long line of wooden houses with corrugated tin roofs. We then approached two men who were talking to each other and introduced ourselves. They responded to our request for an interview by calling a village meeting beneath a thatched shelter on the riverbank.

The villagers explained to us how they struggled to survive through fishing and agriculture, including the cultivation of bananas, pineapples, yucca, and corn. Despite the fact that San Miguel was situated on the Chocó's principal transportation artery, the degree of poverty was extreme, and the government didn't provide the village with any public services. There was no school, no health care, no electricity, and no indoor plumbing. The children endured serious health problems, including malaria and diarrhea, the latter of which was aggravated by the fact that the villagers used the Atrato River as a toilet as well as a place to wash dishes, clothes, and themselves. It was difficult to believe that San Miguel was in the same country as some of the wealthy neighborhoods in north Bogotá. Terry and I had been out for dinner and drinks in the capital's relatively posh Zona Rosa district only days earlier, and the contrast between that experience and life in San Miguel was astonishing. Colombia has one of the most unequal distributions of wealth in the world, and that divide is no more evident than in the contrast between the luxury apartment buildings, ritzy shopping malls, and BMWs of north Bogotá and the Chocó's extreme poverty.

During our time in Bellavista, Terry and I had noticed a few indigenous people in the town. We learned that the Embera tribe maintained an office in the barrio of Pueblo Nuevo that served as a point of contact between the group's twenty-two remote communities and government institutions. After making our way to the office—little more than a simple two-room wooden house on stilts overlooking the river—we introduced ourselves to one of the three indigenous men who were engaged in a conversation inside and asked whether it would be possible for us to visit one of their villages. One of the men introduced himself to us as Loselinios. He had black hair, stood about five feet seven, appeared to be in his late twenties, and wore a T-shirt and shorts but no shoes. Loselinios pointed out that the nearest Embera communities were situated on the Opogodó River, a tributary of the Atrato—six hours away by motorized canoe. He told us it was dangerous to visit them because both the guerrillas and the paramilitaries were active in those territories. When we insisted, Loselinios asked, "Why do you want to visit our communities?"

"We would like to investigate how the conflict is affecting the Embera," I answered.

"You want to visit the villages to speak with the people? Nothing more?" he asked, leaving me a little puzzled about what else he thought we might want.

His next question made clear his concern.

"You aren't going to look for plants or to ask about our medicines?"

It suddenly struck me that he was worried we might be botanists for a multinational pharmaceutical company seeking to learn about the medicinal qualities of plants in the Embera communities. I had heard about indigenous knowledge in Colombia and other tropical regions of Latin America being exploited by pharmaceutical companies that learned about the local medicines and then patented them and made millions of dollars in profits while the indigenous people received nothing. Nevertheless, I was still surprised that groups as remote as the Embera in the Chocó were so aware of the issue of intellectual property rights related to their medicines.

"We're journalists, and we are only interested in the plight of the Embera people," I said, hoping to put his mind at rest.

He nodded his head thoughtfully.

"Have you had problems in the past with people wanting to learn about your medicines?" I asked.

"Yes. Sometimes people say they want to visit our villages, but all they are interested in are the medicinal plants," Loselinios explained, appearing satisfied that we were only journalists. "I have to discuss your request with others. Come back this afternoon and we will have an answer for you."

When we returned later that afternoon, Loselinios told us that we could visit two villages and that the trip would take two days. We were to leave the next morning. He would accompany us, because it would be virtually impossible for us to get there on our own and because the Embera people would not speak with us if we showed up unaccompanied. The only catch, he said, was that we'd have to pay for the cost of the gasoline.

"No problem," we replied.

The next morning, we found Loselinios in front of the Embera office. He was on the river's edge preparing the boat—a dugout canoe equipped with an outboard motor—for our departure. Loselinios and a fellow indigenous man who would pilot our boat were in no apparent hurry to leave, so Terry and I gave Loselinios money for gasoline and then relaxed on the riverbank in the shade of a large tree. Eventually Loselinios and his wife, Liria; another indigenous man and his daughter; the boat pilot; and the two of us all piled into the canoe and set off down the Atrato.

We traveled for two hours before heading west up the Opogodó River, which was much smaller than the wide, fast-flowing Atrato. We passed a small Afro-Colombian village shortly after entering the Opogodó, but after that we journeyed through uninhabited jungle. As we became more intimately encased in the canopy of the surrounding rainforest, the great expanse of cloudy sky shrank down to a sliver directly above our heads. I felt an incredible sense of peace as we glided through the water. Yet juxtaposed against this peaceful setting was the ever-present possibility of running into an armed group.

After more than an hour on the Opogodó, we pulled over to the shore for lunch. We all climbed out of the canoe, and Liria dished up plates of cold fish, rice, and beans that she'd prepared in Bellavista. Soon we were back on the river, feeling increasingly remote from the rest of the inhabited world.

Five and a half hours after leaving Bellavista and three and a half hours up the Opogodó, we rounded a bend and saw several small dugout canoes moored on the riverbank up ahead. As we approached the shore, I suddenly felt as though I were being transported back in time. The canoes were moored at the foot of a dirt embankment that rose about fifteen feet above the river. Perched atop the embankment were several mist-enshrouded dwellings capped with conical thatched roofs. The entire scene had a mystical air about it, and the twenty-first century suddenly seemed worlds away.

We clambered out of the canoe and followed Loselinios up the embankment toward the dwellings. The sensation of having gone back in time intensified as we approached the first two houses, which consisted of wooden platforms mounted on stilts and covered with thatched roofs. Indigenous Embera emerged from the dwellings to greet us, or to be more precise, to greet Loselinios. Most of the women were topless, their faces and torsos decorated with purple paint and their lower halves adorned with traditional, colorful wraparound skirts called *parumas*. The men were also topless, although without the decorative paint, and wore shorts. We were in the village of Egorokera, which was home to about twenty families.

Over the centuries, little has changed in the way the Embera live their lives. This was clearly evident in Egorokera, where there were few modern amenities. A small outboard motor had replaced the paddles on one of the dugout canoes, and several large plastic barrels caught the rain for use as drinking water.

Other than those modern intrusions into the Embera world, everything else remained traditional. There was no running water or electricity. Entire extended families still lived together in open-sided thatched huts in which fires were permanently maintained for cooking purposes. The Embera diet consisted primarily of subsistence crops such as rice, corn, yucca, and banana, as well as the occasional small game caught in the surrounding rainforest. Loselinios explained that the Embera were hunting less frequently for fear of running into the armed groups and that there were few edible fish in the Opogodó River, which this far upstream was too shallow to host any sizable species. As a result, the Embera diet had become overly reliant on starches, and many of the children exhibited signs of malnutrition.

Loselinios spoke with an elder, who then arranged for all the villagers to gather together in one of the larger dwellings. We climbed up a ladder made from a narrow tree trunk, with notches cut out of it to serve as steps, and entered the house. The dwelling was about twenty-five feet long by ten feet wide and had a fire burning at one end. The villagers sat in a circle around the perimeter. The gathering included men, women, children, and babies, all of whom were very friendly. Loselinios addressed the villagers in their native tongue, explaining who we were and asking whether everyone was willing to speak with us about the problems that the village faced. Their democratic process was impressive, and they unanimously agreed to speak with us.

Several villagers explained various aspects of the Embera's social structures and culture. Approximately 3,300 Embera lived in twenty-two communities in the municipality of Bojayá. Each community had a representative serving a two-year term on the Cabildo Mayor, a council that addressed broader issues affecting all the communities and maintained the tribal office in Bellavista. Each village had a governor, who served a one-year term as head of that particular community and was responsible for overseeing sanitation, organizing meetings, and addressing community problems. Only men served as governors; each community also had a governess who addressed women's issues. The Cabildo Mayor's Council of Justice addressed all serious criminal violations committed by the Embera, while governors determined punishment on the community level. For example, if a person stole someone else's belongings, killed someone else's animals, or cut down someone else's crops, the perpetrator would receive a sanction, such as a fine paid with labor, animals, or crops. In some cases, a perpetrator might also be ordered to sit in the stocks, not unlike those used in medieval Europe, that were situated in the center of the village.

The Embera in Egorokera engaged in their own religious rituals and did not recognize Catholicism. Catholic missionaries had evidently visited Egorokera in the past, but the Embera had made it clear that they were not interested in Catholicism. The village had a wise man, called El Jiguana, who communicated with the spirits. When there were problems in the community or someone became ill, El Jiguana would chant to the spirits at night.

Terry asked the gathering about health problems in the village. An elderly man responded that there were many, including diarrhea and fevers, but the most serious was malaria. He told us about a one-year-old baby girl who had died only a month earlier when her malaria developed complications. He then pointed out an elderly man across the room who was suffering from malaria.

"The epidemic is very strong; it's everywhere," the man continued. "If one doesn't have money, how can one get medicine? We need help from the institutions because we cannot take care of this alone. We make something simple, some remedy, and sometimes it stops the malaria and sometimes it doesn't."

Each question that we asked led to a long, involved discussion among the villagers in their native tongue, which meant that we couldn't understand. Sometimes the villagers would glance over at us and burst into laughter, apparently at a joke made at our expense. Whenever we asked Loselinios for a translation of these episodes, he would just smile at us and shake his head from side to side.

"What kinds of problems do you have with the armed conflict?" I asked the gathering.

"We have serious problems," said a different elderly man. "The guerrillas are less of a problem because they are more nomadic. Still, the guerrillas recently came and uprooted our maize crops, claiming that the land upon which they were growing was not Embera land."

A younger man interjected, "Fifteen days ago, armed people took two saws from the community. We were cutting some wood over there for a commission we had received from the assembly in Quibdó. Then these men came out of the forest, and they took away the saws."

Loselinios explained that many Embera were afraid to roam far from the village. There were often paramilitary checkpoints on the rivers linking the three indigenous villages located in that part of the Chocó. In order to obtain food and medicine, the Embera had to make a six-hour journey by motorized canoe to Vigía del Fuerte or Bellavista—and oftentimes they didn't have enough money to purchase fuel. Even if they chose to paddle their canoes all the way to Vigía or Bellavista, once they reached their destination they would often face harassment at the hands of the state security forces. Also, Loselinios told us, soldiers regularly prevented them from bringing food and medicine back to their communities, because the army suspected them of giving supplies to the guerrillas.

According to another young Embera man, "Some go to Vigía, but there's a lot of interrogation there, so that scares us. They take away our documents—sometimes they tear them up to illustrate to us that they are not worth anything. As a result, some of us allow our kids or our women to die here because of fear of the military."

After the meeting, Terry and I were invited to wander around the village. We separated, and I hung out with several playful children. After a while I went in search of Terry and found her in the company of several Embera women in one of the houses. She was kneeling on the wooden floor in front of a young woman who was painting Terry's face with the same purple dye that had been used to decorate her own body. The dye is the liquid from a fruit called jagua; it is used to protect the women from mosquitoes and the sun's rays, as well as to paint decorative designs on the face and body for ceremonial occasions. The Embera woman was painting a decorative design on Terry's face, much to the amusement of the other women.

When Terry had been appropriately decorated, Loselinios said it was time for us to leave Egorokera in order to make the thirty-minute journey further upriver to the next village before nightfall. We bid our farewells to the villagers and reboarded our canoe for the trip to the village of Boquiaza, where the family of Loselinios lived. It was on that short stretch of river that we were most likely to run into paramilitaries or guerrillas, according to Loselinios. Thankfully, the journey proved to be uneventful, even idyllic, as the dusk light dulled the lush greens of the surrounding rainforest.

The dwellings and layout of Boquiaza were very similar to Egorokera. Loselinios led us to his mother's house and introduced us to his family before showing us to the empty dwelling in which we would spend the night. He left us there to get settled in, telling us to return to his mother's house when we were ready to eat. We pulled out the double hammock that we had purchased in Bogotá just in case such an occasion were to arise. More than half a dozen Embera children gathered around to watch the two *gringos* attempt to hang a hammock and attach a mosquito net to it by flashlight. The children laughed wholeheartedly as we struggled pathetically over the next thirty minutes to get the hammock-and-mosquito-net combo to function adequately. They were also probably amused at the sight of the decorative dye on the face of a *gringa*.

At the conclusion of the hammock debacle, Terry and I made our way back to the home of Loselinios's mother. We climbed the rustic ladder up to the wooden platform that served as the family's living, eating, and sleeping quarters. Sitting under the thatched roof, we dined on eggs, fried bananas, and a hot chocolate drink in the light provided by two kerosene-fueled lamps. While we ate, Liria and several other women from the village sorted through new cloth material to decide how to use it for an upcoming community dance. We watched a teenage boy giving his mother a difficult time and couldn't help but think about how similar adolescents are, regardless of their culture. Several smaller children were quietly amusing themselves in a corner of the dwelling, some of them sitting with their arms around each other.

We were amazed at the lack of privacy in the life of the Embera. There were no bedrooms in the dwellings; every family member slept in the open space. The houses were situated very close to each other, and without any walls there was no privacy between families with regard to conversations and other activities, such as sex.

Finally we said goodnight to Loselinios's family and made our way in the darkness back to our dwelling. Clambering into the hammock, we tried—and failed—to find a position that was comfortable for both of us and struggled to keep the mosquito net sealed. It wasn't until after six in the morning, as the sun was beginning to rise, that we both finally fell into a deep sleep.

A few short hours later, we got up and went down to the river to bathe. Terry desperately tried to wash the purple dye from her face, but to no avail. An elderly Embera man, who was also bathing, laughed at Terry while shaking his head in a motion that suggested she was wasting her time.

"Doesn't it wash off?" Terry asked the man.

Again he shook his head and smiled.

"How long until it wears off?"

"Perhaps two weeks," the man answered, still smiling.

Following a moment of terror upon realizing that she was going to have to function back in mainstream Colombian society with her face painted purple, Terry resigned herself to her fate.

Before we departed from Boquiaza, several women from the village treated us to a traditional dance. We sat in one of the larger dwellings with the villagers and watched ten women, whose bodies were adorned with colorful *parumas* and purple dye, chant as they danced around and around the post that supported the center of the building. The elderly woman who led the dance, which was intended to "wake up the wild beast," banged steadily on a small drum while the others followed behind her.

After the performance, we were introduced to more than a dozen children who were suffering from various maladies. We were told that the necessary medicines were difficult to obtain because of the army's economic blockade of the region. Like the villagers in Egorokera, those in Boquiaza were caught in the middle of Colombia's armed conflict. The Embera did not want anything to do with any of the armed groups—not the guerrillas, the paramilitaries, or the army. Unfortunately, all three, particularly the army, constantly harassed those peaceful indigenous communities.

It was late morning when we boarded the canoe for the six-hour trip back to Bellavista. The return journey down the Opogodó was as beautiful and uneventful as the one that had brought us into Embera territory. As we left the mystical world of the Embera behind, I recalled the defiant words of one Egorokera resident: "We have been threatened for our territory, but we are still here. We have resisted for five hundred years."

The Opogodó grew wider as it neared the broad and fast-flowing Atrato River. Terry and I lay back and relaxed under the clear blue sky and scorching sun. I thought about how much we in the so-called developed world could learn from indigenous groups like the Embera. Although I had been with them for only a short time, their apparent lack of some factors that plague Western society—like violence, greed, and environmental destruction—was inspirational. It was true that the Embera had resisted for five hundred years, but would they be able to resist for five hundred more?

It was late afternoon when our canoe dropped us on the riverbank in Vigía and we bid farewell to Loselinios and Liria. After dropping our stuff at the Media Luna, we made our way to the small restaurant in which we had dined during most of our stay in Vigía. We ordered a fried fish dinner and cold beers and, seated at an outside table, watched the locals go about their early evening business. More than a few of them were amused by Terry's painted face.

After dinner, while we were sitting there enjoying our beers, an Afro-Colombian from another table joined us for a drink, and we all sat there talking for the next couple of hours. The man, whose name was Luis, was in his mid fifties. He was a lumber salesman who purchased wood from indigenous communities and had lived his entire life in the region. Luis explained how the violence in the region had escalated over the past decade. Surprisingly, given that we were in a heavily militarized town, he openly displayed his sympathies for the guerrillas, claiming that they were the only ones among the armed groups who were interested in the welfare of poor communities. Naturally, we kept our opinions to ourselves. After all, Luis could have been an informer for the army or the paramilitaries, and his alleged sympathy for the guerrillas may have simply been a ploy to determine our political leanings. After a few beers too many, Terry and I said goodnight to Luis and stumbled back to our room.

•　•　•

The following morning, we packed our bags and, after bidding farewell to Henry the spider, departed from the Media Luna. While awaiting our ride back to Quibdó, I decided to get a haircut at a little barbershop one block from the waterfront. It was a small wooden shack occupied by two young Afro-Colombian barbers: twenty-two-year-old Yatuman and twenty-one-year-old Rokaman. When I walked in, Rokaman was playing a battered acoustic guitar. The three of us talked about music while Yatuman trimmed my hair. I told them that I also played guitar, and they said that they wrote and produced hip-hop music. When Yatuman was done with my hair, they asked me to play something on the guitar, so I took the instrument and sang several songs.

Afterward, the two barbers played a tape of some of their original music, much of which addressed the political and social plight faced by Afro-Colombians in the Chocó. One song was particularly powerful in its depiction of the attack that had killed 119 people in the Bellavista church the previous year. It was titled "No More Violence":

> *Most sought refuge in the church,*
> *the mortal church,*
> *when a missile was launched*
> *and on the church it fell.*
> *In this peaceful place, many people died,*
> *and all who died were innocent,*
> *having nothing to do with this problem.*
> *No more violence, no, no,*
> *I don't wanna hear of it in my region, no, no.*
> *Because of the violence,*
> *many will die.*
> *If we were all brothers,*
> *we wouldn't commit these sins.*
> *Because of this, our country is out of control.*

Although the plight of the Afro-Colombian and indigenous peoples in the Chocó was truly tragic on many levels, Yatuman and Rokaman allowed Terry and me to depart the region with a healthy dose of hope. It was inspiring to hear young people speaking out on behalf of peace in the midst of such violence, no matter how daunting the obstacles to achieving peace and prosperity.

That same year, U.S. satellite imagery revealed that increasing amounts of coca were being cultivated in the Chocó, having been displaced from Putumayo and other southern regions. I hoped that the people of the Chocó wouldn't be the next target of Plan Colombia's aerial fumigations.

The Ninth Hour

6:00 p.m., August 16, 2006

It's beginning to get busy in this little farmhouse. Not only has the father-and-sons guerrilla team returned home, but so has the four-year-old son of my host and the mother of the small baby. Apparently the baby belongs to one of the guerrilla sons and his wife; the teenage girl who has been around the house all day is my host's daughter. I also discover that four of the coca pickers live on the farm.

This flurry of activity is a welcome distraction from the endless hours spent reflecting on my predicament. I look on as the older woman, who has been cooking for most of the day, dishes out plates of chicken, beans, and yucca for everyone. My guard and I, the two guerrilla sons, and one of the coca pickers eat dinner inside the house while the rest dine at the table by the kitchen. Although everyone is polite to me, nobody is willing to engage in serious conversation. I know from past experience that this behavior is normal when an outsider is initially detained by the FARC. The local peasants and guerrillas are wary of engaging with a stranger until the status of that individual has been clarified.

I finish my dinner and take another walk around the outside of the house as the last sliver of daylight begins to fade, watching my host and his son work on a small gasoline generator in a clump of trees. After several minutes it bursts into life, and two bare light bulbs, one in the kitchen and one in the center of the house, suddenly illuminate their immediate surroundings. My host invites me back into the house to watch the news on a small television mounted on the wall above the seat that my guard occupied for much of the day.

I again sit in the white plastic chair, and everyone except the older woman and the teenage girl gathers around to watch the news on Colombia's Caracol channel. As usual, the leadoff story relates to the conflict. A reporter is interviewing an army commander, who is describing the progress of a massive military operation called Plan Patriota. The operation, he explains, is successfully targeting "terrorists" based in southern and eastern Colombia. I glance over at the face of my guerrilla host to see whether there is any reaction to the army commander's claims or his use of the word "terrorist" to describe the guerrillas, but there is none. Perhaps he has become immune to the perspective presented by Colombia's television networks, which overwhelmingly rely on sound bites from government and military officials.

The Plan Patriota operation being discussed is a U.S.-supported military offensive involving almost twenty thousand Colombian troops—the largest counterinsurgency operation in Colombian history. It was initiated in early 2004 in the department of Caquetá before being expanded to include parts of Putumayo, Guaviare, and Meta. The objective was for the Colombian military to seize control of territory in the FARC's traditional strongholds.

For the U.S. government, a subgoal of Plan Patriota is to locate and rescue three U.S. civilian contractors who are being held prisoner by the FARC. The three contractors, along with a fourth contractor and a Colombian pilot, were flying a reconnaissance mission over the jungles of Caquetá in February 2003 for the U.S. Department of Defense when their plane was allegedly shot down by FARC guerrillas. One of the contractors and the pilot were shot to death at the crash site, and the other three Americans were taken captive. It's believed that the Americans are being held in FARC camps deep in the jungles of Caquetá.

The contractors who are being held captive worked for Northrop Grumman, one of seventeen military contractors operating in Colombia under U.S. Defense Department and State Department contracts. U.S. military contractors—who typically are retired military personnel—are responsible for a wide array of activities in Colombia, including piloting Black Hawk helicopters and spray planes and conducting intelligence-gathering missions. Critics claim that the contracted corporations have little accountability to U.S. taxpayers, since the personnel are no longer employed by the U.S. military, and that contractor casualties do not receive the same degree of media coverage as the deaths of U.S. soldiers. The critics seem to have been right in the latter case, as there was no significant U.S. mainstream media coverage of the death of one contractor and the capture of three in Caquetá.

I visited Caquetá in February 2004 to investigate the displacement of rural communities by the Colombian army's Operation New Year, which turned out to be the initial phase of Plan Patriota. I flew from Bogotá to the city of Florencia with my friend Eric Fichtl, whom I'd met four years earlier when we both were working at the North American Congress on Latin America. We found a driver to take us to the town of El Paujil, located on the region's main road about a third of the way between Florencia and San Vicente del Caguán. We decided to try to locate some of the peasants who had been displaced from the village of La Unión Peneya during Operation New Year. Soon after it had secured the village, the army's 12th Brigade flew in journalists from mainstream national and international media outlets, who then dutifully reported the army's version of events. It was apparent in their coverage that none of the reporters had ventured beyond virtually abandoned La Unión Peneya to locate the displaced villagers or to find out how residents of other, soon-to-be-targeted communities felt about the army's offensive.

It was early afternoon when we arrived in El Paujil, where we planned to spend the night before visiting remote villages lying in the path of Operation New Year. We found that El Paujil was heavily militarized with not only soldiers but also an armored unit that was participating in the offensive. Eric and I checked into a *residencia* and decided to spend the afternoon investigating the local situation. We located the commander of the armored unit on a small farm on the outskirts of town.

"I cannot discuss Operation New Year without authorization from brigade headquarters in Florencia," he explained. "I also would advise against trying to visit rural communities, because I cannot guarantee your safety once you leave El Paujil."

His refusal to be interviewed represented one of the rare occasions when a field commander was uncooperative. It also appeared to signify a shift in the military's approach to journalists under President Uribe: reporters were now required to obtain permission from the highest levels before conducting interviews.

Since we'd gotten nowhere with the army commander, Eric and I decided to request an interview with the mayor of El Paujil. The mayor himself was in Bogotá, but the deputy mayor, Oscar Ochoa, was happy to meet with us. Ochoa invited us into his office and began to explain how the national government had provided increased security in El Paujil since President Uribe had assumed office eighteen months earlier. Despite the positive changes he'd seen, however, Ochoa was critical of the government's single-minded focus on security. He explained that in 2002 a FARC mortar attack launched against the police station had missed its target and instead destroyed the town's medical clinic, located across the street. Under Uribe, the national government was funding military operations in the region but had repeatedly refused to contribute to the building of a new clinic. Such complaints were common in rural Colombia, and I mused that Plan Patriota's counterinsurgency strategy appeared to be replicating Plan Colombia's counternarcotics strategy in that most of the funding and resources were being used for military operations and very little was being spent on social and economic programs.

We heard from several locals that many of the villagers displaced from La Unión Peneya were being temporarily housed in a village called Bolivia, so the next morning we got a ride from Jorge, a landowner who was heading out to his property near the village. The initial part of the trip wove through cattle-ranching country, where the rainforest had been cleared to create grazing land, but after a while the fields gave way to increasing numbers of trees and the cattle ranches were replaced with smaller farms. Jorge owned a medium-sized farm near Bolivia, in what had traditionally been FARC-controlled territory, and claimed that he'd never had any problems with the guerrillas. As we made our way along the bumpy road, Jorge told us that a new round of aerial fumigations had been launched in the region to coincide with Operation New Year.

"The fumigations have made life difficult for people, because they have destroyed food crops and harmed animals," he explained.

It was shortly after ten o'clock in the morning when Jorge dropped us off in Bolivia, a small village of several hundred peasants situated on top of a hill and surrounded by a combination of farms and forest. Eric and I approached two men who were talking to each other in front of a small restaurant. After introducing ourselves as journalists, we asked whether they knew how we could locate the peasants who had been displaced from La Unión Peneya. The two men looked at us, then shifted their gaze to something behind us; when I turned around I saw three men crossing the street and walking directly toward us. I could see no weapons, but the three wore camouflage pants and were undoubtedly members of the local FARC militia. They shook our hands but did not introduce themselves.

"We would like to interview peasants who have been displaced by the army's Operation New Year," I told them.

"We will have to contact some people to see if that is possible, because the displaced peasants are not here in Bolivia," explained the guerrilla who appeared to be in charge.

We sat down and waited. Eventually the guerrilla leader came back with the news that he'd submitted our request and was waiting for an answer, but had no idea how long it would take. And so we continued to wait. One hour passed, and then a second, and then a third. I decided to try to take a walk around the village. I told Eric I'd be back shortly and strolled down the main street—a dirt road lined with basic wooden structures. The guerrillas seemed unconcerned with my walkabout; but then again, where was I going to go? We were stuck in the middle of Caquetá without any transportation.

The problem of transportation was one of the reasons for my little walk. It was early afternoon, and if we didn't hear anything soon I wanted to find a ride back to El Paujil, because nobody would be willing to drive after dark. I encountered a truck with a cow in the back parked on the main street and asked the driver whether he was going to El Paujil. He answered in the affirmative, but said that he wouldn't be leaving until later.

"Could we get a ride with you if we are ready to leave by then?" I asked.

"Okay, but like I said, I don't know when I will be leaving," he responded.

I thanked him and continued walking along the street. Within two minutes the truck's engine started, and our potential ride pulled out of town without us. How strange, I thought.

Looking down a short dirt road, I saw a man working under the hood of a jeep. I approached to ask how we could arrange a ride back to El Paujil. He said that he'd be heading that way in the next hour. But when I asked whether we could go with him if we hadn't received a response to our request to interview the displaced peasants by then, he shook his head slowly and said, "Sorry, I can't do it."

"Why not?" I sensed that something peculiar was going on.

He smiled at me and then clamped each of his hands onto the opposite wrist as though he were placing handcuffs on himself. He appeared to be suggesting that the guerrillas might want to kidnap Eric and me, and I realized that nobody was willing to even contemplate giving us a ride out of Bolivia until the FARC had decided our fate. Although this scenario unnerved me, I placated myself with the thought that the three FARC militia members had so far been friendly and had not overtly detained us.

I returned to Eric and told him about my discovery that we weren't going anywhere without the FARC's permission. We continued to wait. Four hours after we had arrived in Bolivia, the guerrilla leader again came over to see us and asked whether we had a video camera. We told him we didn't, that we had only cameras that took still photos.

Finally, at almost five o'clock, the rebel leader told us that we wouldn't be able to interview the displaced peasants because the army's ongoing offensive rendered the security situation too dangerous. He also told us that we'd have to wait until the next morning to return to El Paujil, because it was too late to leave that day, and that he'd arranged a place for us to sleep. Although we were disappointed at not being able to meet with the displaced villagers, Eric and I were relieved to know that we were free to leave the village.

The guerrilla took us to meet Alejandra, a single mother with two children who'd agreed to put Eric and me up in her home for the night. We walked the short distance to her house, a small wooden structure with three enclosed bedrooms and an open-sided section in the rear that served as a living area and kitchen. Alejandra showed us to our bedroom, which contained three beds draped in mosquito netting for protection against malaria and yellow fever. We set our bags down and went out to the living space to meet Alejandra's sons, Jairo and Francisco, who were eight and six years old. Eric and I sat talking to the children while Alejandra busied herself in the kitchen.

Jairo and Francisco told us that they attended a small school in the village and that neither of them had ever traveled further away than El Paujil. Jairo then described an incident that had occurred a week earlier, which we assumed was probably related to Operation New Year. He explained that the two brothers were fishing in the local river, not far from the village, when an army helicopter descended from the sky and began firing its machine gun and dropping bombs near them. Terrified, they scrambled out of the water and ran home. The experience had obviously left a deep impression on them.

I walked over to the kitchen to speak with Alejandra, who was cooking on a stove fueled with gas from a long, cylindrical metal canister. Gas canisters are the most common source of cooking fuel in rural Colombia. They're also popular with the guerrillas, who cut the tops off and use the remainder of the cylinders as mortars to launch projectiles against police stations in rural towns. These homemade mortars—known locally as *cilindros*—are notoriously inaccurate and have killed many civilians throughout Colombia, leading human rights groups to repeatedly condemn the FARC for its use of the weapons. Fortunately, there was nothing deadly about the gas canisters in Alejandra's kitchen—in fact, the delicious smell of the food she was cooking made me realize just how hungry I was. I asked Alejandra about life in the village.

"Life is difficult; most of the people survive on subsistence farming and coca cultivation," she explained.

"Does the national government provide any help for the people here?"

"No. The government has no presence here. The only time we see the government is when the soldiers come or when the planes drop bombs." It was a refrain that I had heard repeatedly in rural Colombia.

"What do you think about the army's Operation New Year?" I asked.

"We are afraid that what happened in La Unión Peneya will happen here."

I found it unsurprising that Alejandra felt as many rural Colombians did: after decades of governmental neglect and fear of the military, she remained distrustful of the state.

Alejandra served up a tasty plate of chicken, fried bananas, yucca, and rice, and we all sat around the living area talking and eating. Not long after dinner, the guerrilla leader stopped by to see whether everything was okay. He then sat and talked with us awhile, although he wouldn't discuss political issues in depth without authorization from his commander. He did explain that the community lacked the resources to support the displaced people who had arrived there, which is why they were relocated to another place. On a similar note, he also pointed out that the economic situation made it difficult for peasants to survive and that the escalating violence was causing some to abandon the region.

The next morning we said goodbye to Alejandra and the guerrilla leader, who had shown up early at the house, no doubt to ensure that we'd leave. We walked out of the house to find that the bus we were to take was a Chiva, the traditional mode of public transportation throughout rural Colombia. A Chiva bus has a colorfully decorated wooden body perched on top of a truck chassis. There is no glass in the windows, and the seating consists of rows of benches. We climbed aboard, along with a handful of locals, and the bus slowly made its way in the pouring rain along the dirt road out of Bolivia. The journey was uneventful; our last sight of the FARC was a lone, partially uniformed guerrilla walking alongside the road with his AK-47 slung over his shoulder.

From El Paujil, we caught a ride back to Florencia, where we visited the headquarters of the Colombian army's 12th Brigade and met with Major Edgar Ortega. Whereas the FARC and many peasants in the region believed that the poverty caused by the government's social and economic policies lay at the root of the conflict, Major Ortega placed the blame elsewhere.

"Colombia's problem is not poverty; Ecuador and Peru are poorer than Colombia and they don't have these problems. Nor is narco-trafficking Colombia's problem; Bolivia, Ecuador, and Peru also have narco-trafficking. The problem is authority. We haven't had real leadership until now. We haven't had security until now," he said, referring to the policies of President Uribe.

According to Major Ortega, twenty-seven FARC militia members were captured in the villages of San Isidro and La Unión Peneya during Operation New Year. He said that the army had also seized weapons, communications equipment, and rebel propaganda, including CDs containing "communist" music. I couldn't help but think of the army's notorious history of falsifying battlefield reports, including exaggerating body counts and even dressing dead civilians in rebel uniforms, and the many mass arbitrary arrests of alleged guerrillas that had occurred under the Uribe government.

The mainstream media's accounts of Operation New Year had failed to question why the guerrillas would leave behind all that weaponry and communications equipment when they had known about the military offensive more than two weeks in advance. Or how the army, after facing no resistance when it took the village, knew that those arrested were in fact FARC guerrillas, given that they were all dressed in civilian clothing.

"How can the army determine whether or not people clad in civilian clothing are guerrillas?" I asked the major.

"They have pistols tucked into their waistbands, and they also have walkie-talkies," he replied.

Essentially, Major Ortega was claiming that, despite knowing well in advance that the army was coming, FARC militia members had simply waited, with their guns tucked into their trousers and walkie-talkies in their hands, for the military to come and arrest them. More and more frequently under President Uribe, some, if not all, of those captured were unarmed civilians accused of being guerrillas by soldiers who were under increasing pressure to show results on the battlefield; I imagined that in Operation New Year, things were much the same.

The next morning, Eric and I took a plane from Florencia to Puerto Asís in Putumayo, where we checked into the Hotel Chilimaco. I called my regular driver, Miguel, and he agreed to meet us in the second-floor restaurant later that afternoon. My purpose in Putumayo was twofold: to research the aerial fumigation of coca crops and to investigate the oil industry in the region. After witnessing the U.S. military escalation in oil-rich Arauca under the Bush administration's war on terror, I wanted to see to what degree Plan Colombia had provided security for multinational oil companies operating in Putumayo. Given that Eric had only one day before he had to return to Bogotá, we decided to first see how difficult it would be to locate coca, in light of recent declarations by the U.S. and Colombian governments that Plan Colombia had "virtually eradicated" coca cultivation in Putumayo.

Meeting us in the restaurant, Miguel agreed to take Eric and me to view coca crops the following day and to drive me to the town of Orito later in the week to investigate the oil situation. Meanwhile, he invited us to his house to eat dinner with him and his wife, Marcela.

After dinner, we were sitting in the living room of Miguel's small two-bedroom cinder-block house when a woman in her early thirties appeared at the open front door. She was clearly upset. Through her tears, she explained to Miguel that the paramilitaries had threatened to kill her because they believed that her boyfriend was a guerrilla. She pleaded with Miguel for help, but he just listened to her calmly and then, with resignation, said that there was nothing he could do for her. Still crying, she turned and left. Eric and I looked at each other, stunned at what had just occurred. We asked Miguel about her problem, but he quickly changed the topic. A little while later, as we drove back to the hotel, I wondered about the fate of that woman. She might well have been killed already, for all we knew.

The next morning, Miguel picked us up at the hotel at eight o'clock, and we headed out of town in the direction of the village of Santa Ana, thirty minutes away. Miguel explained that although the paramilitaries were still dominant in Puerto Asís, they were much weaker overall throughout the region. He claimed that the FARC had defeated the paramilitaries in several large battles over the previous eighteen months, thereby regaining some of the territory the rebels had lost in the late 1990s.

Not far from the army base in Santa Ana, we stopped in a clearing that contained several small houses next to a river, and Miguel arranged for one of the residents to take us downriver in a motorized canoe. We all climbed in and motored away under the watchful eyes of the soldiers stationed on the bridge above us.

Ten minutes downriver, our driver pulled over to the shore, and Miguel beckoned us to follow him up the muddy embankment. Behind a row of trees lining the top of the embankment sat a small farmhouse and several fields used for pasture. Miguel introduced us to the farmer who lived there, a man in his late twenties named Javier. We walked through the fields around the farmhouse and through a clump of trees to a smaller field that was full of coca bushes—as were four other clearings that Eric and I visited. More than three years of Plan Colombia's aerial fumigations had forced growers to cultivate coca on smaller plots carved out of the rainforest in order to make them more difficult to locate. Although those fields were significantly smaller than the ones I had witnessed on my first trip to Putumayo three years earlier, their very existence undermined official claims that coca had been "virtually eradicated."

The last two fields that Eric and I visited were particularly interesting, because the coca plants stood nine feet tall as opposed to the more conventional height of five feet.

"How come these bushes are so much taller than other coca plants I have seen?" I asked Javier.

"They are a new strain that is more resistant to the spraying and that grows faster than other varieties," he explained.

I snapped several photos of Eric as he strolled among the coca bushes that towered over his five-foot-seven frame. Several months later, British journalist Jeremy McDermott, in an article for the *Scotsman,* revealed the existence of a new crossbred, herbicide-resistant "super strain" of coca that was capable of yielding four times as many leaves from the same acreage. The implications of the new strain, which Eric and I had apparently seen in Putumayo, were enormous for Plan Colombia. With the new variety, growers could achieve the same level of production in their smaller fields as on the larger plots they had previously farmed. Consequently, although the U.S. and Colombian governments claimed that Plan Colombia was working because the fumigations were reducing the number of acres under cultivation in Putumayo, in reality coca production had remained relatively stable. This helped explain why the cost, purity, and availability of cocaine in U.S. cities hadn't changed after more than three years of Plan Colombia's spraying operations.

After visiting the five coca fields, we headed back to Puerto Asís. In the restaurant in our hotel, Eric and I encountered two representatives from international human rights organizations:

the International Organization for Migration (OIM) and the office of the United Nations High Commissioner for Refugees (UNHCR). Both representatives had been working in Putumayo to investigate the flow of refugees across the border to Ecuador. The UNHCR representative, a man who appeared to be in his mid fifties, confirmed what Miguel had told us about the weakening of the paramilitaries in Putumayo over the previous couple of years, although he pointed out that they were still responsible for many selective assassinations. He also claimed that the fumigations were hurting the farmers more than the guerrillas. The thirty-something female representative of the OIM told us that there were more than one thousand refugees in Ecuador and that some had fled from the violence and others from the fumigations. It appeared to me that little had changed for the people of Putumayo in the four years since I had investigated the consequences of Plan Colombia's initial fumigation campaign.

Eric caught his flight to Bogotá the next morning, and I went to meet with several local journalists. The New York–based Committee to Protect Journalists had asked me to interview local reporters in some of the rural regions to learn about the difficulties they faced. More than thirty reporters had been killed in Colombia over the previous decade, making it one of the most dangerous countries in the world in which to practice journalism. All of those assassinated were Colombian journalists; although foreign reporters had received threats, none had been killed. Because of the high risk they ran by working in rural conflict regions, Colombian journalists had, in large part, learned to avoid serious investigative journalism. They'd become selective about what stories to report and how to cover them, effectively engaging in self-censorship in an effort to avoid being targeted by armed groups.

Miguel took me to the home of Carlos, a former reporter who'd agreed to speak with me about how he used to go about his work in such an intimidating environment. While sitting in his living room drinking *tinto,* the traditional Colombian coffee, Carlos explained that he used to write for a regional newspaper but had recently quit his job because he was tired of the constant risks.

"The situation is complex," he began. "For example, it is difficult to report selective murders in the urban areas of Puerto Asís, because if you don't mention the perpetrators, then you are omitting part of the story. But if you do, then you are getting directly involved with the perpetrators. The Self-Defense Forces commit most of the selective murders in Puerto Asís, but that is information that can't be openly stated. You know that they are always monitoring the news, especially on the radio and in the newspapers. Some of my associates have been killed. Sometimes you decide not to write about the armed groups because you fear for the life of the person who gave you the information."

"How would you present a story related to the violence here in Puerto Asís?" I asked.

"Because most of the selective murders in Puerto Asís are committed by paramilitaries, you have to present that information in an indirect manner. When you publish the information, it is better to use an official source, like the police or the army, and let them say that it was this or that armed group. It is one of the most complicated topics to handle, so you avoid naming the perpetrator as much as possible and just describe the incident itself."

"It would seem that working under these conditions makes it virtually impossible to conduct any serious investigative journalism," I pointed out.

"Yes. Most of us prefer to practice social journalism. We mainly cover social and political life in the region. Most of us prefer to handle public-order issues in a cautious and precise manner."

Ultimately, because of the risks they face, many local journalists in Colombia do not see it as their responsibility to investigate violence related to the conflict; they prefer to leave that task to the police and the army. This is another reason why the official perspective on Colombia's conflict dominates media coverage. I thanked Carlos for his time and candor and wished him luck.

Miguel then drove me to a community radio station, where I met with two news reporters, Jorge and Fernando. Jorge didn't mince words, immediately declaring, "There is no freedom of the press. You can report information, but not say the truth. It is impossible to report the real news."

Fernando described how they go about their work, reiterating the point that Carlos, the former reporter, had made earlier.

"If there is an attack in Puerto Asís, obviously we have to say that an attack just happened," Fernando explained. "But our job is not to assign responsibility for that attack to X, Y, or Z. We state that this happened, at this time, in a car like this, and this many people were hurt. We have to be careful how we present the information. Believe me when I tell you that the armed actors are the people here who have the decision-making power, and they know who we are."

"Because of the difficulties faced by local reporters, do you think foreign journalists have a responsibility to more thoroughly investigate the violence related to the conflict?" I asked.

"The foreign journalists are paid to do that. But sometimes they'll get information from any useful fool around here, and later it can cost the source his life," Fernando said. "We are careful about this. We have learned how to live with the conflict. We have learned to build a protective shield around our families and ourselves."

Sitting alone in the hotel's restaurant later that afternoon, I wondered how I would function if I were a local journalist facing the risks that Colombian reporters confront daily. It is easy to say that journalists have a responsibility to inform the public, but at what point does the risk to one's own life outweigh that responsibility? Foreign journalists have maintained immunity because we primarily inform an overseas audience. Colombian reporters, on the other hand, directly affect public opinion among the very population that the armed groups are attempting to control. In my mind, the immunity that foreign correspondents have so far enjoyed in Colombia means we have an even greater responsibility to cover those stories that pose such a threat to the lives of our Colombian counterparts.

I also couldn't stop thinking about Fernando's claim that foreign journalists sometimes recklessly endanger the lives of their sources. I thought about my own modus operandi in Colombia. Had I endangered the lives of my sources and the drivers I worked with? I know I did in Arauca when the paramilitaries detained both my driver and me. But when I hired a driver, I always tried to make it as clear as possible what I wanted to do and to explicitly state any risk. In my articles, I often changed the names of my sources if they could be targeted for what they had told me. Still, I have never been completely comfortable with the potential risk to others that results from my work. It is something I'm always conscious of when working in Colombia.

The next morning, Miguel picked me up at the hotel and we drove to the town of Orito. We passed several coca fields situated within plain view of the road, further discrediting claims that coca had almost been eradicated in Putumayo.

When we reached Orito, we made our way to the small oil refinery on the far side of town. Four pipelines interconnected at the refinery, making Orito the hub of Putumayo's oil operations. Two pipelines carried oil from nearby fields being exploited by three companies: the state oil company Ecopetrol, U.S.-based Argosy Energy, and Petrominerales, a subsidiary of Canada's Petrobank. Another pipeline brought oil from the Ecuadorian Amazon, where U.S.-based Occidental Petroleum and Canada's EnCana had operations. The fourth was the

Transandino pipeline, which transported oil from the other pipelines across the Andes to the port of Tumaco, on Colombia's Pacific coast, for export to the United States.

At the entrance to the refinery—which was guarded by heavily armed National Police officers—I requested an interview with an Ecopetrol official and was told that all on-the-record interviews had to be conducted at the company's headquarters in Bogotá. However, I was informed that a representative at the refinery was willing to meet with me to provide background information about oil operations in Putumayo. I entered the refinery and was directed to an office building, where I met with a female representative who provided me with a brief history of oil in Putumayo.

Texas Petroleum, a subsidiary of U.S.-based Texaco, originally owned the rights to the oil in the region but sold them to Ecopetrol in 1980. Oil production in the remote Amazon region declined throughout the 1990s, in large part because of the growing military strength of the FARC, which often bombed the oil infrastructure. Although production had still been low in 2003, the outlook for 2004 was hopeful; a slew of new contracts signed between multinational companies and the Colombian government promised dramatic increases. Under those contracts, multinational companies obtained the rights to Colombian oil on favorable terms as a result of the neoliberal economic reforms demanded by the International Monetary Fund, whose loans constituted the economic component of Plan Colombia.

The new contracts reduced the royalty rate that foreign oil companies had to pay to the Colombian government to 8 percent per barrel, down from 20 percent four years earlier. They also permitted foreign companies to operate without going into partnership with Ecopetrol, thereby allowing them to retain ownership of 100 percent of the oil. Previously, foreign companies had to operate in partnership with the state oil company and owned rights to only 50 percent of the oil. As a result of these changes, the Colombian people were now receiving a much smaller percentage of the wealth derived from the country's petroleum resources.

Although it was clear that Plan Colombia had established favorable economic terms for foreign oil companies, the question remained whether it was also providing the necessary security for oil companies to successfully operate in Putumayo. In order to answer that question, I left the refinery and visited the adjoining military base, where I was introduced to Lieutenant Colonel Francisco Javier Cruz, commander of the twelve hundred army troops stationed in Orito.

Colonel Cruz was candid in admitting that his principal responsibility—in a region where the armed groups routinely attacked the civilian population—was protecting the oil industry.

"Security is the most important thing to me," he said. "Oil companies need to work without worrying, and international investors need to feel calm."

He explained that FARC attacks against the oil infrastructure had been reduced from 110 in 1999 to 43 in 2002, but leaped to a record 144 the following year. The majority of those attacks, according to Cruz, had occurred during a rebel offensive against the oil infrastructure the previous November.

"Some foreign oil companies in Colombia," I pointed out, "allow the army to use company helicopters to transport troops. Do you have access to company helicopters here?"

"Yes. We have the use of one Russian-made Mi-17 helicopter and one Bell 206 Ranger. Those helicopters are based here permanently."

"Do they belong to Ecopetrol?"

"They belong to Ecopetrol and Petrominerales," he replied, apparently unconcerned with the implication that the provision of a company helicopter to transport combat troops meant that the foreign company, in this case Canada's Petrobank, had become enmeshed in the conflict.

"Has Plan Colombia helped provide security for oil operations in Putumayo?" I asked him bluntly.

"Sure. We are conducting better operations now because we have tools like helicopters, troops, and training provided in large part by Plan Colombia," the colonel explained.

His response confirmed that Plan Colombia's military aid was being used not only to combat drugs but also to further foreign economic interests in the country. U.S. Secretary of Energy Bill Richardson had alluded to that objective when Plan Colombia was initially being formulated. During a visit to the Colombian city of Cartagena in 1999, the energy secretary declared, "The United States and its allies will invest millions of dollars in two areas of the Colombian economy, in the areas of mining and energy, and to secure these investments we are tripling military aid to Colombia."

I asked the colonel whether I could view some of the surrounding oil infrastructure from one of the helicopters. He agreed and, after making a quick call to arrange my tour, led me out of his office and toward the helipad in the center of the base. Colonel Cruz ordered a lower-ranking officer to accompany me on the Bell 206 Ranger. I climbed into the seat next to the pilot, who was an oil company employee. The helicopter took off, and we were soon flying above the lush green canopy of the rainforest. We quickly located a Petrobank oil well, with a tall derrick and several small structures, situated in a clearing. Flames shooting into the air from the burning of excess gases stood in stark contrast to the verdant rainforest around the site. We flew over several other drilling sites, the only scars on an otherwise magnificent vista. The pilot flew me back to the base, and after thanking the colonel, I rejoined Miguel, who was waiting outside the main gate.

It was difficult to find the benefits from oil royalties that were supposed to be improving the lives of the residents of Orito, Putumayo's largest recipient of oil revenue; the degree of poverty and underdevelopment was no less stark than in other comparably sized towns that received no oil funds. Miguel drove me to the large, modern recreation area near the center of town; it contained basketball courts, picnic and games areas, a modern hall for social gatherings, and a huge swimming pool with a winding plastic waterslide, but only Ecopetrol and Petrobank employees stationed at the refinery could use it. A tall wire and steel fence ensured that the residents of nearby shantytowns didn't stray into the fortresslike complex, which wouldn't have looked out of place in the middle of a Caribbean tourist resort. In the Colombian Amazon, it was an anomaly. Across the street I saw the small run-down wooden shacks, with no running water, that served as homes for local residents. The dramatic contrast between the lifestyle of the oil workers and that of local residents evoked Colombian novelist Gabriel García Márquez's portrayal of the foreign fruit company's presence in the mythical town of Macondo in his famous novel *One Hundred Years of Solitude*.

Miguel and I found a café and went inside to grab a cold drink and eat a late lunch. Two residents of Orito who knew Miguel were already in the café and joined our table. When I suggested to them that there was little evidence of the oil wealth benefiting local residents, one replied, "That is because the oil leaves Putumayo, and the royalties go into the wallets of the administrators."

"The politicians steal the money," the other man bluntly added.

The men explained that, whereas the guerrillas had regained control of several small towns in the region, the paramilitaries still controlled Orito. Interestingly, although President Uribe had cut off royalty payments to oil-rich Arauca because corrupt municipal governments were allegedly sympathetic to leftist guerrillas, he had continued to allow the money to flow to corrupt local officials in Putumayan towns such as Orito and Puerto Asís—towns that were controlled by the paramilitaries.

One of the men explained that the paramilitaries were ruthless in their efforts to maintain control over Orito. "They kill innocent peasants just because they might be guerrillas."

The man's claim was driven home the next day when I discovered that paramilitaries had assassinated a local peasant leader, Alirio Silva, in Orito at the same time that I was interviewing Colonel Cruz.

As we drove back to Puerto Asís, I reflected on my visit to that virtually abandoned indigenous village in the Ecuadorian Amazon fifteen years earlier. Although oil production in Colombia's Amazon region hadn't yet proven to be as devastating to local peasants as it had been to many indigenous peoples in Ecuador, it certainly wasn't benefiting them in any significant way. Given the levels of violence in Putumayo, oil exploitation appeared to be further fueling the conflict in order to ensure that multinational oil companies maintained access to a steady supply of the valuable commodity. Once again I was leaving the Amazon rainforest struggling to comprehend why the preservation of our lifestyles in North America and Europe had to prove so destructive to the lives of so many others.

Two days later I was back in Bogotá, where I visited Ecopetrol's headquarters but failed to obtain an interview with a company official. I had better luck at the north Bogotá offices of Calgary-based Petrobank, where I met with company representative Steven Benedetti.

"We believe there is a big prize in Putumayo," Benedetti told me.

He also admitted, not surprisingly, that Petrobank was excited about the economic reforms that had provided more favorable terms for oil companies. And even though some of the company's oil wells and storage tanks had been damaged by the FARC the previous November, Benedetti declared, "We believe the benefits outweigh the risks."

As I exited Petrobank's offices, I couldn't get those words out of my head. The words of a man in Puerto Asís with whom

I had spoken three days earlier came back to me: "Everyone knows the conflict in the Middle East is because of oil, and Colombia's problems are no different. Maybe the coca is going, but there's still oil. And if there's oil, then the armed groups won't leave, because they are interested in places where there is money and power."

The Tenth Hour

7:00 p.m., August 16, 2006

It's beginning to look like I might spend the night on this farm, and I'm wondering why it's taking so long for someone to respond to my request to investigate the aerial fumigations of coca crops in this region. More than nine hours have passed since I was detained in Santo Domingo. Perhaps I've already been kidnapped and they just haven't told me yet. My anxiety level begins to rise again, and I try to clear my mind of all negative thoughts. I've had my fill of the waiting game, but there is nothing I can do about it.

Most members of the household are seated in the main room watching television. The Caracol network repeatedly runs promotional spots for the premiere of its new *telenovela,* a combination soap opera and drama, which will be broadcast later this evening. Most of my fellow television viewers appear to be excited about the event. The new show, titled *Sin Tetas No Hay Paraiso—Without Tits There Is No Paradise—*is based on a Colombian novel and has been a controversial topic of discussion in the country for weeks. *Sin Tetas* is about a seventeen-year-old girl named Catalina who believes her flat chest is a barrier to her escaping poverty by becoming a drug trafficker's pampered playgirl. Catalina turns to prostitution in order to raise the money needed to pay for the operation that will give her the large breasts preferred by drug traffickers. In a country that has been labeled the plastic surgery capital of the world, the show clearly reflects some aspects of the national culture. Critics claim that it demeans women, since it reduces them to men's playthings, and feeds into the negative stereotypes of Colombia.

I get up and walk to the bathroom under the watchful eye of my guard, wondering which broadcast he would prefer, Radio Resistencia or *Sin Tetas*. Exiting the bathroom, I walk along the fence and peer up at the increasing brightness of the emerging stars in the clear sky above. Standing outside in the darkness, with the faint sound of the television in the background, I reflect on this latest sojourn to Colombia. I said goodbye to Terry and Owen almost three weeks ago. My first stop, after changing planes in Bogotá, was the city of Valledupar in the northern department of Cesar. My objective was to visit the region containing the Pribbenow coal mine, which is owned and operated by the Alabama-based Drummond Company.

Upon my arrival in Valledupar, I quickly found a driver willing to take me two hours south of the city to the town of La Jagua de Ibirico, where I spent the night. The next morning I located a local driver, Enrique, to take me on a tour of the region surrounding the Pribbenow mine. We left the paved road in La Jagua and headed west on a dirt road toward the town of La Loma, located on the edge of Drummond's mine.

As we drove through cattle-ranching country, Enrique told me that he'd lived in the region his entire life and that his father had been killed by paramilitaries four years earlier. Evidently the paramilitaries dominated the lowlands, where numerous coal mines were situated, while the guerrillas maintained control of the mountainous region east of La Jagua.

It was the paramilitaries whose actions had turned the international spotlight onto Drummond's Pribbenow mine five years earlier. In the late 1980s, Drummond took advantage of the deregulation that was occurring under economic globalization—a process, dominated by the ideology of free market capitalism, that has made it easier for corporations to set up shop anywhere in the world. Drummond purchased the open-pit Pribbenow mine, as well as a Caribbean port from which the company could ship its coal to the United States and other countries. In the ensuing years, the company boosted the Pribbenow mine's coal production to more than twenty million tons annually, making it one of the largest coal-mining operations in the world and the most significant contributor to Drummond's $1.7 billion in annual revenues.

It cost less for Drummond to mine Colombian coal than U.S. coal, partly due to low wages and favorable concession terms from the Colombian government. As a result, Drummond closed five mines in Alabama and laid off seventeen hundred U.S. miners. The payroll savings for the company proved substantial, since Alabama mine workers who earned eighteen dollars an hour were replaced with Colombian miners who earned an hourly wage of only two dollars and forty-five cents. The payroll savings alone boosted Drummond's profits by more than a quarter of a million dollars annually—not including the additional savings from no longer having to provide expensive health insurance and other benefits to U.S. workers.

By choosing to do business in Colombia, however, the company became enmeshed in the country's civil conflict. In March 2001, a paramilitary death squad stopped a company bus carrying workers from the Pribbenow mine, pulled two men off, and executed them. The victims, Valmoré Locarno Rodríguez and Victor Hugo Orcasita, were the president and vice-president of the local chapter of the Colombian union Sintramienergetica, which represents the mine's workers. Drummond had recently refused a request by the two union leaders, who were engaged in contract negotiations with the company at the time, to be allowed to sleep at the mine due to paramilitary threats. Seven months later, the union local's new president, Gustavo Soler Mora, was also taken from a company bus and killed by paramilitaries.

In 2002, a suit was filed in U.S. Federal Court on behalf of Sintramienergetica, claiming that the Drummond Company had "aided and abetted" the paramilitary perpetrators of the murders. Although Drummond denied the allegations, a sworn statement by former Colombian intelligence officer Rafael García supported the union's claims. In his statement, García said he was present at a meeting where Augusto Jiménez, president of Drummond's Colombian operations, handed over a briefcase containing two hundred thousand dollars in cash to be delivered to Colombian paramilitary leader Rodrigo Tovar. García stated that the money was to pay for the killing of labor leaders and identified the targets as two of the three unionists killed in 2001.

For the past twenty years, Colombia has been by far the most dangerous country in the world for those who fight for workers' rights. Almost 75 percent of the union leaders killed in the world during the previous two decades were Colombian. Since 1985, more than four thousand Colombian labor leaders have been assassinated by paramilitaries, and in only a handful of cases have those responsible been convicted in court. The paramilitaries, with the help of the Colombian military, have waged a dirty war against Colombia's unions with virtual impunity. Because they engage in a struggle to improve the life of Colombia's workers, union leaders are assumed to be guerrillas by the government, the military, and the paramilitaries. The links between multinational companies and the paramilitaries were made evident when Cincinnati-based Chiquita pleaded guilty in a U.S. court to funding AUC paramilitaries in northern Colombia. Between 1997 and 2004, Chiquita paid $1.7 million to the AUC, even though the company knew that the group was on the State Department's list of foreign terrorist organizations.

In 2003, President Uribe began negotiations with the AUC with the goal of demobilizing the paramilitary organization's fighters. The two parties agreed that in return for demobilizing their troops and confessing to their crimes, paramilitary leaders would serve no more than eight years in prison. By March 2006, more than thirty thousand paramilitaries had demobilized and were receiving monthly payments from the government under the Justice and Peace Law, which established the legal process for the demobilization. Despite the official face of the demobilization, human rights organizations claimed that many paramilitaries hadn't actually laid down their weapons and that the process represented more of a restructuring than an actual disbandment of the AUC. Amnesty International reported in late 2005 that paramilitaries in Medellín were still active in the city's poor barrios almost two years after they had supposedly demobilized. In 2006, the Colombian nongovernmental organization INDEPAZ (Institute for Development and Peace Studies) revealed that forty-three new paramilitary groups had formed in twenty-two of the country's thirty-two departments.

Many of those who demobilized were not even paramilitaries, according to documents discovered on the laptop of AUC commander Rodrigo Tovar. The information showed that the AUC had paid unemployed peasants in northern Colombia to act like paramilitary fighters and to participate in the demobilization process, while the real paramilitaries continued committing crimes. This helped explain the reports that thirty-one thousand paramilitaries had demobilized, when their numbers were estimated to be only fifteen thousand prior to the government's negotiations with the AUC. As for AUC leader Carlos Castaño, he never benefited from the demobilization process, because he was killed by rival paramilitaries in April 2004.

One thing that the demobilization process did achieve was

mainstream media coverage of paramilitary atrocities. Prior to 2003, U.S. and Colombian mainstream media outlets reported mostly on the FARC's role in the conflict, even though most of the violence was being perpetrated by the paramilitaries. The media all but ignored the paramilitaries until the Colombian government began negotiations with the AUC—at which point the mainstream coverage focused on the paramilitaries, emphasizing that the demobilization agreement would disband the armed group that was responsible for the majority of the massacres and other gross violations of human rights in the country. Suddenly the AUC's atrocities began appearing on the mainstream media's radar screen, because the government was eager to portray its peace talks as a means to improve the country's human rights situation. Human rights groups and independent media had been reporting paramilitary atrocities for years, but Colombian and U.S. government officials tended to ignore their findings.

On the drive to La Loma, I asked Enrique about the demobilization process and whether there were still paramilitaries active in that part of Cesar.

"The demobilization of the paramilitaries here hasn't achieved anything. Everything is still the same," he replied, echoing statements I had heard in various parts of the country over the previous two years.

Shortly after Enrique and I entered La Loma, the dirt road turned into smooth concrete; it was the only paved street in town, and was paid for by Drummond. It was difficult to tell that the road was paved merely by looking at it, because it had a thick layer of dust coating its surface—dust generated by Drummond's giant and ever-expanding 25,000-acre open-pit mine. The dust permeated everything in La Loma: roads, vehicles, homes, clothes, and people. When I asked a few local residents about the mine's effects on the community, a middle-aged man named Francisco said, "Many people here suffer from respiratory ailments due to the dust in the air."

I pointed out to him that Drummond claims to fund health and education programs for local residents; he acknowledged that they did, but said that the programs didn't even begin to offset the social and health consequences of the mine. A slightly younger man jumped in and declared that prostitution had gotten worse as the mine increased in size. Evidently the mine's overwhelmingly male workforce had attracted increasing numbers of bars and prostitutes to the once quiet farming town.

"Some of the prostitutes are children," Francisco acknowledged, looking ashamed.

Enrique and I returned to the truck and headed out of town to the Pribbenow mine. The entrance to the mine consisted of two eight-foot-high gates with huge billboards on either side of them. One of the billboards boldly declared, "We are committed to the preservation of the environment"; the other displayed beautiful color photos of wild animals and warned that killing those creatures on company property was prohibited. I found it ironic that the operator of one of the world's largest open-pit coal mines was portraying itself as environmentally friendly and a protector of animals, even as its ever-expanding operations were devouring every tree and plant that constituted the natural habitat of the local wildlife.

Fully aware that company officials working in rural regions are usually reluctant to give interviews to independent journalists, I decided that we should locate the local army battalion responsible for protecting the mine's operations. Perhaps I could parlay an interview with the army commander into an entrance ticket to the mine.

Enrique turned back onto the highway in the direction of Bucaramanga. We had gone no further than twenty yards when we were stopped at a checkpoint manned by two armed guards, who appeared to be protecting the railroad crossing used by coal trains entering and leaving the mine. A uniformed man with a revolver strapped to his hip was speaking into a hand-held radio as he approached our vehicle. I could tell right away by his uniform that he was neither a Colombian soldier nor a police officer. As he drew closer to Enrique's window, I noticed the words "private security" emblazoned on his uniform in Spanish and a name badge hanging from his breast pocket identifying him as an employee of the Drummond Company. The guard told us that he had received orders to detain us until the mine's chief of security arrived on the scene. It was then that it hit me: we'd been detained on a public Colombian highway by the private armed security force of a U.S. corporation.

Enrique and I got out of the vehicle, and I couldn't help but think how most Americans would feel if they were detained on a public highway in the United States by armed guards working for a foreign corporation. I honestly couldn't imagine many U.S. citizens tolerating it, but Enrique appeared nonplussed; most likely he was accustomed to it.

Within ten minutes, Drummond's security chief pulled up with a truckload of Colombian soldiers, asked us for identification, and inquired about what we were doing in the area. Identifying myself as a journalist, I asked whether it would be possible to interview a Drummond official at the mine. The security chief said that such a request would have to be authorized by corporate headquarters, but agreed to my follow-up request to ask the army commander responsible for protecting Drummond's mining operations for an interview. The chief and I climbed into his vehicle and drove into the mine, passing between the two billboards that almost implied we were entering a nature preserve.

Several minutes along the road that ran inside the mine, we pulled up at a small army base. Drummond's security chief introduced me to the army commander, Captain Wilfredo González, who agreed to be interviewed. We stepped inside his air-conditioned office, and I soon realized that Captain González liked to talk. More specifically, he liked to talk about what a wonderful job he and his two hundred troops were doing protecting mining operations from the "terrorists" and how his success was possible only because of President Uribe's security policies. He explained that the guerrillas primarily stayed in the mountains, but would descend to the lowlands occasionally to try to blow up the railroad tracks used by the coal trains. When I asked the captain whether Drummond provided helicopters for his troops, he stated that his soldiers used army helicopters but the company provided the fuel. In response to my question about the demobilization of paramilitaries in the region, Captain González said that the army hadn't focused on that process because it was primarily concerned with the guerrillas.

I finally managed to extricate myself from Captain González, and I even welcomed the oppressive heat and humidity that hit me when I stepped out of his office. As we climbed back into the vehicle, I asked Drummond's security chief whether I could tour the mine, but he refused and drove me back to the gate.

Enrique and I left the mining region and made our way to Valledupar, where I stayed overnight. The following morning I caught a taxi to the offices of Sintramienergetica, the union that represents Drummond's Colombian workers. There I met with Estivenson Avila, the union's president, and Alvaro Mercado, a member of the executive committee.

The three of us began our meeting by eating breakfast and exchanging stories about our mutual friend Francisco Ramírez, the president of the state mine workers' union Sintraminercol, who had worked closely with Sintramienergetica. I'd known Francisco for years, having spent time with him in Colombia, the United States, and Canada. He was then, and continues to be, an outspoken critic of the government's links to the paramilitaries and of the neoliberal economic policies being implemented under the globalization process. These policies have made Colombia's valuable natural resources available to multinational companies on terms that, according to Francisco, represent a theft of the national wealth. As a result of his outspokenness, Francisco had become a target of the paramilitaries. He'd miraculously survived seven assassination attempts made against him during the previous fourteen years and had gone into temporary exile on several occasions, but he always insisted on returning to Colombia to continue his work.

The topic of conversation eventually shifted from Francisco to Drummond. Avila talked about the company's failure to adequately address the health problems experienced by workers. He also claimed that Drummond was increasing the percentage of the mine's workers that were contractors in an effort to break the union.

I told them about my encounter with Drummond's private armed security guards on the public highway. "How is it possible for them to have jurisdiction on a public highway?" I asked.

"The security guards, the army, and the paramilitaries are all the same," Mercado explained. "They all work with the company. Drummond provides vehicles and gasoline to the paramilitaries inside the company's installations, including the Pribbenow mine."

"But haven't the paramilitaries demobilized?" I asked.

"It is an illusion; they have not demobilized," Mercado replied. "They are still here doing the same things. We have to be careful here in Valledupar and when we go to the mine. We are in the eye of the hurricane, and they can kill us at any moment. It's still dangerous."

"They tried to kill Alvaro in June," said Avila, pointing to his colleague.

"Yes. I was arriving home to my house when I heard a motorcycle come around the corner," Mercado said. "I looked around and saw two men with guns on the motorcycle. I yelled at my wife to get inside the house, and they missed us because we made it inside in time."

I thanked the two union leaders and took my leave. Several weeks later, I made several phone calls to the Drummond Company's Colombian offices and its headquarters in Alabama requesting an interview. I never received a response.

• • •

The next day I departed Valledupar, bound for the semiarid department of La Guajira, in a *taxi colectivo*—a long-distance taxi that leaves when it has four passengers. It was my third visit to the region to investigate the social and economic effects of El Cerrejón, the world's largest open-pit coal mine, on Afro-Colombian and indigenous communities. As was the case with oil, the Colombian government had lowered the royalty rates for coal at the urging of the International Monetary Fund and World Bank, allowing foreign companies to keep a greater share of the country's resource wealth. It was difficult for me to see how the implementation of such policies was benefiting rural Colombians who lived in resource-rich regions of the country; although some jobs were created, they were rarely filled by members of the local communities. Yet those communities were usually forced to endure the environmental degradation and violence that often accompanied the exploitation of the country's natural resources, which weren't even being extracted for domestic consumption. And although most of the wealth went to multinational companies, the rest ended up in the pockets of national elites, thereby maintaining the social inequalities that have long plagued Colombia and lie at the root of the conflict.

In the 1980s, U.S.-based Exxon, which became Exxon-Mobil after merging with Mobil in 1999, formed a partnership with the Colombian state-owned company Carbocol to extract coal from the Cerrejón mine. In 2000, the Colombian government sold Carbocol's 50 percent share to a consortium of multinational mining companies—Anglo American, BHP Billiton, and Glencore—as part of the economic reforms demanded by the International Monetary Fund. In March 2002, Exxon-Mobil sold its 50 percent share in the mine to the consortium. With the growth of both Drummond's Pribbenow mine and the Cerrejón mine, coal soon became Colombia's second-largest legal export after oil, and Colombia became the number one foreign supplier of coal to the United States. The initial construction of the Cerrejón mine, as well as a private railroad and port, in 1983 displaced more than 1,100 indigenous Wayuu. By the late 1990s, the Cerrejón mine had become a massive hole in the ground measuring thirty miles long and five miles across.

In 1997, in order to further expand, the mine's owners convinced the Colombian government to displace the Afro-Colombian farming community of Tabaco, a town whose residents were descendents of escaped slaves and had survived on subsistence farming for generations. Realizing that their displacement was inevitable, the residents of the town requested that the company negotiate a collective relocation of the community so that they could keep their livelihoods and social networks intact. The company refused, insisting on negotiating with individual property owners. Some residents settled with the company out of fear that they wouldn't receive anything if they continued to demand a collective negotiation. Some seventy families, however, continued to resist and on August 9, 2001, were forcibly evicted from their homes by state security forces and the mine's private guards. The entire town was then bulldozed and incorporated into the mine.

I first went to La Guajira one year after the displacement of Tabaco to meet with former residents and to visit other communities threatened with future displacement. While traveling on the dirt roads that linked the communities located on the perimeter of the mine, I was constantly followed by the mine's private security guards. At one point the guards stopped their vehicle and glared menacingly at residents of the village of Chancleta who chose to speak to me about their plight. Most of Chancleta's residents had already been forced to abandon their homes due to an inability to support themselves. The mine had purchased much of the land surrounding the remote village and then denied residents access to it; as a result, villagers could no longer hunt and fish, and their goats had nowhere to graze. The mine was effectively starving the villagers out.

Juana Arregoces, a seventy-three-year-old Afro-Colombian woman, told me that she had lived in the region her entire life and in her current house for the past nineteen years. From the front of her humble mud and wood hut, the edge of the giant mine could be seen little more than a hundred yards away. She told me that the dust and noise from dynamiting were intolerable and caused many respiratory problems for her and other residents, and she claimed that the mine's private security personnel and the army regularly harassed residents.

On a subsequent visit, my wife Terry and I experienced some of that harassment. As we departed the mining region, we passed through a checkpoint manned by the mine's private security guards. Just beyond the checkpoint, we stopped the car and took a photograph of a large, colorful billboard that the company had erected beside the road to inform people about the social projects that the Cerrejón mine funded. Fifteen minutes further down the road, we were stopped by the Colombian army. The soldiers searched the car and our belongings and asked us why we were taking photos. Clearly, the mine's security guards had notified the army that we had taken the photograph of the billboard.

In 2002, I visited the office of the Cerrejón Foundation, located an hour and a half from the Cerrejón mine in the city of Riohacha. I met with the organization's executive director, Yolanda Mendoza, who explained that the foundation was established in 1984 by the mine's owners to address the needs of local communities affected by the mine's operations. Mendoza said that the foundation provides microcredit programs to small businesses and indigenous communities, and a field staff helps teach the communities new farming technologies. But when I asked her what the foundation was doing to help communities displaced by the mine, she replied, "They are not really displaced. They are not displaced because there are no communities where the mine is at this time. There was a process a long time ago, but now there are no communities there."

"But what about the community of Tabaco, which was forcibly displaced by the mine last year?" I asked.

"I don't think that is true," Mendoza declared, becoming visibly tense. "It is a topic that you will have to speak about with the Cerrejón mine company, because I don't have the authority to talk about it."

When I contacted Cerrejón, spokesperson Ricardo Plata Cepeda said that the company was waiting for the Colombian courts to determine how much it had to pay to those forcibly evicted from Tabaco. Unfortunately, there seemed to be little likelihood of any judicial rulings in favor of the residents of Tabaco being effectively enforced by Colombian authorities. Meanwhile, the Colombian government extended the company's operating contract until 2034, at which time the dominant feature in the landscape of southern Guajira will likely be an ecologically devastating seventy-mile by twelve-mile hole in the ground. This expansion will undoubtedly displace more Afro-Colombian and indigenous Wayuu communities in order to supply coal to power plants in the United States, Canada, and Europe.

The reason for my third and most recent visit to La Guajira was to attend a conference on mining and human rights that I'd helped to organize. At the conference, I met up with several friends who'd also been working to help the displaced people of Tabaco and other communities affected by the mine. Those friends included union leader Francisco Ramírez, Tabaco community leader José Julio Pérez, and history professor and activist Aviva Chomsky, who had introduced me to the Tabaco issue four years earlier. The conference was held on August 9, 2006, which was both the fifth anniversary of the displacement of Tabaco and World Indigenous Day. The objective of the conference, as well as the related international solidarity campaign, was to pressure the mine's owners into negotiating a collective relocation of the displaced villagers of Tabaco and of any other community to be displaced in the future. I became involved in the campaign when Terry and I moved to Nova Scotia in 2004 so that she could teach international politics. Shortly after arriving in Nova Scotia, I discovered that the province's electricity was being generated by power plants burning coal from the Cerrejón mine.

At the mining conference, I met Alirio Uribe, a leading Colombian human rights lawyer who worked with the José Alvear Restrepo Lawyers' Collective. Members of the collective had been labeled as terrorist sympathizers by the government and threatened by the paramilitaries due to their criticism of President Uribe's security policies. Consequently, Alirio always traveled with international accompaniment for protection. I sat down with him to discuss the demobilization of the paramilitaries.

"We have a list, name by name, of more than three thousand people assassinated by the paramilitaries during the demobilization talks," Alirio said. "The government is complicit in this process. There are forty-three new paramilitary groups, but according to the Ministry of Defense, these new paramilitary groups have nothing to do with the old ones. But the truth is, they are the same. Before, they were the AUC; now they are called the New Generation AUC. They have the same collusion with the army and the police. It's a farce."

"What about claims made by the UN that the number of human rights abuses directly attributable to the Colombian military has increased under President Uribe?" I asked.

"Under this government, killings by paramilitaries have decreased, and murders and attacks by public forces have increased. There is an explanation for this. Historically, the paramilitaries represented the privatization of the dirty war. The government created these dark forces to carry out the repression, to kill civilians, journalists, and others, and then the state could say that it has nothing to do with it because the paramilitaries are responsible. But the paramilitaries have never been independent from the state. They have never fought against the state. They have always been allied with the civil authorities, the public forces, the army, and the police, with all the security organizations of the state. But during the past four years, as paramilitary violence has diminished, official violence by the police and the army has increased."

"What sort of violence is being perpetrated by the state security forces?" I asked.

"Under this government, a million people have been forcibly displaced by violence. And under this government, there have been ten politically motivated assassinations a day: peasants, indigenous people, human rights defenders, and social leaders. And under this government, more than four hundred union leaders have been assassinated. And under this government, there have been, more or less, six deaths a day in combat between the army and the guerrillas. However, the president is telling the international community that there is no armed conflict in Colombia."

After speaking with Alirio, I met with Debora Barros Fince, an indigenous Wayuu woman in her early thirties who lost several family members in a massacre perpetrated by paramilitaries in April 2004. Debora was dressed in a bright orange full-length *manta*, a traditional Wayuu dress. She had grown up and lived most of her life in the village of Bahía Portete, which is located next to the Cerrejón company's private port in northern Guajira. She said the community had always been peaceful, surviving on fishing and artisanry, until one morning in April 2004, when paramilitaries entered the village and massacred twelve indigenous Wayuu, including two young children. Another thirty members of the community, including three of Debora's cousins, were "disappeared," and more than three hundred were displaced. Some locals have speculated that the massacre was part of a paramilitary strategy to ensure control of drug trafficking routes; others have suggested that it was motivated by land speculation due to rumors that the Cerrejón mine wanted to expand its port.

As we sat there with the turquoise waters of the Caribbean serving as a majestic backdrop, Debora described the massacre.

"The paramilitaries arrived in the area several months before the massacre," she began. "The police knew they were there, because the paramilitaries would walk around in their uniforms at night and the police wouldn't do anything. And then the paramilitaries began saying that they were going to start killing people. Two days before the massacre, my uncle called the army base in Riohacha and asked them to send troops to protect the community."

"And what happened?" I asked her.

"They didn't send any troops. Instead, they called the paramilitaries," Debora explained. "We know this because thirty minutes after he had called the army, my uncle received a call from the paramilitaries, who said they were going to kill him because he had called the army."

"Can you describe what happened the day of the massacre?"

"About one hundred and fifty soldiers entered the village on the morning of the eighteenth; they were from the army, so people didn't react. But then the soldiers started attacking people. They broke my grandmother's legs. They tied one boy to the back of a Toyota truck and dragged him along the street. When people realized what was happening, they tried to run away. Most of them escaped. But the soldiers caught some of them and turned them over to men in civilian clothes. Those men were the paramilitaries who had arrived in the community a few months earlier. It was the paramilitaries who did the killing."

Debora's description of the links between the paramilitaries and the army was a clear illustration of the ongoing collusion that Alirio had alluded to only half an hour earlier. On the same day that Debora described the massacre to me, another massacre occurred, in the southern department of Nariño, in which five indigenous leaders were killed. On this World Indigenous Day, it was clear that the situation for Colombia's indigenous peoples remained as dire as ever.

• • •

The next day, I flew from Riohacha to Nariño in order to investigate the massacre. I spent the night in a hotel in the city of Pasto, where I watched an army general being interviewed on a nightly news show. When asked about the massacre of the five indigenous leaders, the general stated unequivocally that the FARC was responsible.

The following morning, I located a driver to take me to the small town of Ricaurte, halfway along the road that winds its way from eight thousand feet up in the Andes down to the Pacific port city of Tumaco. Only half an hour into our two-hour journey, we were stopped at a joint army and police checkpoint. A soldier told us that all vehicles traveling from that point on had to travel in a caravan under military guard due to guerrilla activity in the area. The next caravan wasn't scheduled to depart until three o'clock in the afternoon, which meant that my driver wouldn't be able to make it to Ricaurte and back before nightfall. After my driver agreed to drive to Ricaurte without military accompaniment, I asked to speak with the officer in charge. I got out of the car, introduced myself to the army commander, and presented my press card.

"I have an interview scheduled for two hours from now with the mayor of Ricaurte," I lied. "Could we please go on ahead of the caravan?"

"We can't be responsible for you if you are not traveling in the caravan," the commander explained. "Go ahead if you want to, but you are responsible if anything happens to you."

I thanked him and got back into the car, and my driver and I resumed our journey on the eerily deserted highway, which descended spectacularly from the high-altitude temperate zone to the tropical rainforest that blanketed the lower elevations of the Andes.

Ricaurte was a small town situated next to a river in the bottom of a ravine, with three main streets running parallel to the river. Several very steep roads ran up and down one side of the ravine, connecting the three main streets to each other. There was a heavy army presence in the town, including several tanks.

The five indigenous leaders had been killed in the village of Ataquer, thirty minutes farther along the road to Tumaco. The massacre victims were among the seventeen hundred indigenous Awa, including more than four hundred children, who had been forcibly displaced from their remote villages a month earlier. Twelve hundred of the displaced indigenous people were living as refugees in Ricaurte; the rest were in Ataquer.

After checking into a hotel, I went in search of the displaced Awa and soon found some of them camped out in a school. More than a dozen children were playing in the school yard as their parents looked on, while off to the side of one of the school buildings several women were preparing food in large pots on open fires. I asked one of the men watching the children playing whether there was a representative I could speak with about their situation, and he pointed me in the direction of a community center across the street.

The dark and dingy community center stood in stark contrast to the bright openness of the school. Its small rooms and narrow hallways were so full of indigenous refugees that an overwhelming sense of claustrophobia enveloped me. A nun who was helping the Awa cope with their dilemma greeted me and showed me into the only brightly lit room in the building. A couple of dozen children were excitedly receiving fresh mangoes, which two other nuns were handing out; the fruit was part of a care package that had just arrived from an aid agency.

I was introduced to an elderly Awa woman who was a member of the Cabildo Mayor, a council that oversaw eleven indigenous communities in that part of Nariño. She told me that they had been living as refugees for a month and that it was difficult to adjust to the concrete environment after having lived in the rainforest their entire lives.

"We don't want to abandon our land or lose our land. We want to live in peace," she said. "We did not have problems with the illegal armed groups in the past. It was about four years ago that they came to the Awa territory. We are not friends with these groups; we are neutral. We are caught in the middle of the fighting between the armed groups, including the army, which has threatened us."

"Who was responsible for the massacre in Ataquer two days ago?" I asked her.

"I believe it was the Self-Defense Forces that massacred the five indigenous leaders. They have previously threatened our communities."

After leaving the community center, I found a taxi to take me to Ataquer in search of the rest of the displaced Awa. I learned from the driver that there wasn't a significant paramilitary presence in that part of Nariño—a claim that was confirmed by several more sources over the next couple of days. Apparently the FARC dominated the rural areas, where it had maintained a presence for decades, and the military controlled the towns and villages along the highway, including Ricaurte and Ataquer. In that light, the elderly Awa woman's claim that the paramilitaries were responsible for the massacre was curious, to say the least.

Ataquer was smaller than Ricaurte, but just as militarized; I saw soldiers, police, and two tanks on the streets of the village. A local resident pointed me in the direction of a small school where the displaced Awa had set up camp, and my driver waited while I entered the property. Next to one of the buildings, more than twenty Awa were gathered under a large black tarpaulin cover that served as a giant makeshift tent. Several women were stoking two large fires, and another was mixing rice in a giant pot. The men, women, and children greeted me warmly; the children were particularly curious, possibly having never seen a *gringo* before. I was told that no other foreign journalist had visited them to discuss either their displacement or the massacre—the foreign press had covered the massacre from Bogotá.

I sat down with a young Awa leader named Jairo, who told me the story of his community's displacement.

"We were displaced from Chaguichimbuza one month ago, and now, during this difficult time, we are living here in Ataquer."

"Who displaced you?"

"We were displaced by government forces conducting military operations, and now we don't have any security here either, as five of our friends were massacred two days ago. This massacre occurred while the public forces were here. We need the government to end its military operations, because their helicopters, planes, and soldiers enter our territories to search for armed groups, but they terrorize our people and displace many communities. This has been happening for the past three years."

"How did the massacre occur?"

"When the massacre happened, the army was stationed five hundred yards away and the police were also here in town. Some of us were sleeping here in the school, and others in people's homes. They came in the morning and took them out of the houses and shot them like animals. I don't know if it will happen again."

Jairo introduced me to several other Awa, and I listened to their stories. Most of them reiterated Jairo's version of events and pointed out that the killers wore black T-shirts and camouflage pants. Others spoke about how they missed their homes and how they were worried about what was going to happen to their animals and crops while they were in Ataquer. A few of them were considering returning home; the massacre had made it evident that they weren't safe in Ataquer, and since they were going to live under the threat of violence, they preferred to do so on their own land. It pained me to hear their stories. I couldn't imagine living in such a state of insecurity, especially with children. The Awa had been threatened on their lands, and now they were being threatened as refugees. And most of the world was oblivious to their plight.

After I'd spoken with a few of the Awa refugees, Jairo introduced me to Ernesto Moreno, a coordinator with the government's Social Action Agency. Ernesto was helping the Awa in Ataquer and Ricaurte cope with their situation.

"We arrived in the region on July thirteenth in response to the displacement," Ernesto said. "The displacement was caused by army operations seeking to recapture areas historically controlled by the guerrillas."

Ernesto told me that the displaced Awa lacked everything— they'd left all their belongings behind when they fled their homes. They needed food and water, but most of all, they needed to be able to return to their homes safely.

"They have a culture that is closely connected to the land, the land and animals that they have been forced to abandon," Ernesto explained. "This is a humanitarian tragedy. They need humanitarian assistance from the state that guarantees them food, health care, and social assistance in all areas. What they are receiving isn't sufficient."

"How are the children coping with the displacement and the massacre?" I asked.

"The whole community is suffering, but particularly the children. We need to understand what they are feeling and thinking and to help them express themselves. It's a very complicated situation; they have been collectively threatened."

It was late afternoon when I returned to Ricaurte, where I spoke with several soldiers in an attempt to request an interview with their commander. Unfortunately, none of them knew his whereabouts. Evidently the Grupo Cabal Mechanized Battalion was responsible for security along the entire length of the Pasto-Tumaco highway, so the commander moved around a lot. One soldier thought the commander would probably be in Ricaurte the next day. The following morning, I again spoke with soldiers patrolling the town's streets, but they had no idea when their commander might arrive. I decided to wait around for that day; if he didn't show up, I'd return to Pasto the next morning.

I spoke with several locals throughout the day about the situation in that part of Nariño. Apparently the conflict had intensified during the previous few years. Plan Colombia had displaced coca cultivation from neighboring Putumayo to Nariño, and President Uribe had implemented security policies in the region that called for the army to launch offensives against the FARC. A middle-aged man I spoke with on a street corner said that Ricaurte and the surrounding area had been peaceful before the army arrived to target the guerrillas. When I asked him about the massacre, he nodded in the direction of several soldiers sitting on a tank and whispered, "They did it."

I was beginning to draw the same conclusion myself. Although the army was publicly blaming the FARC for the massacre, the evidence on the ground didn't appear to support that claim. In order to perpetrate the massacre, armed guerrillas wearing camouflage pants would have had to walk brazenly through the village, opening fire on multiple occasions—all while essentially surrounded by soldiers and police. It was certainly an unlikely scenario. Also, despite the police and army's close proximity to the killings, they were remarkably slow to respond. Many of the soldiers I saw from the army's Grupo Cabal Mechanized Battalion wore black T-shirts under their camouflage uniforms, which matched the description given by Awa witnesses. Although the elderly Awa woman believed the Self-Defense Forces had perpetrated the massacre, many paramilitary groups consist of partially uniformed off-duty soldiers, which might explain her confusion. And finally, according to several displaced Awa, it was the army, not the guerrillas, that had threatened them in the past and was responsible for their displacement.

The army was undoubtedly aware that I was investigating

the massacre, so I was becoming a little concerned for my safety. I knew that the Grupo Cabal's soldiers were in total control of both the town and the highway that served as my only escape route. I decided to send the information implicating the army in the massacre to my friend Cecilia Zarate, who headed a human rights group in Madison, Wisconsin, called the Colombia Support Network. I hoped the army would have less incentive to make any move against me if the information had already been disseminated. Fortunately, because Ricaurte was situated on the main highway, which was paralleled by telecommunications and power cables, there was Internet access in the town. I located a small Internet office and e-mailed my findings to Cecilia, then nervously passed the rest of the day in Ricaurte waiting for the army commander to show up. He never did. In the meantime, I visited the local indoor market, where I purchased several dozen shirts and pants for the displaced children and delivered them to a nun at the community center.

Thankfully, the drive back to Pasto the next morning was uneventful, although it did prove to be fascinating. Within a three-hour time span, I experienced three different political viewpoints. As we left Ricaurte, my driver, Alvaro, told me that he'd lived in the area for all twenty-six years of his life. We struck up a conversation about the conflict in Nariño. Alvaro said that the FARC had been in the region for as long as he could remember and that many households had family members who'd joined the guerrillas.

"When I was eighteen, the FARC asked me whether I wanted to join them or work in a civilian job. I decided to take a civilian job," he explained. "My brother was a guerrilla, but he was killed two years ago. My cousin is still a guerrilla."

Alvaro echoed the sentiment I'd heard from several others over the past couple of days: there wasn't much violence before the army arrived, and the guerrillas didn't bother the local population.

"Most people don't like having the army here, because the

soldiers think that everyone is a guerrilla and they have killed many civilians," he said.

"Who was responsible for the massacre in Ataquer?" I asked, already guessing what his answer would be.

"The army killed the five indigenous people in Ataquer," he stated without hesitation, then moved on, unprompted, to talking about the president.

"President Uribe doesn't do anything for the people here," he said. "There's no money for health care or education; nothing but the military. Young people join the guerrillas because there is no work here. The guerrillas give them food, clothes, and schooling."

Alvaro explained that the FARC operated in the foothills of the Andes, where there was plenty of rainforest. He said there were no rebels at the higher elevations because the open terrain wasn't conducive to guerrilla warfare.

We'd just left the rainforest behind when Alvaro announced that he could take me only as far as the town of Tuqueres, which was about halfway to Pasto. He wouldn't explain why, but it might well have been a security issue, given his pro-FARC stance. In Tuqueres, Alvaro found another taxi driver, Andres, to take me the rest of the way to Pasto.

We were out of guerrilla country, and the political opinion shifted accordingly. Andres and his brother Jaime—who accompanied us—were critical of both the FARC and President Uribe. They were supporters of the new center-left Alternative Democratic Pole party, and although they were somewhat ideologically aligned with the FARC, they believed that change could be achieved through elections and didn't support the armed struggle.

My first stop in Pasto, after checking into my hotel, was the Avianca office to make a reservation for a flight back to Bogotá. There I became engaged in a conversation with two women who worked in the airline's downtown office and who were noticeably white-skinned. When they found out that I'd been to Ataquer to investigate the massacre, they immediately went on a rant against the guerrillas, then sang President Uribe's praises and claimed that the Colombian people were enjoying security for the first time ever. I cynically wondered whether the five indigenous leaders who'd been massacred four days earlier counted as "Colombians" in the eyes of those women.

In just three hours, I had conversed with a pro-FARC Colombian from a rural region, two nonviolent moderates from a medium-sized town who were critical of the rebels and the government, and two right-wing city dwellers who were avid defenders of President Uribe. There was a clear correlation between where each person lived and his or her political views. Given that my journey began in the lowland rainforest and terminated over eight thousand feet up in the Andes, it appeared that not only did ecosystems change with altitude in that part of Colombia—political opinions did too.

The next morning, I resumed my investigation into the massacre by traveling to the Grupo Cabal's headquarters in the city of Ipiales, an hour and a half south of Pasto and near the border with Ecuador. Again I failed to obtain an interview with a high-ranking officer, but I was able to meet with battalion spokesperson Sergeant Monterroza, who was emphatic that the FARC had perpetrated the massacre in Ataquer.

Only weeks before the massacre, the Bush administration had declared that the Grupo Cabal Mechanized Battalion met the human rights conditions required to receive U.S. aid. Given that the evidence I had uncovered pointed to the Grupo Cabal as the likely perpetrator of the massacre, I was once again left questioning the methods of Washington's war on terror in Colombia.

I flew to Bogotá the next day to prepare for my trip to La Macarena National Park. Almost a week earlier, President Uribe had ordered the first-ever aerial fumigation of coca crops in a Colombian national park. Not one journalist had traveled outside Bogotá to cover this escalation of Plan Colombia, and although a spokesperson for the National Police declared that all of the coca in the park had been successfully eradicated, I decided to visit La Macarena to investigate the reality for myself.

The Eleventh Hour
8:00 p.m., August 16, 2006

Out of the corner of my eye, I glimpse a flash of light from the front of the house and turn to see a pair of headlights coming up the dirt driveway. A dark-colored SUV pulls to a halt next to the house, and voices emerge from its interior. From my vantage point, I can't see who the new arrivals are, but I'm guessing they're guerrillas. Either it's a social visit and they've come to watch *Sin Tetas,* which starts in less than thirty minutes, or they are here for me.

My host has gone out to greet them. He reenters the house alone, grabs two plastic chairs, and signals for me to follow him outside. Three uniformed guerrillas are standing on the grass. My host sets down the two chairs, and he, his two guerrilla sons, and two of the new arrivals stand together in a group. The third new arrival shakes my hand and invites me to sit in one of the chairs as he seats himself in the other. My heart begins to race as I wonder whether I'm about to be interrogated or about to discover my fate, or both.

The guerrilla seated next to me, dressed in full camouflage

uniform and armed with an AK-47, is evidently one of the FARC's commanders in this region; I learn that he goes by the nickname Chiguiro. He waves his hand at one of the guerrillas who arrived with him. The man steps forward and places my blue poncho and all my belongings on the ground at my feet as Chiguiro asks me to check and make sure that everything is there. I do a quick inventory and tell him that everything is indeed there. Realizing that they wouldn't be returning my belongings unless they were intending to release me, I feel a sense of relief and overwhelming joy that I'll be seeing Terry and Owen again soon.

"I understand that you want to investigate the aerial fumigations that occurred last week?" Chiguiro asks.

"Yes," I respond. "I would like to investigate how much coca was destroyed and the consequences for the peasants and the environment."

He nods his head thoughtfully before speaking again.

"I have been authorized to allow you to conduct your investigation," he says, to my amazement. "You can travel anywhere you need to and speak with anyone you wish to speak with. However, you will need transportation in order to get around. A driver and a vehicle will be here at eight o'clock in the morning to take you wherever you want to go. Do you have any questions?"

I can hardly believe my luck—I've received the green light to do exactly what I came here to do. I thank Chiguiro and ask him for his take on the fumigations.

"I can tell you that the fumigations hurt the peasants more than the guerrillas. They are the ones who are most dependent on coca for their survival," he explains.

Chiguiro then stands up, shakes my hand, and wishes me luck with my work. The rebel commander, the two guerrillas who came with him, and my guard all climb into the SUV and disappear into the night. And just like that, my ordeal is over.

I walk back into the house and sit in my plastic chair just as *Sin Tetas* is about to begin. Everyone in the house is excited about the premiere of the *telenovela,* while I'm eagerly anticipating the work I'll do over the next couple of days; the room is filled with positive tension. The opening credits include an advisory that warns viewers of adult content. One of the guerrilla sons turns to his seventeen-year-old sister and jokes, "It's for adults only; you had better go to bed."

I can't help but smile at the ridiculousness of the situation. The television network is advising viewers to protect their children from graphic content while the four-year-old son of a guerrilla fighter is seated only three feet away from two AK-47s. It's all too surreal.

I sleep on the floor of the main room under a mosquito net and wake up at six o'clock in the morning, when the mother of the house begins preparing breakfast. By the time I've showered and dressed, it is fully daylight. I grab my camera, exit the fenced-in compound, and stroll among the coca bushes, relieved to be able to wander around without an armed guard for a shadow. I snap several shots of the green coca bushes that escaped the fumigations of a week earlier, defying the government's claim that all 11,370 acres of coca in La Macarena had been destroyed. I walk down to the coca paste lab, where the coca pickers are already hard at work crushing leaves and soaking them in gasoline in order to turn them into paste. Twenty minutes later I return to the house, where the teenage girl, Luz, serves me breakfast.

My vehicle arrives promptly at eight o'clock. It is a red jeep with a white hardtop and comes with a driver and an assistant—Carlos and Osvaldo, both twenty-two years old. After introductions are made all around, Osvaldo tosses my backpack into the rear of the jeep and climbs in after it. Carlos invites me to sit up front in the passenger seat and asks me where

I want to go. I tell him that I would like to go deeper into La Macarena to view areas that were fumigated last week and to speak with peasants whose crops were sprayed.

We bounce our way along the rough dirt road, which is flanked on both sides by jungle. Carlos and Osvaldo explain that they've both lived their entire lives in La Macarena and work for the Communal Action Council, the local governing structure, which contains both guerrillas and peasants.

When Carlos sees a dark blue SUV approaching from the opposite direction, he pulls our jeep over to the right side of the road. The oncoming vehicle, which contains four uniformed rebels, pulls up beside us, and I see that Hector, the practical joker who stopped by the farm for lunch yesterday, is driving. He beckons for me to get out. When I reach his open window, I notice he's holding a four-inch-thick wad of fifty-thousand-peso bills, each of which is worth about twenty dollars—several thousand dollars in what are large-denomination bills for rural Colombia. It is most likely drug money.

The FARC's role in the drug trade has shifted in recent years from taxing large-scale coca farms—many of which have been eliminated by Plan Colombia's fumigations—to acting as a broker in the deals between smaller coca farmers and the owners of the cocaine processing labs, who are often drug traffickers belonging to the country's cocaine cartels. I learned much of what I know about the FARC's role in the coca trade from my colleague Oscar Jansson, a Swedish anthropologist who has conducted extensive field research on the political economy of coca in Putumayo. According to Oscar, the FARC establishes a set price that the farmers receive for a gram of coca paste, as well as a higher price that the processors have to pay; both prices are higher than in areas controlled by the paramilitaries. When the FARC purchases the coca paste from the farmers and sells it to the processors at the higher price, it earns a profit that helps fund its insurgency.

Although the FARC earns a profit from the coca trade, it guarantees that coca farmers receive a greater share of the profits than they would under the paramilitaries. Because paramilitaries look out for the interests of the cocaine processors, and by extension the drug traffickers, they ensure that farmers will receive the lowest possible price for the paste. From the perspective of the drug traffickers, the more coca-growing territory controlled by the paramilitaries, the better. If farmers in FARC-controlled areas are caught trying to sell their coca paste to a non-FARC broker, the rebels often punish them by forcing them to leave the region. This isn't a common occurrence, however; since coca farmers make more money selling their product to the FARC, there's little incentive to sell to someone else. On the other hand, if farmers in paramilitary zones are caught selling to the higher-paying FARC, the growers are often killed.

Ironically, by making the FARC the principal target of Plan Colombia, the United States is undermining its primary counternarcotics objective of eradicating coca crops in order to reduce the amount of cocaine produced. Using the logic of supply and demand, a shortage of cocaine will drive up the street price in the United States; this increase in the street price of cocaine will, or so the argument goes, lead to a reduction in use. But by aiding the Colombian military and targeting coca growers in FARC-controlled regions, the United States is increasing the possibility that the paramilitaries will gain control of these areas. If the paramilitaries gain control of areas previously controlled by the FARC, the cost of cocaine production will decrease, because drug processors and traffickers will pay farmers less for their coca paste. Consequently, the street price of cocaine in U.S. cities will most likely remain unchanged or, if anything, decrease.

Hector's wad of cash is undoubtedly money that he has received from cocaine processors, and some of it will be used to purchase coca paste from local farmers. He counts off five of the fifty-thousand-peso bills, approximately one hundred dollars, and offers them to me.

"For your meals and drinks and anything else you might need while you are here," he says.

I decline his offering, explaining that it is not necessary, since I have my own money.

"Okay," he says with a shrug of his shoulders and drives away.

About fifteen minutes later, Carlos, Osvaldo, and I pull into a farm, whose owner comes out of the house to greet us. As we walk through the coca field closest to his house, the farmer tells me that the fumigation planes sprayed his crops a little over a week ago. He points at the rows of stems sticking out of the ground and at the brown tops of bushes lying in the dirt.

"These are what are left of my coca bushes," he explains. "I was lucky because I cut them in time, before the chemicals killed them."

One tactic coca farmers use to save their crops is cutting off the tops of sprayed coca bushes about six inches above the ground. If they do so in time, the chemicals don't kill the roots, and the bush grows again and produces four or five harvests of coca leaves annually.

We continue across the field to the coca paste lab, which is devoid of activity. The farmer has had to lay off his coca pickers because of the spraying, which is causing economic hardship for both him and his workers. Ultimately, however, the fumigations will prove to be only a temporary setback. In several months, the coca bushes will again be ready to harvest and coca paste production will resume.

We leave the farm and continue further along the bumpy road, passing several coca fields that the fumigations missed, and enter a small village—a community consisting of some fifteen wooden dwellings at its center and several farms in the surrounding area—that will remain nameless for the security of its residents. Carlos pulls over next to three middle-aged women and one elderly man sitting in front of a small store in the center of the village, and I introduce myself to them. One of the women invites us to sit down. She serves us cold sodas while the man tells me that no journalist has ever visited the village before.

"They don't care what happens to us," he complains. "The army comes here and kills some peasants and then says that the guerrillas did it, and the media repeat the lies. Nobody ever comes here to find out the truth."

I ask whether they were targeted by the recent fumigations, and they tell me that they were. The old man explains that the wind blew the sprayed chemicals over the entire village. When I ask him to point out the crops that were targeted for fumigation, they all lead me outside and point beyond the community soccer field to a farm on a small hill.

"Can I visit that farm?" I ask.

Suddenly the four people from the store, along with several other villagers who gathered around following our arrival, are excitedly leading me across the soccer field toward the farm.

As I approach the farm, I can see entire fields full of coca bushes with brown leaves; this farmer failed to cut the tops off the plants following the spraying. A woman emerges from the small wooden house when she sees the crowd of people approaching and introduces herself as Cecilia. She's the mother of two young children, who are watching events unfold from the safety of the front porch. I realize that I must be a strange sight to many of these people, particularly the younger ones; my six-foot-one frame towers over most of them, and many have probably never seen a *gringo* before, since outsiders rarely venture into this region.

Cecilia leads me around to the rear of her home, pointing to the banana and papaya trees and yucca plants that were killed by the fumigations, and describes how the chemicals blanketed not only the coca crops that she and her husband cultivate, but also their food crops and their two children.

"The children suffered from diarrhea and vomiting for several days," she says. "They were also terrorized by the helicopters."

The dead coca bushes come all the way to within six feet of one side of the house; it would have been impossible for an airplane to spray them without the chemicals also blanketing the house. Only ten feet from the other side of the house, several banana trees were also sprayed. The large leaves are wilting and discolored, and the bananas are mostly black, rotting from the chemical deluge. Not far from the banana trees, the narrow trunks of two papaya trees reach majestically toward the sky, their leaves hanging limp at the top. And in the back of the house are yucca plants and several other food crops that have also been destroyed. The scene is devastating.

"Are these the crops you depend on for food?" I ask Cecilia.

"Yes," she answers.

"How are you feeding your family now?"

"We are dependent on friends who still have food."

"And what about the children; did they need medicine when they got sick?"

"Yes. The FARC gave us money to buy medicine for them."

One of the villagers tells me that another farm nearby was fumigated, so we head off across Cecilia's farm and through a thicket of trees to her neighbor's property. As we approach the farmhouse, I feel like the pied piper with the growing crowd following me—a crowd that now includes Cecilia and her two children. Once again I'm immediately struck by the number of food crops in front of the house that have been killed by the fumigation.

Two women come out to greet us, followed by two shirtless teenage boys carrying machetes. I explain why I'm here, and they begin describing the day that the planes came to spray, taking me around the side of the house to a field full of dead coca bushes. One of the boys points with his machete to a line of holes in the dirt, each of which is about five inches in diameter and several inches deep. I must look puzzled.

"From the bullets fired by the helicopters," he explains, saying that the helicopters appeared first and fired their machine guns at the ground to deter any guerrillas that might be waiting to shoot at the spray plane. And then the spray plane came and fumigated everything. The second boy starts picking up the empty shell casings scattered on the ground, some of which are disturbingly close to the house. No wonder Cecilia's children were "terrorized by the helicopters."

The two machete-wielding boys take me back past the house and through another fumigated coca field to the coca paste laboratory, which has a row of small holes in the corrugated tin roof. I realize that the soldiers in the helicopters fired into the roof of the lab, and look down to see a corresponding line of holes in the light brown dirt.

"Are the bullets still in the dirt?" I ask.

"Yes," replies one of the boys as he drops to his knees and starts digging around one of the holes with his machete and his bare hands. A couple of minutes later, he produces several small metal fragments: shrapnel from one of the bullets.

As I exit the coca paste lab, I find myself again looking out across a fumigated coca field. I turn to one of the boys and ask, "What will you do now that the coca has all been destroyed?"

"We will plant more," he answers.

"Will you replant in the same fields or cut down more rain-forest?"

"I don't know. If we start cutting down trees to plant more crops, the FARC will fine us. We must obtain permission from the guerrillas before we can cut down the rainforest," he explains.

Evidently, because La Macarena is a national park, the FARC is trying to carry out a delicate balancing act between funding its insurgency from coca cultivation, allowing peasants to earn a living, and limiting the destruction of one of the country's most exquisite ecological treasures.

We leave the farm and make our way back to the village, to a small community recreation building. Inside are a television showing a Kung Fu movie and nine uniformed FARC guerrillas, evidently a patrol taking a break. Eight of the guerrillas are men and one is a young woman; they seem unconcerned with my presence, which suggests that Commander Chiguiro alerted all rebel units that I would be working in the region. While Carlos is getting drinks for us, I ask the guerrillas whether I can take some photographs of them. Several of them shake their heads. I try unsuccessfully to engage a couple of them in conversation; they're either too engrossed in the movie or are under orders not to interact with me.

We return to the jeep and head off down the road to a similar village forty-five minutes away. During the journey, Carlos and Osvaldo gladly answer my many questions about life in La Macarena. They explain that the local peasant population constructed all the roads—little more than muddy trails, incredibly rugged and rut-filled, and only traversable in a four-wheel-drive vehicle—that allow both peasants and guerrillas to move from village to village with relative ease. Osvaldo says that the government has never provided education, health care, or public services of any kind, and explains that the FARC has always been the governing body here, both establishing and enforcing the laws. Carlos says that disputes between people are resolved by the FARC: when two people have a disagreement, the rebels listen to both sides and impose a settlement if the two parties cannot reach a satisfactory resolution on their own. He and Osvaldo tell me that there are no prisons; those convicted of crimes either pay reparations to the victims or are sentenced to perform public works, such as working on farms or fixing the roads. As I'm shaken by another bone-jarring rut in the road, I can't help but think that crime rates in this region must be ex-

tremely low. When I ask about more serious crimes, like murder, Carlos says that such crimes are rare, but when they do occur, the perpetrator is forced to leave the region. I point out that
the FARC has the death penalty for serious crimes, but they
both claim it hasn't been implemented in this region.

I am unable to determine how closely connected Carlos and
Osvaldo are with the FARC. Are they actual guerrillas or just
sympathetic peasants? I figure it has to be one or the other, because there appear to be few people in this region who are critical of the FARC. Perhaps that is due in part to fear of the rebel
group; on the other hand, the guerrillas are the only ones who
have ever done anything to help the peasants in La Macarena.
The only thing the government has ever done for these people is
to launch sporadic military operations and carry out aerial fumigations of their crops.

Carlos struggles to maintain control of the jeep as we slide
sideways in the mud on an exceptionally poor uphill stretch of
road. We finally reach the crest of the hill, and as we begin our
descent down the other side, I can see a village situated at the
bottom. Much of the rainforest has been cleared around the village. I ask Carlos to stop halfway down the hill. I get out of the
jeep and look out across the rolling fields that spread for at least
a mile. For as far as I can see, most of the land is brown from
the fumigations. Several large trees scattered throughout the
area have retained their green leaves, but the coca bushes and
all the other small vegetation have been killed.

I snap some photos and climb back into the jeep. After interviewing several peasants in the village about the fumigations, we drive toward a town called Cooperativa, where I will
spend the night because it's the only place that has *residencias*.

We arrive in Cooperativa, close to the outer edge of La
Macarena National Park, in the late afternoon. The town's
long main street is unpaved and lined with stores, restaurants,
and other small businesses. Cooperativa is a vibrant town,

abuzz with people going about their daily business, much of which is most likely related to coca. Beyond the main street are numerous other dirt roads lined with small wooden houses and the *residencia* in which I'll spend the night. Carlos introduces me to the proprietor and takes his leave, telling me that he'll be back to pick me up at seven the next morning.

The proprietor shows me to a small, very basic room of four rough-hewn wooden walls and a bed beneath a mosquito net. I set down my backpack and take a shower in one of the two stalls in the rear of the building. As I'm getting dressed back in my room, I hear a flurry of activity and step out of my door to see a number of FARC guerrillas settling into several of the other rooms.

"*Hola,* Garry," bellows a voice from down the hall behind me.

I turn and see Hector walking toward me with a big smile on his face. Evidently he and the rest of his rebel unit are also going to be spending the night in the *residencia.* As Hector and I begin talking in the hallway, other guerrillas pour out of their rooms to listen in on the conversation. There is a lot of good-humored banter back and forth as Hector and a rebel named Iván begin questioning me about my life.

"How old are you?" Hector asks me.

"I'm forty-six."

"Do you have a woman?"

"Yes, I have a wife."

"How many children?" Iván asks.

"I have a son; he's three months old."

"Only one child?" Hector asks in disbelief.

"Yes, only one," I answer.

Pointing to Iván, Hector asks me, "Guess how many children he has?"

"I don't know." I'm wondering where this conversation is going.

"Six. He has six children, and he's only twenty-two years old," Hector explains as he and the other rebels smile.

"Really?" I respond, not believing him.

"Yes. Iván's only twenty-two and has six children, and you are forty-six and only have one child. That's why Colombia is going to become more powerful than the United States, because we fuck more." The rest of the guerrillas burst into laughter. I also laugh and tell him that he might have a point.

I excuse myself from Hector and his fellow rebels and walk around to the front of the *residencia* in search of a bottle of water. I find the proprietor, his wife, four male guerrillas, and two female rebels seated in a room watching a television on which several women dressed in camouflage combat fatigues are hiking through the jungle. The proprietor responds to my water request by dispatching his daughter to a local store.

"What are you watching?" I ask him.

"It's the movie *Guerrilla Girl,*" he responds, referring to the recently released documentary by Danish director Frank Poulsen. "Do you want to watch it with us?"

"Yes, thanks." I settle into a plastic chair.

The documentary, filmed in a FARC training camp, follows a girl who has just joined the rebel group as she goes through her indoctrination and training.

"Is the training in the film similar to what you went through?" I ask the guerrillas sitting around me.

They look at me and then at each other before one of them hesitantly nods in affirmation; perhaps they're not sure to what degree they are authorized to engage with me.

After the documentary is finished, I walk down toward the main street in search of a place to eat dinner. As I'm walking past a mix of civilians and uniformed FARC guerrillas, I run into my driver, Carlos. I invite him to join me for dinner. We enter a small restaurant and find an empty table not too close to the television, which is broadcasting the news at a volume far

too high for my liking. About half of the ten tables are occupied, two of them by guerrillas. I order chicken and rice and a
cerveza; Carlos orders the same without the beer.

I'm sitting drinking my beer and waiting for my food when
a man in civilian clothes gets up from one of the rebel-occupied
tables and comes over to join us, introducing himself as Mateo.
He's about five feet eight, with white skin and light brown hair.
As he sits down, I notice a 9mm automatic pistol tucked into
the rear of his waistband. Mateo has a rough edge about him
and an air that suggests he is a man to be feared.

Mateo explains that he speaks some English and French in
addition to his native Spanish. He tells me in broken English
that he has spent a lot of time in Europe, particularly Switzer-
land. He orders a beer, and we engage in friendly small talk.
When I ask him what he does, he pauses and then says he's a
businessman. But his tone and the look he gives me clearly indi-
cate that I shouldn't pursue that avenue of discussion. He tells
me how much he loves Europe before finally excusing himself
and rejoining the table of guerrillas. I suspect he's engaged in
some sort of covert activity. Perhaps he's a FARC representative
overseas, or perhaps a trafficker of weapons or cocaine or both.

After dinner I return to the *residencia* and enjoy a relatively
good night's sleep. When I wake shortly after daylight and walk
out to the front porch, I'm surprised by a mildly familiar voice
from behind me that addresses me in English.

"Good morning," says the mysterious man I met in the
restaurant last night. Mateo is standing shirtless in the open
doorway of his room with his pistol in his right hand, which is
hanging down at his side. Behind him, inside the room, I can see
a young woman getting dressed.

"Good morning," I reply.

Hector is the next one to appear, and he's in a very serious
mood—in fact, for the first time in my several encounters with
him, he's not smiling or joking. Either he has some serious
business at hand or he simply is not a morning person. He and

the other guerrillas pile into the SUVs and disappear down the street.

Minutes later, Carlos and Osvaldo arrive, and after saying goodbye to the proprietor, I toss my backpack and myself into the jeep. We visit another small remote village and hear the testimonies of peasants whose lives have been devastated by the fumigations in much the same way as those I spoke with yesterday.

In fact, it seems to me that little has changed for peasants throughout Colombia who are forced to grow coca in order to survive economically. Seven years of Plan Colombia has failed to significantly reduce the amount of coca being cultivated and cocaine being exported; it has only further intensified the hardships endured by peasants. As long as demand remains strong in North America and Europe, and the overwhelming majority of rural Colombians remain in poverty, there is little reason to believe that targeting cocaine at its source will prove successful.

A little before midday, we arrive back in Cooperativa and locate a *taxi colectivo* to take me out of La Macarena and back to government-controlled Colombia. I bid farewell to Carlos and Osvaldo and climb into the back of a jeep with six other passengers for the two-and-a-half-hour journey to Vista Hermosa. The road is in horrendous condition, thanks to the torrential rains that fell during the night, and several times we go off-road to bypass vehicles that are stuck in the mud-filled ruts. Miraculously, we don't get stuck or tip over.

I'm leaving La Macarena by a different road than the one on which I entered the region. Instead of reentering government-controlled territory at Vista Hermosa, we cross a river guarded by Colombian soldiers and enter a small town called Piñalito. Soldiers stop our jeep as soon as we enter the town; they order us out, frisk us all, check our identification, and ask me where I have been and what I was doing. I tell them that I'm a journalist and that I was investigating the fumigations in La Macarena.

After receiving the all clear from the soldiers, I ask the driver to wait a minute while I run into a store to buy a cold drink. As I'm leaving the store, one of the soldiers who stopped our vehicle approaches, hoping I'll provide him with information now that I'm out of earshot of my fellow passengers. He asks me whether I saw any guerrillas in La Macarena.

"No, I didn't," I lie.

"Not even in Cooperativa?" he persists.

"No," I lie again. "I only saw peasants and lots of coca."

He just nods his head, turns, and walks away.

I return to the jeep, and we exit Piñalito. Thirty minutes later, the driver drops me off in Vista Hermosa at the street corner that is the departure point for the buses that make the four-hour journey to the city of Villavicencio. There is a bus leaving in a few minutes that I'm eager to board, having no desire to spend the night in Vista Hermosa, given that it's crawling with paramilitaries who are most likely aware of the fact that I just returned from FARC-controlled territory.

I run across the street to the corner where several days ago I located Javier, the driver who initially took me into La Macarena. Because we were separated when I was detained in Santo Domingo, I haven't been able to pay Javier for his services. I ask the group of drivers hanging out on the corner whether Javier has returned safely and whether they know where he is. They tell me that he returned without a problem, but isn't around right now. Knowing that the bus is about to leave, I hand a wad of Colombian pesos to one of the drivers and ask him to make sure that Javier gets it. I then climb aboard the air-conditioned bus and slump down into an incredibly comfortable reclining seat, exhausted but happy to finally be heading home to Terry and Owen.

Epilogue

June 2007

The canoe that Terry and I have been traveling in for the past hour pulls up to the muddy riverbank. We climb out, walk down a narrow jungle path to a small clearing, and wait while our two female FARC guerrilla guides stash the canoe and its outboard motor. When the two rebels return to the clearing, they each pick up two planks of wood measuring six feet long, ten inches wide, and two inches thick. They insist on also carrying our backpacks for us, in addition to their own bags. The sun is setting when we all set off along a muddy trail through the jungle on a one-hour hike to the FARC camp. It's taken us over two days to get here from Bogotá, and I'm not only tired, I'm also feeling slightly emasculated by my failure to keep up with these two female guerrillas even though they're loaded down and I'm not carrying anything.

We stumble and slide along the muddy path, traversing streams on fallen logs with only the narrow beams of our small flashlights to illuminate the way. Miraculously, I manage to avoid falling into this quagmire that passes for a trail. Almost an hour into the hike, I hear the female guerrilla in front mumble something to a shadowy figure in the darkness. A fully uniformed, AK-47-toting male guerrilla greets Terry and me as we pass him.

I notice a small white light through the trees up ahead, and as we reach the perimeter of the camp I see a uniformed man with a gray beard working on a laptop computer. It is FARC commander Raúl Reyes, a member of the rebel group's seven-person Central Command. According to many analysts, Reyes is the second-highest-ranking member of the FARC.

Reyes greets us both and, after an introductory conversation, invites us to join him and several other guerrillas for dinner. We dine on fish and potatoes while several dozen rebels, seated on rows of wooden benches, watch a film in a large tent-like edifice. After dinner, Terry and I are shown to our bivouac —identical to the ones the guerrillas use—which contains a bed with wooden planks for a mattress, a mosquito net, and a plastic camouflage canopy that hangs above everything to provide protection from the frequent tropical rains. Over the next three days, Terry and I will live as the guerrillas live: we'll bathe with them in a nearby stream, go to the bathroom in their rainforest latrines—trenches dug in the ground—and eat what they eat, ample servings of basic Colombian food.

Terry and I have come to this remote FARC camp for different reasons. She's planning on interviewing female guerrillas as part of her research on women engaged in social struggle in Colombia. I'm here to interview Reyes. More specifically, I want to discover the FARC's perspective on the prospects for achieving peace in Colombia.

During our time in the camp, we've been given free rein to speak with all the guerrillas, about one-third of whom are women. In fact, one of the most impressive aspects of life in the camp is the degree of gender equality. Everybody takes a turn in the rustic kitchen cooking meals for the entire unit, and everybody does laundry, stands guard duty, and goes out on patrol.

I'd heard that this sort of equality was part of the FARC's philosophy, but I wasn't sure to what degree it had actually been implemented. Of course, I'm still not sure to what degree it applies in other FARC units throughout the country, but there is little doubt that the guerrillas in this particular camp have achieved an impressive level of gender equality. It's evident not only in their sharing of duties and in their discourse but, more importantly, in their way of being.

Surprisingly, for me at least, gender equality is more evident in the behavior of the men than the women. The softness of the energy exhibited by the male rebels toward their female colleagues, their absolute lack of machismo, their acceptance of their *compañeras* as equals, are all quite astounding. And for their part, the women exhibit many feminine qualities, which is something I have observed in my past dealings with the FARC and always find surprising given their rugged lifestyle. In fact, maintaining their femininity is important to the female guerrillas. During off-duty hours, the women often get together to apply makeup or to braid each other's hair. Evidently equality in the FARC is not about women acting like men.

It quickly becomes clear to Terry and me that the guerrillas are all dedicated to their revolutionary cause, contrary to accusations made by many analysts that the FARC is nothing more than a criminal organization. These critics claim that the FARC was ideologically motivated many years ago, but now is interested only in profiting from its criminal activities, which are primarily related to the coca trade. However, James LeMoyne, the UN's special envoy to Colombia, warned in 2003 that it would be "a mistake to think that the FARC members are only drug traffickers and terrorists." Nevertheless, President Uribe has repeatedly declared that there isn't an armed conflict in Colombia and that the government is simply combating criminals who engage in terrorism, a strategy meant to delegitimize the FARC as a political entity.

It's difficult for me to accept such a simplistic analysis of the

FARC, given my experiences with the rebel group and knowing how the guerrillas live. Unlike Colombian soldiers and paramilitary fighters, the guerrillas don't get paid. And if FARC leaders are little more than the heads of a criminal organization, then they must be considered miserable failures. After all, other Colombian criminals live in luxury. The leader of the former Medellín cocaine cartel, Pablo Escobar, lived lavishly in magnificent mansions, as have many other Colombian drug traffickers over the past thirty years. Paramilitary leaders have also lived well on their vast cattle ranches in northern Colombia, enjoying the riches wrought from their criminal activities. And now they're demobilizing so they can legally enjoy their ill-gotten wealth. In contrast, the FARC's leaders live as Reyes lives. They receive no personal material gain, despite the guerrilla group's financial wealth. For them, it is a hard life spent sleeping on wooden planks, bathing in rivers, fighting off tropical diseases, coping with separation from family and loved ones, and constantly moving from camp to camp to avoid U.S. intelligence-gathering efforts and the Colombian army. Reyes has lived in the jungle in this manner for twenty-six years, and the only comforts he enjoys are a laptop computer and the camp's television. It is hardly the lifestyle of a criminal whose principal objective is the attainment of wealth.

The FARC could demobilize under the same terms as the paramilitaries, and after a short spell in a custom prison cell, its leaders would be able to live out the rest of their lives in comfort. But the rebel group refuses to demobilize, because the process would not address the structural problems that lie at the root of the conflict—further evidence that the guerrillas do indeed maintain a political ideology. Of course, this doesn't justify the FARC's violations of human rights of civilians through such tactics as kidnapping and selective assassinations, nor their use of landmines and notoriously inaccurate homemade mortars. It does, however, discredit claims that the FARC is nothing more than a criminal organization.

With all this in mind, I sit down with Reyes to talk about the future possibilities for peace. We begin our conversation by discussing the country's new center-left political party, the Alternative Democratic Pole. Many critics of the FARC point to the Alternative Democratic Pole's successes in the electoral arena over the past four years as evidence that there is no longer any justification for engaging in armed struggle in Colombia. But according to Reyes, the Alternative Democratic Pole is not a true leftist party because social democrats, not socialists, dominate its ranks.

"These people have accepted the establishment, the state, because they calculate—and it's a miscalculation—that they will be able to attract the revolutionary left," he explains. "But it so happens that the revolutionary left cannot be attracted to the social democrats, because we are conscious that social democrats end up favoring the right, the bourgeoisie."

According to Reyes, it is because the Alternative Democratic Pole has maintained a relatively moderate political stance that the paramilitaries have not assassinated the party's members in the same way that they slaughtered the Patriotic Union's members in the 1980s. "Nevertheless, it should be noted that they do continue murdering people, but they are selective murders of the people who truly are on the left," he adds, suggesting that he believes the ongoing dirty war against the left justifies the continuance of the armed struggle.

Finally, I ask Reyes whether he thinks there is any possibility of the FARC negotiating peace with the Alternative Democratic Pole should the party win the presidency in the 2010 elections.

"It would depend on their policies," he replies.

I return to my bivouac, and as I sit here watching the guerrillas go about their daily activities, I can't help but think how little the situation has changed for most rural Colombians in the seven years since the launching of Plan Colombia and my first interview with a FARC commander, Simón Trinidad. Although President Uribe's security policies have reduced violence in the cities and made life safer for middle- and upper-class Colombians by reducing the risk of their being kidnapped, his policies have done little to help those who live in the rural conflict zones. If anything, they have made life worse for many peasants, who are targeted by the Colombian military and accused of being guerrillas simply because they live in FARC-controlled regions.

One of the original objectives of Plan Colombia was for the Colombian army to take the military offensive against the FARC and force the rebel group to engage in negotiations from a position of weakness, as has occurred with the ELN. While seven years of Plan Colombia, five years of President Uribe's security policies, and more than five billion dollars in U.S. military aid have placed the FARC on the defensive in many regions, there is little evidence that the rebel group has been significantly weakened in its traditional strongholds. Consequently, with the FARC too strong to be defeated on the battlefield and not strong enough to take power by force, a negotiated settlement seems the only possible route to achieving peace. Because of the FARC's political commitment, any negotiated peace would require a restructuring of Colombia's political, social, and economic system to allow for a much more equitable distribution of the country's wealth and land. But such a negotiated settlement would require the acquiescence of the country's political and economic elite, as well as the U.S. government. Even if the Alternative Democratic Pole did prove victorious in 2010 and the party did attempt to implement such redistributive policies, Colombia's history suggests that the country's elite, and foreign countries with interests in Colombia's natural resources, wouldn't tolerate them. Consequently, at least for the near future, it appears that the conflict will continue to rage. And tragically, the civilian population will continue to bear the brunt of the violence.

On our final morning in the camp, Terry and I bid farewell to Reyes and the other guerrillas. Along with our rebel guides, we make the return trek through the rainforest to the river and board a canoe. As we cruise along this jungle river, I think about the many Colombians I have met during the last eight years who, against seemingly insurmountable odds, continue to fight for social justice. I can only hope that my work will contribute in some small way to ensuring that U.S. policies aid, rather than hinder, their struggle to finally achieve the democracy, peace, and justice they so deserve. Colombia's long, dark past suggests that the attainment of such noble objectives is an impossible dream. However, the inspiring optimism of the Colombian people has instilled in me the belief that anything is possible in this magical country. Clearly, it will not be easy. But then, nothing ever is in Colombia.

Postscript: March 2008

Eight months after my meeting with FARC leader Raúl Reyes, he and nineteen other guerrillas were killed in a predawn air strike launched against their jungle camp by the Colombian military. It was the first time in the decades-long civil conflict that the Colombian government had succeeded in its attempts to capture or kill a member of the FARC's seven-person central command.

One week later, a second member of the central command, Iván Ríos, was killed by his bodyguard, who then surrendered to the Colombian army. And, on March 29, the FARC's Supreme Commander Manuel "Sureshot" Marulanda reportedly died of a heart attack. While Plan Colombia has clearly failed to achieve its counternarcotics objectives, it has proven successful as a counterinsurgency initiative, forcing the FARC to retreat to the country's most remote regions and safeguarding U.S. economic interests in this troubled nation. Tragically, these successes have been achieved at the expense of the welfare of rural Colombians, who continue to endure repression, human rights abuses, and economic marginalization.

Timeline (1948–2007)

1948 The assassination of popular Liberal Party dissident Jorge Eliécer Gaitán on April 9 ignites an uprising in Bogotá. The uprising spreads throughout the country, igniting a decade-long civil war between Liberals and Conservatives known simply as *La Violencia,* or the Violence, in which more than 200,000 are killed.

1950–1953 The Liberal Party boycotts elections that bring hard-line Conservative Party candidate Laureano Gómez to power. The Gómez administration launches a reign of terror against Liberal Party and communist insurgents and their sympathizers.

1953–1957 A military coup overthrows the Gómez government, and General Gustavo Rojas Pinilla seizes power. Rojas Pinilla implements major public works projects to win support while simultaneously repressing protests against his dictatorship.

1957 Liberal and Conservative party elites sign a power-sharing agreement and support public protests and a military coup that overthrows Rojas Pinilla.

1958 The National Front government assumes power under the power-sharing agreement, which calls for the Liberal Party and Conservative Party to alternate the presidency every four years and to evenly split all government posts. The National Front lasts until 1974.

1958–1964 The level of violence diminishes under the National Front as partisan conflict is replaced by government repression against communist peasants.

1964 Government forces bomb the rural community of Marquetalia, and the surviving peasants respond by forming the Fuerzas Armadas Revolucionarias de Colombia (Revolutionary Armed Forces of Colombia), or FARC. The FARC announces its agrarian reform agenda and begins its campaign to overthrow the government. Urban intellectuals influenced by the Cuban Revolution found another rebel group, the ELN (Ejército de Liberación Nacional, or National Liberation Army).

1970 Supporters of newly established opposition party ANAPO (Alianza Nacional Popular, or National Popular Alliance), whose presidential candidate is former dictator Rojas Pinilla, claim that the National Front "stole" the election.

1972 Disgruntled socialist members of ANAPO form the M-19 guerrilla group.

1974 The National Front comes to an end as the Liberal and Conservative parties field candidates against each other. However, government posts remain evenly divided between the two parties.

1978–1982 Liberal government of Julio César Turbay Ayala intensifies repression against the expanding guerrilla movements.

Cocaine traffickers become increasingly powerful and, along with large landowners and the Colombian military, begin forming right-wing paramilitary groups to combat the growing strength of the guerrillas.

1985   M-19 guerrillas take over the Palace of Justice, which houses Colombia's Supreme Court. The army kills more than one hundred people, including eleven Supreme Court justices, in its two-day offensive to retake the building.

1985   The Conservative government of Belisario Betancur reaches a cease-fire agreement with the FARC and engages in peace talks. The FARC, the Communist Party, and other leftists form the Patriotic Union (Unión Patriótica, or UP) party in order to participate in elections. Paramilitaries intensify their dirty war against leftists and assassinate more than two thousand members of the UP—including two presidential candidates and four elected congressional representatives—over the next five years.

1986–1990   Under pressure from the U.S. government, the Liberal administration of Virgilio Barco cracks down on cocaine traffickers, who, led by drug kingpin Pablo Escobar, respond by launching a massive bombing campaign to protest the government's extradition treaty with the United States. The government negotiates a peace agreement with the M-19 and several smaller guerrilla movements, the members of which demobilize under an amnesty.

1990   In August, newly elected president César Gaviria of the Liberal Party begins implementing neoliberal economic reforms in return for increased military and drug-war aid from the United States. In December, the military launches a surprise attack against the headquarters of the FARC, bringing an end to the five-year-old peace process.

1991   A new constitution promulgated in July prohibits the extradition of native-born Colombians and leads to the surrender of Pablo Escobar.

1992 In September, Escobar escapes from his luxury prison and again wages a bombing campaign against the government.

1993 In December, government forces track down and kill Pablo Escobar in Medellín.

1994 President Ernesto Samper of the Liberal Party assumes office. Relations with the United States deteriorate during his four-year term due to accusations that his campaign was funded by the Cali cocaine cartel.

1996 The United States decertifies Colombia for providing insufficient support in the war against drugs. Tens of thousands of farmers protest against government repression and fumigations of drug crops. The FARC attacks and seizes an army base in southern Colombia.

1997 President Samper reauthorizes the extradition of Colombians accused of drug trafficking to the United States. Regional paramilitary groups form a national organization called the Autodefensas Unidas de Colombia (United Self-Defense Forces of Colombia), or AUC, and intensify the dirty war in FARC-dominated southern Colombia.

1998 The FARC inflicts further defeats on the army in southern Colombia. In November, newly elected president Andrés Pastrana of the Conservative Party withdraws two thousand soldiers and police officers from five municipalities in southern Colombia and turns the zone over to the FARC as a safe haven in which to conduct peace talks. There is no cease-fire agreement during the peace process, and the war continues to rage throughout the rest of the country.

2000 U.S. President Bill Clinton announces a new multibillion-dollar antidrug initiative called Plan Colombia, making Colombia the third-largest recipient of U.S. aid. The initiative calls for an intensification of aerial fumigations of illicit drug crops, particularly in regions of southern Colombia controlled by the FARC. Plan Colombia is launched in the southern department of Putumayo in December and in the ensuing years spreads throughout much of Colombia.

2002 In February, the peace process ends when President Pastrana orders the military to invade the FARC-controlled safe haven. In July, the Bush administration begins providing counterterrorism funding to the Colombian government. In August, President Alvaro Uribe, an independent, assumes office after waging a hard-line antiguerrilla campaign. He immediately begins strengthening the military in order to take the offensive against the FARC.

2003 A new center-left party, the Alternative Democratic Pole, wins the mayoral election in Bogotá and numerous other local offices throughout the country. The AUC and the government begin negotiations to establish the terms under which paramilitary fighters will demobilize. Meanwhile, state security forces become more directly involved in the dirty war against leftists through extrajudicial executions, arbitrary arrests, forced displacements, and disappearances.

2005 In July, the enactment of the controversial Justice and Peace Law provides the legal framework for the demobilization of the paramilitaries. FARC attacks against the military throughout the country raise questions about the effectiveness of President Uribe's security strategies. The Colombian Congress amends the constitution to allow President Uribe to run for reelection.

2006 President Uribe is reelected. The Colombian attorney general's office uncovers evidence of extensive collusion between paramilitaries, government officials, military officers, and multinational corporations in what becomes known as the parapolitics scandal. Dozens of new paramilitary groups emerge, many headed by former midlevel AUC commanders.

2007 In response to the parapolitics scandal, Democrats in the U.S. Congress block a free trade agreement negotiated by the Bush and Uribe administrations and force a 10 percent reduction in U.S. aid to Colombia.

Acknowledgments

I owe a huge debt of gratitude to my family and friends who have helped me along the path that has brought me to where I am today. My parents, Norma and Gerry, as well as my brother, Don, and sister, Karyn, have all provided unwavering support and inspiration to me throughout my life. I am indebted to my longtime friend Stephen Paul for keeping me honest and for contributing significantly to my becoming the person I am today. I will also always be indebted to my former wife, Jacqueline Gentile, for her selflessness and generous support in helping facilitate my return to university and in my early years of working as a journalist. I would also like to acknowledge Thomas C. Wright, who is not only an excellent professor of Latin American history but also a friend, who provided me with the political and historical context that helped me to begin making sense of my early experiences in Latin America.

I am also grateful to all those who helped me get my story down on paper. Steve Law and Evelyn Jones pushed me to step outside of my comfortable journalistic role as a disconnected observer and to reveal more of myself in the pages of this book. It was not an easy process for me, but it proved to be both rewarding and therapeutic, and I will be eternally grateful to them for their advice, friendship, and the much-needed kick in the ass. I also owe a debt of gratitude to my friend Aviva Chomsky for her help with the manuscript and for being such an inspirational colleague in our work related to human rights in the Colombian mining sector. I thank my editors at Beacon Press, Gayatri Patnaik and Tracy Ahlquist, for their insightful editing and their faith in the book. Additionally, I am grateful to Lisa Sacks and Kathy Carter for their editorial contributions. I would also like to acknowledge Suzanne MacNeil for her dedicated work with *Colombia Journal,* which helped provide me with the time to write the book.

I would like to thank my Colombian friends—whose names will remain anonymous for reasons of security—for their generosity, compassion, support, and inspiration over the past seven years. I greatly appreciate the patience they have shown me as I have struggled to better understand both the positive and negative aspects of their fascinating and beautiful country. I am also grateful to the journalists I have been lucky enough to work with in Colombia and who appear in the book—Jason Howe, Scott Dalton, Eros Hoagland, and Eric Fichtl. Finally, I am eternally indebted to my wife, Terry Gibbs, for her unfailing support and faith in both my work and me. She has not only worked alongside me in Colombia but has also endured the anguish of worrying about my well-being when I am there alone. She is a wonderful mother to our son, Owen, and an inspiration to me.

Index